WITHDRAWN

CRITICAL STUDIES IN BLACK LIFE
AND CULTURE
VOL. 21

NTOZAKE
SHANGE

GARLAND REFERENCE LIBRARY
OF THE HUMANITIES
VOL. 1441

CRITICAL STUDIES IN BLACK LIFE AND CULTURE

C. JAMES TROTMAN
General Editor

**BLACK IS THE COLOR
OF THE COSMOS**
by Charles T. Davis

WOLE SOYINKA
An Introduction to His Writing
by Obi Maduakor

THE HARLEM RENAISSANCE
Revaluations
by Amritjit Singh, William S. Shiver,
and Stanley Brodwin

RICHARD WRIGHT
Myths and Realities
by C. James Trotman

THE RHETORIC OF STRUGGLE
*Public Address by African
American Women*
by Robbie Jean Walker

NTOZAKE SHANGE
A Critical Study of the Plays
by Neal A. Lester

**JAZZ REFERENCE
AND RESEARCH MATERIALS**
by Eddie S. Meadows

FROM HARLEM TO HOLLYWOOD
*The Struggle for Racial and Cultural
Democracy, 1920–1943*
by Bruce M. Tyler

THE BLACK UNDERCLASS
*Critical Essays on Race
and Unwantedness*
by William A. Darity, Jr.,
and Samuel L. Myers, Jr. with
Emmett D. Carson and William Sabol

THE GREAT WHITE WAY
*African American Women Writers
and American Success Mythologies*
by Phillipa Kafka

NTOZAKE SHANGE

A Critical Study of the Plays

Neal A. Lester

GARLAND PUBLISHING, Inc.
New York & London / 1995

Library of Congress Cataloging-in-Publication Data

Lester, Neal A.
    Ntozake Shange : a critical study of the plays /
Neal A. Lester.
      p.   cm — (Critical studies in Black life and cul-
ture ; vol. 21) (Garland reference library of the humanities ; vol. 1441)
    Includes bibliographical references (p.) and index.
    ISBN 0–8153–0314–9
    1. Shange, Ntozake—Criticism and interpretation.
2. Afro-Americans in literature.   I. Shange, Ntozake.
II. Title. III. Series. IV. Series: Critical studies in
Black life and culture ; v. 21.
PS3569.H3324Z77   1995
812\.54—dc20   94–36113
                                      CIP

Printed on acid-free, 250-year-life paper
Manufactured in the United States of America

General Editor's Preface

Critical Studies in Black Life and Culture is a series devoted to original, book-length studies of African American developments. Written by well-qualified scholars, the series is interdisciplinary and global, interpreting tendencies and themes wherever African Americans have left their mark. The ideal reader for the series is one who appreciates the combined use of scholarly inquiry with a focus on a people whose roots stretch around the world.

Critical Studies is also a window to that world. The series holds out the promise of fulfilling the ideal of all scholarship by uncovering and disseminating the sources of a people's life-line. In relationship to this series, the untranslated Ghanaan narratives offering the earliest perspectives on African life and thought illustrate a scholarly need in this area. If and when they are published, we might have a clearer view of the past and of the consciousness of blacks in antiquity. The clarity would almost certainly contribute to a more detailed basis for understanding what the roots of "culture" and "civilization" are for African Americans in particular and for all of us in general.

Sometimes, however, the scholarly works published in Critical Studies remind us that the windows have not always been open or, if they were, the shades were pulled down, making it difficult if not impossible to see in or out. The series reaffirms forerunners who, by talent and determination, refused to be unseen or unheard: the aesthetic and intellectual foundation created by Phillis Wheatley, Anna Julia Cooper, Frederick Douglass, William E.B. Du Bois, Zora Neale Hurston, Langston Hughes, Ralph Ellison, and the Nobel prizes awarded to Ralph Bunche, Albert Luthuli, Desmond Tutu, Martin Luther King, Jr., Wole Soyinka, and Toni Morrison. In addition to individual achievements, the outstanding examples of organized and permanent group life are to be found in the historic black church, black colleges and universities, and the NAACP; none of these, I might add, has received a comprehensive historical treatment, leaving sizeable gaps in any effort to conceptualize a total picture of multicultural America.

All of these achievements suggest a promising future in African American developments, pointing to a great deal of activity—some from those who have successfully peeked around pulled down shades to look out, while others have found ways to peep in. Critical Studies in Black Life and Culture is committed to publishing the best scholarship on African American life.

C. James Trotman

CONTENTS

FOREWORD

The excitement I feel about Neal Lester's study of my works for the stage is equalled only by my anticipation that some day a group of African American scholars will emerge whose concern is not simply to prove that we as a people have a literature but to explore it. Neal Lester has evinced an analysis of choreopoetry, performance art from the black-hand side, and of our feminism that is of great assistance.

I have been asked if I write or speak English, if I consider myself black or female, if what I write is for the stage or publication. All these questions are designed to minimize the significance of what I do as well as to humiliate me for stepping out of my place. The nature of this scholarship refuses condescension or cultural chauvinism.

I can sustain my work, for the moment, with my body and a rigorous touring schedule that broadens audiences. But work such as Neal Lester's provides a longer, more studied examination of the whole of my endeavors that will be available to generations I can only imagine.

> Ntozake Shange
> 26 October 1993
> Crossroads Theater
> New Jersey

PREFACE

With the Broadway debut of *for colored girls who have considered suicide/ when the rainbow is enuf* at the Booth Theater
(September 1976), Ntozake Shange announced her arrival upon the
American stage and her distinct presence in African American
literature. As an African American, as a woman, as an African
American feminist, and as an African American artist, Shange
proved black females as worthy of heroic stature and literary exploration as are white males and females and black males. Since the
phenomenal commercial success of *for colored girls*, Shange has
continued to write poems, short stories, novels, dramas, and other
performance pieces that proclaim the unlimited creative potential of
blacks and women toward optimal self-worth and self-realization in a
sexist, racist, and capitalist society. Reaching back to the myths and
rituals of her own private and often painful experiences, Shange
emerges on the literary forefront steadfast in her mission to raise the
consciousness of people of color and women. This study of five
published plays—*for colored girls who have considered suicide/ when
the rainbow is enuf* (1976); *spell #7* (1979); *a photograph: lovers in
motion* (1979); *boogie woogie landscapes* (1979); and *From Okra to
Greens/ A Different Kinda Love Story: A Play/ With Music & Dance*
(1985)—reveals Ntozake Shange as an important contemporary artist
whose dramas are complicated, original, forthrightly political, and
entertaining. While experimental in form, they clearly connect with
African American and feminist literary traditions.

Since substantial literary criticisms in African American drama
seem relatively few as compared to criticisms on poetry and fiction,
and since Ntozake Shange's name is relatively new in literary scholarship—either because few critics understand the format of her dra-

matic presentations, or because she writes of "marginal" experiences, or because of her radical attacks on racism and sexism—this investigation does not propose to be a definitive analysis of Shange's theater pieces. Instead, it examines critically Shange's contributions to the American stage, suggests aspects of her work for further inquiry, and contextualizes Shange's drama within appropriate literary traditions. A number of critical approaches—formalist, biographical, historical, feminist—demonstrate that Shange's experiments in form result in effective poetic drama.

ACKNOWLEDGMENTS

This project has undergone considerable transformation since its early presentation as my doctoral thesis. Largely because of various encouragements, I am finally bringing this phase of my life and this work to fruition. Indeed, I owe hearty thanks to many who have cheered me on to this moment.

First, my dissertation committee members—particularly Jenny Spencer, Ellen Caldwell, and Phyllis Frus—offered invaluable and fundamental criticism that enabled me to know why and how I was to approach this subject and author confidently and critically. To Jenny, I am especially grateful for her insistence that I meet Ntozake Shange personally. I thank Zaki for graciously responding to nine months of letters requesting an interview, and for her steadfast interest and assistance in getting permissions, addresses, and phone numbers; for providing me with her unpublished materials; and for keeping me abreast of her latest works.

Here at the University of Alabama, I am indebted to colleagues Francesca Kazan, Elizabeth Meese, Sharon O'Dair, and Harold Weber for their initial guidance in broadening my critical range. I owe a special thanks to my former Chair, Claudia D. Johnson, who first suggested that these ideas be shared with a larger audience.

Additionally, I am grateful to the University of Alabama Summer Research Grants Committee for funding that freed me to work intensely on this project for one summer. I am indebted as well to Lisa Hammond Rashley, my typesetter, and to Dana Barnett, my Research Assistant, for their diligence and conscientiousness in getting my raw text into a technically appropriate form.

Above all, I owe my wife, Adelina Zottola, my deepest thanks for keeping me spiritually intact and emotionally grounded throughout this project—from its conception to its birth.

Grateful thanks are due the following publishers who gave permission to reprint from the following:

For colored girls who have considered suicide/ when the rainbow is enuf, by Ntozake Shange. Copyright 1975, 1976, 1977 by Ntozake Shange. Reprinted by permission of Macmillan Publishing Company and of Russell and Volkening as agents for the author.

From *My House*, by Nikki Giovanni. Copyright 1972 by Nikki Giovanni. Reprinted by permission of William Morrow and Company, Inc.

From *Nappy Edges*, by Ntozake Shange. Copyright 1972, 1974, 1975, 1976, 1977, 1978 by Ntozake Shange. Reprinted by permission of St. Martin's Press, Inc. (New York, NY) and of Reed Book Services, Sanders Lodge Industrial Estate (Rushden, Northants NN10 9RZ).

From Okra to Greens/ A Different Kinda Love Story, by Ntozake Shange. Copyright 1984 by Ntozake Shange. Reprinted by permission of Russell and Volkening as agents for the author.

Three Pieces, by Ntozake Shange. Copyright 1981 by Ntozake Shange. Reprinted by permission of St. Martin's Press, Inc. (New York, NY).

I also thank the College of Arts and Sciences for its financial support in obtaining copyright permissions and in preparing this manuscript for publication.

Ntozake
Shange

INTRODUCTION

The Choreopoem

Shange's "choreopoem" is her most significant contribution to the stage. Defined simply, the choreopoem is a theatrical expression that combines poetry, prose, song, dance, and music—those elements that, according to Shange, outline a distinctly African American heritage—to arouse an emotional response in an audience. As a theatrical expression, the choreopoem emerges from an African tradition of storytelling, rhythm, physical movement, and emotional catharsis. First encountering the choreopoem when she joined the Broadway company of *for colored girls* in 1977, actor-author Robbie McCauley comments on its form:

> The form demands that the performer have an organic, physical relationship to the words and images of the poems/ narratives. . . . In order to perform Shange's text, the actor has to personalize her relationship to it. (I mean personalize as an acting process wherein the actor involves herself experientially and imaginatively with the text . . . to play it through herself.) I'd say that the form is musical—that a broad range of Black classical music (Jazz, Blues, Rhythm and Blues) informs the work. By this I mean that the performer brings her own musical sense to the text and she will find that the music lives there. . . . Note that I'm describing an actor's work to come to it with some knowledge or strong instinct about how to give it voice.

3

And, of course, there is a physical life in the
text. The actor deals with inner rhythms in giving
voice to text. Shange's work demands that inner
rhythms be physicalized. And of course each actor
finds her own way of doing this.[1]

Definitively, Shange's theater emerges from her own experiences as
a poet and dancer, and she empowers her actors to experience and to
communicate her dramas personally and individually.

An element of improvisation also characterizes the choreopoem
format, again highlighting actors' own emotional and personal responses to the text. Choreographer Dianne McIntyre, with whom
Shange has both danced and collaborated on a number of theater
pieces, highlights the improvisational dimension of choreopoem:

Choreopoem is an ancient [African] form—words
and movement happening simultaneously. It's natural. Zaki made a name for it. The uniqueness of the
form as I know it and have worked with it, is that
the words are not separate over there and danced to.
The words and dance become one—intertwined so
you couldn't imagine one without the other. It feels
very natural to me—but it is somewhat daring. You
have probably seen other people use the form, but it
often doesn't work as well as with Zaki's poetry.
Her words have the music and the dance in it and
the words also have space that is open for the dance
(like abstract music) whereas some other poetry
may be so explicit that movement with it is redundant.[2]

It is precisely this improvisational dimension, with its conscious
crossing of alleged genre boundaries, that separates Shange's theater
from traditionally western verse-drama forms of such playwrights as
Christopher Frye, T.S. Eliot, and even Shakespeare.

Shange uses an unconventional American form to present more
accurately what she offers as her own African American culture.
Toward this end, she rejects standard English in favor of black

vernacular and profanity and declares open war on the patriarchy by
creating her own rules of spelling, punctuation, capitalizations, word
usage, and even syntax. As suggested by Dianne McIntyre, what
Shange presents is not necessarily a new form for African Americans
who had integrated performance, voice, dance, and ritual into serious
aesthetic expressions of truth for the stage.[3] While Shange's deliberate meshing of creative modes alienated mainstreamers, the form has
found commercial legitimacy in Shange's dramas. Actor Laurie
Carlos adds:

> [Ntozake Shange] comes to you with all the things
> that you've ever felt in your life as a colored person
> in America. She comes to you with all your dreams
> and all of your fears, and she manifests them on a
> page—which is something that you don't find ever
> in terms of a script for a black woman, for black
> actors; therefore, it's a blessing.[4]

Shange's theater pieces work to raise consciousness individually,
socially, and artistically and center around the complex notions of
identity politics. In presenting a range of human experiences of
blacks, females, black females, black artists, and black female
artists, Shange reexamines oppressive stereotypes, incorporates role-
playing, and highlights sexual and international politics, all with
keen insight into the impact of verbal communications and miscom-
munications. Transferring her own private experiences and political
voice into a form accessible to a public audience, Shange demands in
her work an emotional internalization of experiences offered, insisting that ". . . a poem shd fill you up with something / cd make you
swoon, stop in yr tracks, change yr mind, or make it up. a poem shd
happen to you like cold water or a kiss."[5] The manipulation of
language to achieve raw emotion—passion, rage, anger, resentment,
ecstasy, and pain—characterizes all of Shange's work. Acknowledging this role of emotion, Shange posits: "I'm committed to the idea
that one of the few things human beings have to offer is the richness
of unconscious emotional responses to being alive. . . . [Y]ou cannot
exclude any human being from emotional participation."[6] The
success and impact of her theater pieces and her poems come from an

audience's experiential identification with and emotional and verbal responses to actions and characters set before them. Shange's language and her daringness to speak about the alleged unspeakables—a single black mother, hooked on crack, who sells her seven-year-old daughter for a hit; a father who drops his two young children from a fifth-story window; a woman who details the sexual pleasure of masturbating—force readers and audiences into an urgent moment of poetry; her theater pieces are thereby extended poetry moments. Single voices in her poems become many speakers in her choreopoems. Each expression demands immediacy and engagement.

A self-proclaimed race poet-playwright, Shange documents and legitimizes the particular experiences of African Americans—their unique political and social oppressions, their cultural rituals, their language, their fantasies, their efforts toward psychological survival individually and collectively.[7] Yet Shange's theater pieces move far beyond the experiences of her intended audience; in her presentations, the personal, social, and political issues, while emphatically particular to the experiences of oppressed people, also move beyond racial, gender, and cultural boundaries.

for colored girls announces the choreopoem format, and each subsequent published drama utilizes this combination of poetry, performance, music, movement, imagery from black popular culture, as well as socio-political and historical images. Although the form, content, and ideas remain virtually the same in each of the five plays,[8] each represents a development of the choreopoem in terms of broadening themes and issues toward more complicated presentations. Examined chronologically, the pieces also reveal Shange's move to present more complex human experiences.

for colored girls who have considered suicide/ when the rainbow is enuf celebrates being a black female in modern America. Originating as a series of monologues which Shange alleges she arbitrarily divided into seven character parts, the play reveals a structurally unified account of seven black women who come together in a singular, gender-segregated moment to voice their fears, pain, griefs, losses, and joys—experiences that are sometimes gender-specific, race-specific, and gender and race-specific. Although each woman brings to the group her own experiences, the varied experiences collectively become the voice of a black female. Their gender experi-

ences, while distinctly particular to black females, potentially connect with all females: rape, abortion, pregnancy, and motherhood.
Through the women's experiences with rejection, infidelity, and
physical and psychological abuse, they—through a kind of spiritual
though not a Christian rebirth—emerge triumphant, full of joyous
independence and greater self-knowledge.

As Shange's first commercial piece, *for colored girls* presents a
playwright whose ideas are as revolutionary as her form is innovative. At the heart of the criticism of the play's particular feminist
perspective is Shange's presentation of black men. Close examination
or re-examination of the piece reveals clearly that Shange does not
condemn black men;[9] nor does she prescribe lesbianism or a swear-
ing off of men altogether. While she attacks the behavior of some
men, she also recognizes women's own responsibilities for their
sufferings at the hands of abusive men. An exploration of the black
woman's sexual, social, and artistic identity, this first published
choreopoem is Shange's most philosophically optimistic and idealistic
despite its realistic foundations.

spell #7 is not so much about individual or personal identity as
about accepting the realities of being black collectively in modern
America. This second published play offers no optimistic resolution
to perceived and internalized problems of being black. Less abstract
in terms of character and action and less idealistic, *spell #7* offers a
poignant statement about the inescapability of racial and gender
stereotypes. It also demonstrates the need for individual fantasy as a
tool for survival in a bigoted society and shows the definitive need
for racially segregated experience to dispel oppressive and often
internalized myths about black culture and celebrates positive aspects
of black identity. Rather than find an inner rainbow after sufferings
as do the women in *for colored girls*, the characters in *spell #7*
acknowledge a potentially futile and often hostile reality of on- and
off-stage role-playing. After a series of sometimes humorous, sometimes amusing, and sometimes frightening improvisations, the actors/
characters resolve to enjoy "being colored." Beginning with the
particular experiences of these black artists, the play expands to
address society's entrapment of blacks by limited social roles.

spell #7 offers an interesting tension that derives specifically
from the presence of a grotesque minstrel mask suspended from the

stage ceiling before and after the production. While the minstrel mask documents a particular moment in American history—when whites blackened their faces with burnt cork and dramatized blacks as lazy, unintelligent, uneducable, and self-mocking—it also recalls the early formal theatrical experiences of blacks like Bert Williams who blackened their own black faces to get work on the commercial stage. The legacy of nineteenth-century minstrelsy presents itself in the dramatic roles these black actors continue to find most available. The mask symbol also reiterates the play's focus on racist mythologies about black Americans created in the western world. Using the choreopoem form and a play-within-a-play structure, *spell #7* presents an interplay between actors and characters whose temporal boundaries are deliberately indistinguishable. With characters that have conventional names and professions and with a geographically localized setting, the play is more naturalistic than *for colored girls*. Additionally, while focusing on issues of racial and gender identity, the inevitable sexual politics in black male-female relationships, and the line between creative and self-destructive fantasy, *spell #7* climaxes in a less spontaneous, consciously willed celebration of blackness.

Shange's third published play, *a photograph: lovers in motion*, explores the ambiguities of male-female sexual identity. Using photography as a metaphor for life, Shange presents black men and women entangled in a web of destructive romance. This play moves further from Shange's earlier mood of celebration to one of tense uncertainty in heterosexual relationships. Shange presents individuals working toward defining and endeavoring to resolve conflicts between their own sexual and social selves. More naturalistic than *for colored girls* and *spell #7*, this play ends without resolving the multilayered problems that plague Sean David, the aspiring young black photographer struggling to define his manhood in the context of a racist society and in the context of three women who allow him to mistreat them and who are themselves trying to reckon with their own confused identities.

In *boogie woogie landscapes*, Shange experiments extensively with expressionistic techniques. More complex than *for colored girls* theatrically, *boogie* dissects the psyche of a black "all-American colored girl." Using characters that enter and exit through walls of the set, Shange creates a dream play where a black female's conscious and subconscious desires are visibly personified. While resembling *for colored girls* most in content and subject matter, this play moves deeper into a black female's psychological identity. That the play is structured as a dream is central to both the play's meaning and structure. As in *a photograph*, this play does not resolve racial and sexual tensions set forth but dramatizes the complexities within an oppressed mind. Issues of racial and sexual identity reveal that Layla, the central character, exists as a product of her immediate environment. *boogie* is an in-depth character analysis and Shange's foremost effort to define and legitimize a black female's ever-threatening realities.

From Okra to Greens/ A Different Kinda Love Story: A Play/ With Music & Dance is perhaps the most structurally complicated of Shange's published theater pieces. Taking almost verbatim poems from an earlier poetry collection and dividing them seemingly arbitrarily into two voices—in much the way *for colored girls* emerged as a drama—Shange presents a metaphoric love story between a black male (Greens) and a black female (Okra) that engages broader gender and political issues. The action of the play involves the couple's meeting, becoming lovers, separating over his infidelity, courting, marrying, and ultimately parenting. The piece moves consistently from personal to political and develops through graphic images of sexuality. With her focus on the role of the black artist, particularly the black female poet, Shange presents a traditional tale unconventionally rendered from a distinctly black cultural perspective.

While each of these five plays is linked through form and content, each evidences a move toward broadening complex issues. Indeed, the development of the choreopoem parallels Shange's own development as a feminist writer of color committed to presenting and celebrating her identity culturally while simultaneously attacking her socio-political realities. Characterizing herself as a black person's writer[10]—a writer primarily concerned with the particular experiences of and issues affecting blacks and third world peoples—Shange recognizes her challenge as a black poet-playwright on the American stage:

> I really resent the idea that we still have to have not
> "race" plays but "issue" plays, or "point"
> plays. . . . The commercial people tell me that one
> of the reasons my work hasn't been as commer-
> cially successful as *for colored girls* is that it has no
> point that they could sell. That's because there's
> going to be no more point. *for colored girls* doesn't
> have a point either, but they made a point of it.
> Those girls were people whom I cared about, peo-
> ple whom I offered to you for you to see and to
> know. Black and Latin writers have to start de-
> manding that the fact that we're alive is point
> enough![11]

Clearly, Shange's theater pieces have a point, if nothing more than to
present race and gender experiences as she perceives and experiences
them. For Shange, the experience is the point; for her characters,
their complicated lives are the point. And Shange achieves these
impacts with no leanings toward moralizing or sermonizing. She
simply, though not simplistically, allows the pieces to exist on her
aesthetic terms.

* * * * *

That Ntozake Shange invests much energy in names and naming
is evidenced in her own name change in 1971 from her christened
name, Paulette Williams. Adopting the Zulu names, *Ntozake*, meaning "she who comes with her own things," and *Shange*, meaning
"who walks like a lion," was a conscious move to renounce European connotations and to celebrate the Afrocentric core of her identity. Shange explains her cultural ideal:

> A name means a lot more than just a signature on
> your MasterCharge. It's who you are. I didn't want
> to be defined by a heritage that infuriates me. I
> didn't want any kind of Anglo-Saxon name because
> European culture has nothing to do with me. And I
> didn't want my first name because I was named

> after my father [Paul T. Williams]—I didn't want a
> man's name either. I had a violent resentment of
> carrying a slave name. Poems and music come from
> the pit of myself, and the pit of myself isn't a
> slave.[12]

Though Shange does not offer this comment to separate herself from
a slave past, her resistance to being named by a patriarchal and racial
Other symbolizes her steadfast efforts toward self-definition, self-
awareness, and a conscious embracing of her African past and
present. An attack on Eurocentricism clearly motivates this
"revolutionary" move. Reborn spiritually and metaphorically after
accepting names given her by friends from the Xhosa tribe in South
Africa who also took her to the Pacific Ocean and baptized her,
Shange reveals her determination to be heard distinctly as a black
feminist and to explore and present with brutal honesty and piercing
accuracy the lives of blacks and women in her theater, poetry,
fiction, and her installation art or "built metaphors."[13]

Shange's attention to names and naming is of utmost importance
in her label "choreopoem," the genre that she feels best suits the
subject matter of her dramatic writing, the form that best allows the
resources of her African American heritage to be fully integrated into
a unified theater piece. While she defines the choreopoem as a series
of poems, with occasional music and dance, that when put together
become one statement or voice[14]—Shange's use of this form is complex and innovative. C.W.E. Bigsby offers an historical context of
Shange's choreopoem:

> The essence of black poetry, particularly in the
> 1960s and early 1970s, had lain in its public nature,
> its performatics. It was never a closet poetry
> (unless, as LeRoi Jones once observed, the closet
> be "as wide as God's eye"). Sonia Sanchez, Nikki
> Giovanni and many others performed their poetry at
> large public gatherings in which the symbiosis be-
> tween audience and performer was a vital part of
> the aesthetic. Such occasions shared something of
> the atmosphere of the store-front church. They

trembled, in other words, on the brink of ritual and
of theatre. Shange's choreopoem is a natural extension of this. Poems with music and dance, forming
a narrative account, become a play.[15]

Bigby's assessment reiterates the foregrounding of emotion and
audience participation, particularly through verbal responses, in both
Shange's poetry and theater. Further contextualizing Shange's
choreopoem, Robbie McCauley adds:

> I'd . . . theorize that Ms. Shange has named
> and shared a theatrical mode that comes directly
> from the African storyteller, a skilled craftsperson
> whose function is to listen to and carry on the im-
> ages of the culture [and] to be able to do this in a
> way that makes what is important in the culture live
> for the moment. In the United States this form
> could be translated into blues, jazz, and poetry—all
> musical and dance forms. Amiri Baraka is a signifi-
> cant artist of this form. The screams, the laughter,
> the agony, and struggle of our lives as African
> people who were transplanted over here is the mu-
> sic of Baraka's poetry.
>   And the Last Poets, the very first Last Poets—
> Gylan Kain, Felipe Luciana, and David Nelson—
> originated the contemporary mode of having a
> group of poets pouring out from the gut the emo-
> tional socio/political images that infuse the lives of
> Black people in this country.[16]

That Shange is influenced by poets and comes practically and theo-
retically to her theater pieces as a poet forms the central feature of
her choreopoetry. Shange provides a lengthy introduction to the
Bantam edition of *for colored girls* detailing the genesis of the
choreopoem. In that introduction, she highlights dance and music as
integral parts of her theater-poetry; dance and music are independent
units brought together to create one theatrical unit, one particular
poetic moment. As for the label *choreopoem*, Shange offers:

> I made it up because I knew I wasn't a playwright.
> My relation to theater developed as a poet and a
> dancer, not as a person who was an actress or who
> was involved in theater or the conventions of thea-
> ter as we know it. . . . I was very concerned about
> and very passionately committed to the idea of
> creating new rituals and new mythologies for peo-
> ple of color . . . [because] the mythologies that
> were available to us were negative images in James
> Baldwin's work or in Ralph Ellison's work for
> instance, or in Claude McKay's. Their images of
> black people were not necessarily false images, but
> they were certainly images that were concerned
> with our relationship with the Other as opposed to
> our relationship with ourselves. Secondly, I thought
> that one of the primary goals assigned young writ-
> ers of color in the late 1960s was to direct our at-
> tentions inward . . . so that we could discern in our
> own communities what things were or were not
> functioning well for us. From what wellsprings
> could I draw things that might in fact envelop us in
> a sense of ourselves that was rooted to the earth,
> that was *not* rooted to the idea that white people had
> about us, that was *not* rooted to our relationship to
> white people, and that had solely to do with how we
> respond to being alive on the planet?[17]

Shange's move to revise images of blacks' relationship with a world
not centrally focused on white people are further complicated by her
role as a black female artist determined to "write" black women into
this black patriarchal world order.

Shange's form reveals in her interdisciplinary artistry, her
suspicion of the absolute separation of arts from one another. She
offers further clarification:

> the fact that we [African Americans] are an
> interdisciplinary culture/ that we understand more

> than verbal communication/ lays a weight on afro-
> american writers that few others are lucky enough
> to have been born into. we can use with some skill
> virtually all of our physical senses/ as writers com-
> mitted to bringing the world as we remember it/
> imagine it/ & know it to be to the stage/ we must
> use everything we've got.[18]

Ignoring traditional boundaries of the stage, Shange writes as a black person particularly about black people—blacks' experiences, mannerisms, tastes, music, dreams, fears, and uses blacks' language—all toward demonstrating and documenting the complexities of blacks' existence and affording a fuller range of African American experience.

Because of Shange's consistent use of a form that resists artificial categories of traditional theater, critics and reviewers insist that her theater pieces are "roughly structured and stylistically unrefined,"[19] or that "Miss Shange is something besides a poet but she is not . . . a dramatist,"[20] even that "Miss Shange has never even managed to write a real play."[21] In fact, John Simon, in his review of *for colored girls*, asks: "Is this poetry? Drama? Or simply tripe? Can you imagine this being published in a serious poetry journal? Would it have been staged if written by a white?"[22] Simon's assessment reveals not only his misunderstanding of the play but also his inability or unwillingness to accept Shange's presentation on its own cultural and aesthetic terms. His condescension reveals a need for new critical language to discuss and understand this dramatic form.

Indeed, Shange does not write plays in the traditional sense of plots and characters that can be neatly analyzed or even straight prose dialogue between characters. Likewise, the choreopoem, because of its eclectic form, cannot be discussed fully or understood completely with the existing critical vocabulary used to discuss and evaluate conventional theater. Loosely using the notion of Greek chorus as many like units becoming one voice, Shange manipulates Aristotle's basic elements of drama—plot, character, diction, spectacle, thought, and melody. Rather than present a Eurocentric and patriarchal artificiality of linear structurings, Shange offers moments in the lives of black people who often represent ideas rather than traditional characters. Again, dance, song, and music are smoothly conjoined not merely to entertain or to amuse—as black theater has traditionally and historically done from popular minstrel shows of the past to commercially successful musical revues of present day—but to communicate a complexity of black experience.

As a poet making words bend at her command to invade, without warning, a reader's territorial space and emotional consciousness and to render words as a visual dance across a printed page, Shange comes to the stage with this same poetic vision and stylistic command. Her choreopoems expand to create the same effect as her poetry: to move readers or viewers through the vehicle of raw emotion. In her introductory essay to *three pieces*, she offers a final clarification:

> as a poet in american theater/ i find most activ-
> ity that takes place on our stage overwhelmingly
> shallow/ stilted and imitative. that is probably one
> of the reasons i insist on calling myself a poet or
> writer/ rather than a playwright/ i am solely inter-
> ested in the poetry of the moment/ the emotional
> and aesthetic impact of a character or a line. for too
> long now afro-americans in theater have been duped
> by the same artificial aesthetics that plague our
> white counterparts/ "the perfect play," as we know
> it to be/ a truly european framework for european
> psychology/ cannot function efficiently for those of
> us from this hemisphere. . . . theater . . . is an all
> encompassing moment/ a moment of poetry/ the
> opportunity to make something happen.[23]

Shange's presentation of this form on the American stage symbolizes her artistic and political goal of redefining her own identity and the identity of oppressed peoples; her choreopoems render and sustain these ideals.

NOTES

1. Robbie McCauley, personal letter, 27 October 1986.
2. Dianne McIntyre, personal letter, 11 June 1991. McIntyre was Shange's dance instructor in the mid-1970s, and they have worked together in Shange's *spell # 7, boogie woogie landscapes,* televised version of *for colored girls, Mouths,* and *Ridin' the Moon in Texas.* Shange also appeared in the first production of McIntyre's dance drama, *Take-Off from a Forced Landing.* McIntyre has used the choreodrama form in her musical adaptation of Zora Neale Hurston's *Their Eyes Were Watching God.* McIntyre's piece is entitled *Their Eyes Were Watching God: A Dance Adventure in Southern Blues (A Choreodrama).* One difference in McIntyre's choreodrama and Shange's choreopoem, according to Shange, is that the choreodrama begins with a verbal line whereas the choreopoem begins with nonverbal expression (i.e., dance).
3. See Melvin Van Peebles' *Ain't Supposed to Die a Natural Death* (1971), a theatrical event that blends these interdisciplinary African American elements into one unified aesthetic form, is a forerunner of Shange's choreopoem.
4. "A Colored Girl: Ntozake Shange," PBS videorecording (Washington, DC: WGBH-TV, 1980), a documentary profile of Shange in a three-day informal interview, includes brief conversations with Shange's parents, actor Laurie Carlos, late producer Joseph Papp, excerpts from the New York Shakespeare Festival's production of *spell #7,* as well as Shange's own readings from the *spell* text.
5. "Ntozake Shange Interviews Herself," *Ms.* (December 1977), 72. Shange's self-interview also appears as "i talk to myself" in the 1987 Methuen edition of *Nappy Edges* (17-24).
6. Claudia Tate, *Black Women Writers at Work* (New York: Continuum, 1983), 151.
7. Reiterating Shange's insistence that this choreopoem form and the experiences of blacks are interconnected, Robbie McCauley acknowledges:

I'd say that the inner life of Black people, the
collective experience, is the motor for the choreopoem. This is not to say that it does not have appeal
and use for other cultures. But I'd say that the particular way of translating the inside/ outside experience that has been the mode of survival for Black
people is also the basis of our art forms. (McCauley
letter)

8. Shange clarifies that her dramatic pieces are not "plays" in
the conventional sense. However, in this study, because of the
critical vocabulary available, I use "play" interchangeably with
"choreopoem."

9. In my article, "Shange's Men: *for colored girls* Revisited,
and Movement Beyond," *African American Review,* formerly *Black
American Literature Forum* 26 (Summer 1992): 319-28, I argue that
the continued hysteria over Shange's presentation of men is unwar-
ranted and needs to be reconsidered particularly with other theater
pieces after *for colored girls.*

Since this whole debate on black feminist writers' allegedly
vicious portrayals of black men continues, it might prove helpful to
examine Donahue Show #72089, "Black Women Writers" (20 July
1989). The panel consists of Maya Angelou, Alice Walker, Shange,
Michele Wallace, and Angela Davis. Among other things, one of the
central issues of the show is black women writers' presentations of
black men. See Donahue transcript #2733.

10. Tate, 171.

11. Ibid.

12. Laura Berman, "The Last Angry Woman? Playwright-poet
Isn't Running from the Rage That Inspires Her," *Detroit Free Press,*
30 October 1979, C1, 3A.

13. In the 16 April 1985 unpublished letter to Dr. Hill at the
University of Houston (Texas), in application for a Master of Fine
Arts degree in sculpture, Shange defines "built metaphors" as
"areas of poetic symbols that envelop the viewer in one or more
tactile (visual) surroundings. For the most part there is no spoken or
written 'translation' of the installations which appeal to non-verbal
arenas of the viewers' (in some cases the participants') uncon-

scious." Speaking of her particular interest in sculpture in metal and
plexiglass as well as her use of feathers, twigs, dirt, shells, and dried
flowers, leaves, and the like (i.e., outdoor pieces that would disinte-
grate organically), she adds:

> On a more aesthetic or conceptual train of thought,
> I think it is important to mention that I believe there
> are certain images/ ideas that are not adequately
> articulated in verbal genres. This is one more rea-
> son for my desire to explore space, color, weight,
> line and angles, so that my artistic dynamic and
> competence will allow me to execute with precision
> and imagination those creative impulses that de-
> mand non-verbal expression.

14. Ntozake Shange, untitled introduction to *for colored girls
who have considered suicide/ when the rainbow is enuf* (New York:
Bantam, 1981), xx. Subsequent references to this work will be cited
parenthetically in the text by page number.

15. C.W.E. Bigsby, *A Critical Introduction to Twentieth-Century
American Drama (Volume Three: Beyond Broadway)* (Cambridge:
Cambridge UP, 1985), 411.

16. McCauley letter.

17. Personal interview. Portions of this interview, formally titled
"An Interview with Ntozake Shange," appear in *Studies in American
Drama, 1945-Present* 5 (1990): 42-66.

18. Ntozake Shange, "unrecovered losses/ black theater traditions," foreword to *three pieces* (New York: St. Martin's, 1981),
x. *three pieces* includes *spell #7, a photograph: lovers in motion*, and
boogie woogie landscapes. Subsequent references to each play will
come from this edition and will appear parenthetically in the text by
page number.

19. Marilyn Stasio, "Tell It, Sisters!," *Cue*, 26 June 1976.

20. Richard Eder, "Sovereign Spirit," *New York Times*, 22
December 1977, Section C, p. 11.

21. John Simon, "Fainting Spell," *New York Magazine*, 30 July
1979, 57.

22. John Simon, "On Stage: *Enuf* Is Not Enough," *New Leader*

59 (5 July 1976): 21. Not only does Simon's review reveal his own personal racial and gender biases, but he misquotes lines from the play and displays a gross misunderstanding of and disinterest in the issues raised. His own cultural arrogance leads him to dismiss *for colored girls* as "amateur night in Harlem."

    23. Shange, foreword to *three pieces*, ix-xi.

CHAPTER II

"bein alive & bein a woman & bein colored":
*for colored girls who have considered suicide/
when the rainbow is enuf*

When Ntozake Shange wrote the poems that make up *for colored girls who have considered suicide/ when the rainbow is enuf* (1976) during the summer of 1974 and later read them in women's bars in California, she did not envision performing them as theater, let alone for a Broadway audience of predominantly upper middle-class whites. Instead, she intended only to celebrate and share with other women—especially black women—her personal experiences as a black female, and to participate in a community of female poets and artists, nourished by each other's creative renderings of their particular and common experiences. Using poet Judy Grahn's *The Common Woman* (1970)[1] as a structural and thematic model, Shange transformed her own suffering, pain, and eventual joy in a celebration of black female identity. From those early informal readings in workshops and women's bars,[2] the poems emerged as a structured dramatic piece at the Henry Street Playhouse (New York) under the direction of Woodie King, Jr. (April-May 1976), then at Joseph Papp's New York Shakespeare Festival under the direction of Oz Scott (June-August 1976). It eventually arrived on Broadway at the Booth Theater (September 1976-January 1978), and of the 867 New York performances of *for colored girls*, 747 were Broadway productions.[3] The choreopoem also received international exposure, with productions in Kingston, West Indies (The National Theater, December

21

1977-March 1978); Rio de Janeiro, Brazil (Teatro de BNH, July 1978-September 1978); and London (The Royalty Theater, September 1979-November 1979). Although it defied conventional forms of theater in the western world in terms of character creation and stage presentation, *for colored girls* was immediately hailed the "hit of the '77-'78 season." Linda Winer wrote of the Broadway production: "What threatens at first to be a self-righteous, predictable complaint by an angry black woman poet named Ntozake Shange soon blossoms into an extraordinary abstraction on the non-stop, fun-sad world of growing up black and female."[4] Alan Rich, reviewing a production at Joseph Papp's Public Theater, accentuated the choreopoem's appeal to a predominantly black audience:

> Part of the exhilaration in *[f]or [c]olored [g]irls* . . . comes from the way its largely black audience is held in thrall. . . . The audience's reaction may be partly born of pride in an enthralling play; it may also be that, respectable plays by blacks being a comparatively new phenomenon, the apathy that enshrouds Uptown Commercial Theater hasn't yet taken hold. In any case, it has a quality one resists only with the greatest difficulty. Theater, on such a night, glows in all colors.[5]

And Clive Barnes insisted that "[The play] could very easily have made me feel guilty at being white and male. It didn't. It made me feel proud at being a member of the human race, and with the joyous discovery that a white man can have black sisters."[6] Finally, Jessica Harris maintained that *for colored girls* was a "theatrical milestone" in presenting black life upon the stage accurately and respectably:

> It is the first time that a Black woman playwright has dealt with young Black women and their role in contemporary society in such a way that it is a commercially viable production (the idea of Broadway theater is after all to make a profit). Yet at the same time, it maintains such a level of integrity that Black women can agree with it.[7]

Nevertheless, public response to *for colored girls* was not unanimously positive from black women, black men, or white critics. Some critics alleged that *for colored girls* portrayed black men negatively and that its choreopoem presentation was artistically haphazard. Unfavorable reviews came from critics who were unable to make the choreopoem fit their preconceived notions of theater, particularly in terms of its melding of performance media and in its seeming lack of linear development in action and character. Somehow, for these critics, having seven black women voice their experiences was not 'enuf' to meet their aesthetic and literary expectations. Recall John Simon's vicious attack on both the subject matter and the form, calling the play "pathetic nonsense."[8]

The choreopoem's commercial success posed an uncomfortable irony for Shange both professionally and artistically. The immediate fame brought moments of intense alienation and artistic paranoia. In discussing this aftermath of her success, Shange explained her sense of detachment from the intimacy she initially wished to create and to convey in the piece.[9] Not only did the success of *for colored girls* on Broadway initially threaten her creative productivity, but it also removed the play from its intended audience. Off-Broadway, her audience was still segregated racially since whites remained largely ignorant of Shange's work. But commercial success took the play out of "average" black females' reach. Lost was the intended intimacy metaphorically with young black girls that Shange sought as she unraveled some of the mysteries of her own experiences as an adolescent developing into and embracing black womanhood.

* * * * *

Considering the significance of names and naming to Ntozake Shange, her titles allude not only to the content of the pieces but also to their structures. The lengthy title of *for colored girls* . . . reveals Shange's technical traits as a poet attentive to words and their ability to communicate specific cultural realities. Most critical attention to the title centers on Shange's use of the word "colored" and her symbolic use of the "rainbow." Shange responds to questions about the play's title:

I used the words "colored girls" in the title [be-
cause] my grandmother would understand. It would-
n't put her off and turn her away. I wanted to get
back to the brass tacks of myself as a child; I was a
regular colored girl, with a family that was good to
me.[10]

In the December 1977 *Ms.* "interview" with herself, she adds:

i use the terms "colored," "yellow," "negress"
& any other i can think of cuz they have a reality
for me that extends beyond governments & territories. i have always hated being referred to as an
american citizen/ tho i love the western hemisphere.
in the colloquial terms referring to black people is
more history & love & acceptance of our "peculiar
situation" than in the cursory description of someone as "black" or "afro-american" which seem
artificial to me. i cannot sustain myself with inadequate language; that leads to superficial & ambiguous living.[11]

"Colored" renders, for Shange, a cultural identification with black
people and their specific historical and generational past. On the one
hand, it connotatively distinguishes blacks from whites in terms of
skin tone. Additionally, the term is at once a stark reminder of
humiliating Jim Crow moments in American history. "For Colored
Only" signs reminded blacks that they were not equal to whites and
innately unworthy of sharing the same territorial space with whites.
In much the same way, Shange's seven women reclaim their own
space in their move toward realized selfhood. And finally,
"colored" is a term of endearment within the black community. As
opposed to being condescending and derogatory when used by
whites, the word, when used by blacks, brings with it a sense of
community and a unique cultural richness and identity. Carol P.
Christ, in her discussion of Shange's use of "colored" in the choreopoem title, recalls a television interview wherein Shange

> . . . spoke of the importance of self-definition, of
> taking pride in dark skin and African heritage [and
> affirming] her American ancestors. She recalled
> that her grandmother's last words to her were that
> she was a precious "little colored girl." Thinking
> about this made Shange realize that "colored" was
> not only a term used by whites to define Blacks, but
> also a term of endearment in the Black community.
> To reclaim the name "colored girl" was to reclaim
> [and celebrate] her relationship to her grandmother,
> a part of her story.[12]

Shange's use of "colored" also reiterates her ultimate commitment
to writing about women of color—not just African American women,
but other non-caucasian women equally oppressed by racism and
sexism.

As for her symbolic use of the rainbow, Shange recalls the
occasion of returning home to Oakland from a women's studies class
she was teaching at Sonoma State College (Rohnert Park, California). Having taught Gabriel Garcia Marquez's *One Hundred Years of
Solitude* (1970) that day and feeling particularly depressed, she
remembers noticing a rainbow and connecting that occurrence in
nature to women's rightful existence in the planet's cosmic order:

> [Women, especially black women,] have as much
> right and as much purpose for being here [on the
> planet] as air and mountains do. . . . We can mini-
> mize those scars or those sores that we don't want
> in us. We can modulate them to the extent that they
> become at least not malignant. And we forget that.
> So that's what the rainbow is: just the possibility to
> start all over again with the power and the beauty of
> ourselves. . . . Rainbows come after storms; they
> don't come before the storm.[13]

Shange's conventional use of the rainbow symbolizes a movement
toward ideals for these suffering black women. It represents discovered self-worth after a series of metaphorical storms, the reasons

these women or any woman might consider suicide. The rainbow as a symbol works as a visual manifestation of women's spiritual beauty and eventual self-actualization. That a rainbow is not monochromatic by definition affirms the diversity of black females' experiences socially, culturally, and individually. Only in her awareness of the complexity of her experiences can a black girl realize positive selfhood. Shange adds:

> The rainbow is a fabulous symbol for me. If you see only one color, it's not beautiful. If you see them all, it is. A colored girl, by my definition, is a girl of many colors. But she can only see her overall beauty if she can see all the colors of herself. To do that, she has to look deep inside her. And when she looks inside herself, she will find . . . love and beauty.[14]

While the overwhelmingly optimistic presentation might seem philosophically suspect to some critics, Shange consciously validates ideals for these women's survival. While the rainbow works as a metaphor for a collective voice of women of color, it also describes the visual impact of these women moving about the stage in an array of different monochromatic costumes. Visually and aesthetically, these women are a rainbow, and only collectively are they able to dramatize the fullness of black female identity. The rainbow, then, symbolizes a physical beauty in the ethnicity of the black female as well as a spiritual beauty she understands when she becomes aware of her own inner rhythms. And just as there are no distinct lines separating the rainbow's colors, these women are not separated from each other's experiences. Using images of "colored girls" and "rainbow" together reiterates the structural significance of color imagery in the piece and highlights its unconventionality in characterization, as noted by Carol P. Christ:

> The juxtaposition of "colored girl" with "rainbow" enables Black women to see the varied tones of their skin as a reflection of the glorious hues of the rainbow, not as a color to be borne in shame.

And, though colored girls have considered suicide
because they have been abused by white society and
Black men, this need no longer be the case. "The
rainbow" is now understood as an image of their
own beauty, and it "is enuf."[15]

Within the title Shange also clarifies the audience for whom she
writes. While the issues of the play potentially transcend race and
gender, this piece is clearly written by a colored girl "for colored
'girls.'" Shange does not address the piece to colored "women" or
colored "females." Instead, "girls" defines a particular age group:
youths. About the audience for whom she writes, she explains:

I collect dolls . . . because there's a person in me
who's still a little girl and she loves them. I also
collect dolls because I want to give the person in
me who's a little girl things I should have had and
never got. The reason that *for colored girls* is entitled *for colored girls* is that that's who it was for. I
wanted them to have information that I did not
have. I wanted them to know what it was truthfully
like to be a grown woman. I didn't know. All I had
was a whole bunch of mythology—tales and outright
lies. I want a twelve-year-old girl to reach out for
and get some information that isn't just contracep-
tive information but emotional information. . . . If
there is an audience for whom I write, it's the little
girls who are coming of age. I want them to know
that they are not alone and that we adult women
thought and continue to think about them.[16]

Shange offers her piece quite literally to young black girls, hoping
that young girls coming of age will—because of Shange's ability to
present complex issues in their simplest terms—comprehend the full
impact of the issues rendered. *for colored girls* is also a warning to
adolescent girls and the innocent and naive adult female whose
experiences might be the same as or similar to Shange's colored
girls'. While it is doubtful that adolescent girls would be in a Broad-

way audience, Shange offers the piece to the young girl who finds
the choreopoem in a high school or public library:

> I'd like to be part of a collection of books by a
> woman that someone might give a female child. It
> simply didn't exist when I was a child; the books
> weren't there. . . . The mere presence of . . .
> women in print has to be of a moral assistance to
> the young women.[17]

Shange's audience also includes the parents or guardians of an
adolescent black girl, particularly older women, whose task is to
nurture that young girl's emotional and psychological identity.
Referring to Adrienne Rich's *Of Woman Born: Motherhood as Experience and Institution* (1976) and Susan Griffin's *Women and
Nature: The Roaring Inside Her* (1978), Shange defines her role as a
black literary mother-figure as well as a mother to her own adolescent daughter:

> [I]t's the silence of mothers that is so shattering.
> The mothers know that it's a dreadful proposition to
> give up one's life for one's family and one's mate
> and, therefore, lose oneself in the process of caring
> and tending for others. To send one's daughter off
> to that kind of self-sacrifice in silence with no prep-
> aration is a mortal sin to me. To do this without
> telling her that this is a sacrifice is so unnecessary.
> To break this silence is my responsibility, and I'm
> absolutely committed to it. When I die, I will not be
> guilty of having left a generation of girls behind
> thinking that anyone can tend to their emotional
> health other than themselves.[18]

At the same time, *for colored girls* is written for adult women who
have had the experiences of these women but have consequently been
unable to accept themselves as complete individuals. The choreopoem is also for those black women who have literally considered
suicide. For those still troubled by their past experiences, Shange—

having attempted suicide four times—offers personal testimony of survival and spiritual health. Hence, the choreopoem is as much an affirmation of black femaleness sexually and socially as it is a warning against social victimization. She describes her own suicide attempts—once after an attempted rape and another after an abortion —not as desperate actions but as "act[s] of taking control":[19] "I was acting out of the terror. I wanted to see how far I could go in destroying myself. I drank Drano; I took alcohol and valium; I drove my Volvo into the Pacific—all dramatic acts, but ridiculous and humorous even at the time."[20] Shange's emotional and spiritual autobiography is partly revealed in the play's title; the experiences that led to these self-destructive tendencies largely determine the ordering of the poems.

The typography of the title with its slash as punctuation is equally important. The phrase, "for colored girls who have considered suicide," announces the ordering of the choreopoem's scenes, a series of painful female experiences. The second clause "when the rainbow is enuf" presents a temporal move; the "colored girls" move to a different moment in their lives—from moments of despair, depression, anxiety, and frustration, to hope and anticipation. From unpleasant experiences, women emerge triumphant, confident about themselves and "their possibilities" as more self-reliant black females (3). After the Lady in Red tells of lost love and pain, the final moment of the choreopoem is one of ideal celebration deliberately likened to that of a religious conversion at a revival meeting. Rebirth after the storm animates the rainbow vision; and for these black women, a sense of rejuvenated womanhood is indeed "enuf" to make their lives worth continuing. At the end of the play the women are still in the process of self-discovery, of "movin to the ends of their own // rainbows"[21] (67), and the process will continue as long as they are alive and living. Shange does not suggest that their lives will be full of unlimited bliss but that their greater self-knowledge will allow them a fuller existence controlled by their own ideas about the world and themselves. No longer will their behavior and self-perceptions be limited by others' oppressive myths and expectations.

Within the title are at least three other traits that characterize Shange's poetic technique. She not only treats the title as though it were two lines in a poem and substitutes a slash for the standard comma, but she consistently uses lower-case letters and phonetic spellings. Characteristically, Shange, here and across genres, abandons standard English with its rigid rules of punctuation, capitalization, and spelling. In efforts to authenticate her presentation for a black audience, Shange adopts the creative spontaneity and structure of black vernacular with its more flexible syntactic style shaped by oral and aural cadences. The title reveals Shange's style as a poet concerned not only with what words say and mean, but also with how they appear on a printed page. She comments on this emphasis on the visual impact of a word or line:

> It bothers me, on occasion, to look at poems where all the first letters are capitalized. It's very boring to me. That's why I use the lower-case alphabet. Also, I like the idea that letters dance, not just that words dance; of course, the words also dance. I need some visual stimulation, so that reading becomes not just a passive act and more than an intellectual activity, but demands rigorous participation. Furthermore, I think there are ways to accentuate very subtle ideas and emotions so that the reader is not in control of the process. This means that I have to have more tricks than everybody else because I can't let you get away with thinking you know what I mean. After all, I didn't mean whatever you can just ignore. I mean what you have to struggle with, and in this transition the piece becomes special.
>
> The spellings result from the way I talk or the way the character talks, or the way I heard something said. I don't write because words come out of my brain. I write this way because I hear the words.[22]

The colors of the women's costumes identify each character—the Lady in Brown, the Lady in Yellow, the Lady in Blue, the Lady in Orange, the Lady in Purple, the Lady in Red, and the Lady in Green

—and concretize the dramatic impact. Specific names are mentioned in the various women's recitations, but assigning individual names to the characters would undermine Shange's portrayal of a collective black woman's experience. And although our conventional expectations would make a character/ color analysis tempting and often forced upon the presentation, each woman's specific color has little to do with what a character actually says or experiences. Instead, colors represent different experiences and different voices. With this color imagery also comes an ambiguity associated with Shange's assessments of human experience and of male-female relationships.

The unconventionality of *for colored girls* is further evidenced in Shange's inclusion of brown and purple as colors of her rainbow. While purple may represent of indigo and violet, brown is clearly a non-rainbow color. Adding "brown" works effectively on a number of levels. First, brown (or some shade thereof) characterizes the skin color of black people. Secondly, brown connects these colored girls with fundamental elements of earth, evidenced not only in the myriad flower imagery throughout but particularly in the concluding moments of the choreopoem. And finally, brown sets the prevailing mood of the piece, until the closing moment, as one of gloom and despair. The dullness that is also associated with the color brown is transformed into a final moment of natural color—of sisterly communion, communion with nature, and communion of the body and spirit. Self-discovery for the women adds the ultimate spiritual color to their lives, a notion that anticipates Layla's discovery of God— hence her partial escape from a futile existence in "black and white two-dimensional planes"—in *boogie woogie landscapes* (1979).

While the choreopoem is by, for, and about "colored girls," Shange, in another strategically feminist move, uses the word "lady" as opposed to "woman" in defining and re-defining her characters. While Robin Lakoff recognizes the general patriarchal use of "lady" as a sexist euphemism for "woman,"[23] Shange's use of "lady" deliberately redefines a sexist and racist label that simultaneously connotes Eurocentric frivolity, politeness, supposed social elevation, and ultimate unreality. Shange's "ladies" openly renounce the traditional concept of a "lady" as "a woman [implicitly white] whose manners, habits, and sentiments have the refinement

characteristic of the higher ranks of society."[24] Breaking the stereotype of politeness in speech, attitude, and behavior, these females
speak openly and passionately about their experiences, particularly
those deemed social taboo for women—but "mannish" or "manly"
for boys and men—and hence "unladylike": celebrating a female's
loss of virginity in a backseat of a Buick, being pregnant and unwed
and psychologically and socially coerced to have an abortion, and
masturbating. *for colored girls* then is an opportunity for black
women to defy social expectations in their language, actions, and
feelings. To a great extent, their defiance results from their failed
efforts to conform to social ideals for respect, self-definition, and
male companionship. These "ladies," who may lack proper social
graces or fail to exercise prescribed politeness in word and action,
command Shange's respect and admiration because they have survived co-existing gender-race battles, have finally been honest with
themselves, and have found honest living preferable to suicide. The
Lady in Orange admits that conformity has led to self-deception and
anonymity:

> ever since i realized there was someone callt
> a colored girl an evil woman a bitch or a nag
> i been tryin not to be that & leave bitterness
> in somebody else's cup . . .
> . . . .
> . . . i had convinced myself colored girls had no
> right to sorrow/ & i lived & loved that way & kept
> sorrow on the curb. . . . (44-45)

Part of these women's nobility comes in their revisions of their own
self-images. The Lady in Purple is relieved to abandon this game of
lady-like behavior with its goal of male companionship because it
resulted in self-destruction:

> i lived wit myths . . .
> . . . .
> & those scars i had hidden wit smiles & good fuckin
> lay open
> & i dont know i dont know any more tricks

> i am really colored & really sad sometimes & you hurt
> me more than i ever danced outta/ into oblivion isnt far
> enuf to get outta this/ i am ready to die like a lily in the
> desert/ & i cdnt let you in on it cuz i didnt know/ . . .
> . . . .
> . . . lemme love you just like i am/ a colored
> girl/ i'm finally bein real/ no longer symmetrical &
> impervious to pain. (46-47)

Able to acknowledge, accept, and articulate hitherto internalized pain, these black women move toward fuller personal existence. To survive psychologically and spiritually intact the circumstances that led them to consider suicide defines their heroism, the source of their self-respect.

Shange identifies *for colored girls* as a statement of "a young black girl's growing up, her triumphs & errors, our struggle to become all that is forbidden by our environment, all that is forfeited by our gender, all that we have forgotten" (xxi). It is thus dramatically and thematically significant that the black women are each from "outside" a particular metropolis: the Lady in Brown is "outside chicago" (3), the Lady in Yellow is "outside detroit" (3), the Lady in Purple is "outside houston" (3), the Lady in Red is "outside baltimore" (3), the Lady in Green is "outside san francisco" (4), the Lady in Blue is "outside manhattan" (4), and the Lady in Brown is "outside st. louis" (4). Although they are from different geographical regions in North America and bring to the group varied personalities and varying backgrounds and experiences, they have in common their oppression as black females, hence Shange's recognition that the oppression of women is not geographically or environmentally specific. That they are "outside" major cities reiterates their social alienation from the "inside" because of gender and race. This notion of "outside" has been internalized and has become a catalyst for many of the actions in the choreopoem. In addition, they are initially "outside" of themselves, unaware of their true worth. By the end of the choreopoem, the women's negative and externally defined identities as black females are replaced by satisfying inner self-definitions.

* * * * *

While Shange admits that the series of poems now constituting *for colored girls* was rather arbitrarily divided among seven characters, close examination reveals a structurally unified piece on a number of levels. First, as mentioned in the discussion of the title, the ordering of the detailed experiences divides the choreopoem into two parts: the experiences that lead these women to contemplate self-destruction, and the moment that their attitudes about themselves change. Within the two-part structure, the choreopoem can be subdivided into three sections: a young black girl's coming of age, the adult black woman's negative self-image defined by external forces, and the adult black woman's reassessment of her own self-worth. Thematically, the choreopoem moves from innocence to experience, from youth to adulthood, from ignorance to knowledge, from ignorance of self to self-knowledge, from darkness to light, from particular women's experiences to a collective black female experience. Despite the unconventional form of *for colored girls*, it is possible to recognize thematic structure in conventional terms of exposition, rising action, climax, and denouement—a fact that may have contributed to its commercial success.

The Lady in Brown begins the choreopoem with "dark phrases" (1), a poem that functions as the prologue or introduction to the piece. The darkened stage and the propless set reinforce the impact of her monologue about a black girl's plight in a racist and sexist society. The color brown in this opening moment, which contrasts with the revised image of nurturing and fertility at the choreopoem's end, affords an earthiness or rawness of experiences, as well as a kind of social and psychological barrenness. The Lady in Brown's questions form the philosophical foundation of the piece—a search for identity: "Are we ghouls? // children of horror? // . . . are we animals?" (2). With images of fear, emptiness, and confusion, the Lady in Brown begins an investigation of the identity of a black girl for the black girl's own sake. In her talk of a black girl's "interrupted solos // [and] unseen performances" (2), both Shange and the Lady in Brown ask an audience not for pity or sympathy but for compassion and understanding for a black girl's unique predicament. The Lady in Brown begs that the world turn an earnest ear toward a black girl's tune of irregular beats and inconsistent though steady rhythms, irregular and inconsistent defined by others' stan-

dards, of course. Shange's traditionally negative images—irregu-
larities, inconsistencies, dissonance, and disharmony—are, by the
play's end, redefined positively. Not coincidentally, these same
terms are associated with the choreopoem form that Shange envisions
as a unified whole.

A song motif, announced at the outset, is woven effectively
throughout the piece, culminating in the final scene of celebration
through song. While music and song are definitive parts of the
choreopoem, these elements are, for Shange, inseparable from her
existence as a poet, or one who sings. Like musicians, poets are
concerned with rhythms, words, and the aesthetics of sounds.[25] She
even admits typing and composing verse to conscious and unconscious rhythms:

> [S]ometimes I'll hear very particular rhythms
> underneath whatever I'm typing, and this rhythm
> affects the structure of the piece. For instance, if
> I'm hearing a rumba, you'll get a poem that looks
> like a rumba on the page. So the structure is con-
> nected to the music that I hear beneath the words.[26]

Music for Shange also stakes a territorial claim for people of color.
Hence, in a society that reinforces feelings of alienation and displacement for minorities, music is a safe though temporary haven. In
the poem "i live in music" from her poetry collection, *Nappy Edges*
(1978), Shange describes her musical residence:

> i live in music
> is this where you live
> i live here in music
> i live on c [sharp] street
> my friend lives on b [flat] avenue
> do you live here in music
> sound
> falls round me like rain on other folks
> . . . .
> i live in music
>   live in it

> wash in it
> i cd even smell it
> wear sound on my fingers
> sound falls   so fulla music
> ya cd make a river where yr arm is &
> hold yrself
>   hold yrself in a music.[27]

The repetition of "hold yrself" reiterates Shange's belief that people
of color can find a truer identity in the music of their cultures.
Shange does not speak of a particular kind of music. Instead, she
finds music in all sound—from the rhythms of typing, to the particular cadences and intonations of blacks' speech, to the seductive
reticence of a saxophone or bass clarinet. Music, as natural as the
elements, releases and sustains full creative energies, an idea
explored at length in *boogie woogie landscapes*, a companion piece
to *for colored girls*.

Consider the dramatic impact and the cadence of the opening
description—"dark phrases of womanhood" (1). It announces what
for colored girls is about, and the word "phrases" connects both
music and dance to the survival of these black women, to the definition of the choreopoem in general, and particularly to the performance technique of this piece. In dance, "phrases" are "movements
forming a unit in a choreographic pattern," and in music they are
"segments of a composition, usually consisting of four or eight
measures."[28] Shange's consistent use of music terminology at the
opening reinforces the musical theme of the choreopoem:
"half-notes," "rhythm," "tune," "melody-less-ness," "lyrics,"
"solos," "soft strains," "sound," and "melody."[29] Words associated with singing and dance are equally significant thematically:
"dance," "dancin'," "song," "singers," "performances,"
"silence," and "voice." Recognizing that a black girl has a song
and a voice distinctly hers, Shange offers *for colored girls* as that
song, renouncing myths that colored girls are "ghouls," "children of
horror"—"animals."

Not only does each woman's testimony become a complete song
in itself, but each song becomes a note in Shange's entire musical
piece—a piece with varied rhythms, solos, choruses, and crescendos.

Highlighting the significance of music and dance to a black girl's story, the Lady in Brown defines the life of a black girl as "another song with no singers // lyrics/ no voices" (2) and characterizes a black girl as "half-notes scattered // without rhythm/ no tune" (1). While the voices of black men and white women have rung loudly in opposition to their oppression by the white patriarchy, Shange's point is that few efforts have been made to document the very particular plight of black females in North America.[30]

The structural and thematic move from youth and innocence to adulthood and knowledge begins with the women's choral rendition of two traditional black female play songs: "mama's little baby likes shortnin, shortnin" and "little sally walker, sittin in a saucer" (4).[31] These songs represent a kind of cultural and social ideal: trouble-free days of childhood games and complete parental protection from the outside world, times when race and gender are not liabilities for these female children. Appropriately, "little sally walker, sittin in a saucer," a song about dance as an elevated creative expression, is also about escaping from pain and "weepin" through dance. Even in these street play songs, there is often rhythmic physical movement (i.e., dance) and a foremost concern for coordinating rhythmical hand clapping and words. Singing together here represents a bond between these black women whose adult personal lives are diverse but whose childhood and adult experiences as black females are parallel. While Shange does not offer her choreopoem as an exploration of *the* monolithic black girl, she submits these experiences as potentially common to many.

With the Lady in Yellow's memories of her "graduation nite" (5), the choreopoem moves the girls from the playground to the threshold of womanhood and adult life. This move into adulthood adopts the form of a high school commencement ritual. While both male and female adolescents undergo this initiation, the break from parental protection or at least the physical immediacy of that protection is socially different for males and females. Whereas males are expected to be self-sufficient and are socially conditioned to be aggressive in their pursuit of goals, females are traditionally assumed more passive, vulnerable, and in need of parental or male protection and guidance. That the Lady in Yellow speaks positively and una-shamedly about her first sexual encounter renders a daring and important social break in traditional female behavior for Shange's colored girls; it boldly announces Shange's commitment to acknowledging sexuality as a natural dimension of female identity and renounces a traditionally revered notion of female virginity in patriarchal societies. Losing one's virginity, like graduating, is an initiation rite. Yet social responses to males losing their virginity continue to be more celebrated than females' same experience. Women continue to be stifled by social restraints that prohibit sexual freedoms. Uniquely for women in such patriarchal societies, awakening sexuality becomes a social liability.[32] That these two events occur on the same night creates a dramatic transition from childhood and adolescence into womanhood for this female. Coupled with the gaiety of graduation night is the flattery of having a male find her sexually attractive, a detail with which more "radical" feminists might take issue. That this narrator describes her first sexual encounter as "wonderful" (9) reveals uncoerced sexual activity as just as pleasurable for females as traditionally and stereotypically for males:

> bobby started lookin at me
> yeah
> he started lookin at me real strange
> like i waz a woman or somethin/
> started talking real soft
> in the backseat of that ol buick
> WOW
> by daybreak
> i just cdnt stop grinnin. (9)

Shange's focus here is less on Bobby's motives than on this female's decision to lose her virginity. This lost innocence is as celebratory as the graduation night itself. In the Lady in Yellow's account, however, Bobby's motives for seduction are not paramount; instead, Shange emphasizes the unqualified satisfaction that this female experiences after her first sexual encounter. The poem celebrates a woman's conscious decision to act upon her sexual stirrings. She is not raped, coerced, or otherwise unaware of her decisions at the moment—there is no pretense of unwillingness on her part. Moreover, there is no indication that this woman wants lasting romance with this man or any other, as stereotype might have it. She is just as capable of moving on emotionally after this initiation ritual as men allegedly are.

While Shange condones females' sexual liberation both individually and socially, the potential resultant problems are centrally focused in *for colored girls*. First is the black girl's willingness to have her sexuality externally defined, in the above case by the way a male looks at her and desires her. Such a detail in the graduation night story offers another theme that transcends race and gender: allowing one's self-image to be other-defined, a problem painfully voiced later in the Lady in Blue's abortion experience ("abortion cycle #1," 22). A female's awakening sexuality and her deliberate pursuit of such pleasures can lead not only to negative self-image but to emotional and psychological vulnerability and abuse that the sexually active female experiences at the hands of some males. While a female's sexuality defines significant aspects of her personal identity, this same sexuality is potentially the basis of a woman's sufferings and fears.

The choreopoem moves from physical love to a more spiritual love in "now i love somebody more than" (11), a narration of failed expectations. In reconciling her disappointment in Willie Colon for failing to appear at a dance marathon in which she was to participate, she offers an analogy between love and music and love and dance. Music for this Puerto Rican black woman is as spiritually sustaining as honest love. For her, music, like dance, creates momentarily a world removed from all restricting physicalities—skin color, gender, economics, and other environmental constraints. Both dance— "mambo, bomba, merengue" (10)—and Willie Colon's music provide avenues for this woman's total surrender—in music a loss of herself to sound, in dance a loss of herself to sheer physicality. Shange suggests here that dance and music are often as satiating as physical and spiritual love. Despite the differing ancestral and geographic origins of dance—whether the Latin steps of the "mambo, bomba, merengue" or the soulful "bumping" and grinding at the New Carver Homes in "graduation nite"—it is both a liberator and a source of spiritual celebration. This woman's disappointment anticipates the characters' greater disappointments in many of the men with whom they become involved. Her regret and anger are not necessarily self-destructive—in contrast to later episodes—and are soothed by her memory's ability to re-create his music, elevating her despite his individual shortcomings. She explains her love:

> & i love you more than i waz mad
>
> . . . .
>
> & poem is my thank-you for music
> & i love you more than poem
>
> . . . .
>
> te amo mas que   te amo mas que
> when you play
> yr flute. (12-13)

An ambiguous refrain, "i love you more than . . .," repeated by the other characters who have now joined in this recitation and recovery, signals a collective attitude toward black men that the choreopoem challenges. These women have loved men in their lives more than men have loved them, more than these women have loved themselves. As importantly, the phrase might directly address music and its power to liberate this narrator from temporal and physical realities. The music of Willie Colon becomes more celebrated than an attraction to Willie Colon, the person. Through music, the Lady in Blue moves from disappointment, anger, and powerlessness to an inner peace. And this moment of peace, however transient, can be recaptured whenever this woman remembers hearing Colon's flute.

The Lady in Blue's disappointment in Willie Colon—an incident illustrating her inability to control her environment, unlike the Lady in Yellow's actions on her graduation night—prompts "no assistance" (13), a narrative of one-sided romance involving a man who apparently takes for granted a woman's efforts to create and sustain a mutually satisfying relationship. Unlike the Lady in Blue, the Lady in Red, in this instance, takes control of her life by ending this potentially self-destructive relationship. She recalls giving herself earnestly to this man who was either incapable of or unwilling to return her affections:

> without any assistance or guidance from you
> i have loved you assiduously for 8 months 2 wks &

    a day
i have been stood up four times
i've left 7 packages on yr doorstep
forty poems 2 plants & 3 handmade notecards i left
town so i cd send to you have been no help to me
on my job
you call at 3:00 in the mornin on weekdays
so i cd drive 27-1/2 miles cross the bay before i go
    to work
charmin charmin
but you are of no assistance
i want you to know
this waz an experiment
to see how selfish i cd be
if I wd really carry on to snare a possible lover
if I waz capable of debasin my self for the love of
    another
if i cd stand not being wanted
when i wanted to be wanted
& i cannot
so
with no further assistance & no guidance from you
i am endin this affair. (13-14)

This narrative is full of ironies. Most obviously, this woman has not necessarily lost all feelings and attraction to this man, and she is trying to camouflage her hurt. Her head rules, however, and the process of writing a note that expresses both her hurt and anger allows her to better objectify the destructiveness of such a relationship. And while there is implied physical love between the couple, a relationship of mutuality does not exist. By itemizing her efforts to develop this relationship beyond sex, this woman reveals her eventual levelheadedness in ending the destructive affair and by acknowledging the irrational lengths to which she went to create and then salvage what was not meant to be. It is not coincidental that Shange makes both the Lady in Blue and the Lady in Red poets who are empowered by and rejuvenated through words in these unsatisfying relationships. The Lady in Red sarcastically calls herself "selfish" in her repeated efforts to realize spiritual commitment from this man. Her selfishness is her desire for a committed relationship with this man. His implied selfishness is that such a relationship need not move beyond his own physical needs. Despite the feistiness of the monologue, this woman's pain from being emotionally neglected is evident.

The Lady in Red's experience offers a transition into the Lady in Orange's declaration of herself as a poet who, like the Lady in Blue, exorcises painful emotions through dance. This poem further illustrates the power and accessibility of dance, particularly when words become barriers to communication. Dance, for Shange, is a survival tool; and for blacks especially, it is a liberating force. In her novel *Sassafrass, Cypress & Indigo* (1982), Shange redefines the stereotype of blacks' talents for singing and dancing:

> what does it mean that blk folks cd sing n dance?
> why do we say that so much/ we dont know what
>   we mean/
> . . . .
> . . . it
> dont mean we got rhythm/ it dont mean the slop or
> the hully gully/
> or this dance in houston callt "the white boy"/ it
> dont mean just
> what we do all the time/ it's how we remember
>   what
> cannot be said/
> that's why the white folks say it aint got no form/
> what was the form
> of slavery/ what was the form of jim crow/ & how
> wd they
> know. . . .[33]

More than free-style movement and even stylized choreography, dance spiritually elevates and liberates the performer. For the Lady in Blue, dance is an occasion to "forget all abt words// [and] . . . definitions" (14)—her socially defined inadequacies, others' harsh words toward her, and others' negative definitions of her. Like music, dance saves and sustains. Shange recasts this racist stereotype as a black cultural reality and thereby presents it as an instinctive and spontaneous response to the inadequacies of verbal language in expressing experiences particularly of oppressed persons. The Ladies in Yellow and Brown admit this very salvation through dance: "we gotta dance to keep from cryin // we gotta dance to keep from dyin" (15). Shange's irony surfaces particularly in the poem's reference to "the white boy," a dance that mocked a stereotypical awkwardness of white males' dancing. Coupled with stereotyping to combat stereotyping, a bitterness at past injustices and sufferings of African Americans at the hands of white racists prevails in the poem.

Appropriately, dance is also a metaphor for physical lovemaking in the Lady in Yellow's talk of "bump[ing] . . . // up & down—up & down the new carver homes" (8) on graduation night. Shange's choice of music from black popular culture is particularly effective in the Lady in Yellow's reference to the Dells and their popular sixties' tune "Stay." While the tune is lilting and conducive to "slow dancing," the title expresses the character's desire to freeze this moment of physical and spiritual satisfaction. But just as lovemaking is temporally experienced, so too are dance and music and the physical crossover from virginity to "womanhood." While the "bump" was a common free-style dance in the late seventies wherein partners collided rhythmically and usually at the hips, the word can denote "thrusting the pelvis forward, in or as if in a burlesque striptease."[34] Sensuality is further created euphemistically by the Lady in Yellow in "graduation nite" (5)—"doin nasty ol tricks," "hot," "inta some business," and "gettin it." The graduation night monologue overflows with references to those body parts involved in lovemaking— "hips," "legs," and "thighs." Martin's "slipp[ing] his leg round my thigh" and their mutual "up & down" dance movements anticipate the sexual encounter that follows. The Lady in Orange continues the dance/lovemaking analogy when she imagines herself with a dance/love partner:

> our whole body
> wrapped like a ripe mango
> ramblin whippin thru space

>   on the corner in the park
>   where the rug useta be. (15)

For this black woman, dance comforts, consoles, and saves her from self-destruction. It also allows for spiritual expression when words and definitions fail to convey the complexities of her emotional experience. The Lady in Orange explains:

>   i dont wanna write
>   in english or spanish
>   i wanna sing   make you dance
>   like the bata   dance   scream
>   twitch hips wit me cuz
>   i done forgot all abt words
>   aint got no definitions
>   i wanna whirl
>   with you. (14)

Shange explains her own spiritual satisfaction and self-discovery through dance:

>   [W]ith dance I discovered my body more intimately
>   than I had imagined possible. With the acceptance
>   of the ethnicity of my thighs & backside, came a
>   clearer understanding of my voice as a woman & as
>   a poet. The freedom to move in space, to demand
>   of my own sweat a perfection that could continually
>   be approached, though never known, waz poem to
>   me, my body & mind ellipsing, probably for the
>   first time in my life. (*for colored girls* xv)

Dance allows these women to know and accept their bodies, a first step toward reclaiming authority in their lives. Improvised physical dance movements as poems are being rendered[35] as well as the discussions of dance reiterate the extent to which Shange's own background as a dancer moves to the forefront in her choreopoems.

Shange combines dance with still another alternative for an oppressed black female's survival: dream and creative imagination.

Sechita, a young dancer in a rowdy redneck bar in Mississippi, is a black woman able to triumph over social adversity. A progression from the social shame of the woman in the abortion poem, this poem describes a woman who, like the Lady in Yellow in "graduation nite," might by social standards be considered morally loose. Sechita's costume is deliberately that of a stereotypical prostitute:

> her splendid red garters/ gin-stained n itchy on her
> thigh/ blk-diamond stockings darned wit yellow
> threads/ an ol starched taffeta can-can fell abundantly
> orange/ from her waist round the splinterin chair. (24)

Her brightly-colored costume contrasts her mood of despair as she feels degraded and belittled in a job where white men throw coins toward her genitals as she performs. Whatever the circumstances that brought Sechita to this bar in these conditions, she is disillusioned and dissatisfied, believing that "god seemed to be wipin his feet in her face/" (25). The traditional masculine Christian God here contributes to her suffering whereas the final moments of the choreopoem move the women toward an awareness of an inner god of realized selfhood that spiritually satisfies.

Yet Sechita is not without creative resources; during her performance she distances herself from the immediate degradation through imaginings. Thus, when she dances, she is no longer "reglar" Sechita with heavy make-up; dance and imagination transform her into "sechita/ egyptian/ goddess of creativity/ 2nd millennium . . ." (24) and

> she suddenly threw/ her leg full-force/ thru the
> canvas curtain/ a deceptive glass stone/ sparkled/
> malignant on her ankle/ her calf waz tauntin in the
> brazen carnie lights/ the full moon/ sechita/ goddess/
> of love/ egypt/ 2nd millennium/ performin the rites/
> the conjurin of men/ conjurin the spirit/ in natchez/
> . . . .
> . . . sechita's legs slashed furiously thru the
> cracker nite/ & gold pieces hittin the makeshift
> stage/ her thighs/ they were aimin coins tween her

thighs/ sechita/ egypt/ goddess/ harmony/ kicked
viciously thru the night/ catchin stars tween her toes.
(25-26)

Very consciously, she transforms the act of a black woman's dancing
before a rowdy and lustful audience of "crackers" to one of power
over these white men.[36] As an Egyptian goddess, she is no longer
exploited; instead, the men are under her creative spell and have no
choice but to give her their money. Through dance and imagination,
Sechita gives her ritual performance cosmic proportions. Her story
especially anticipates the thematic foundation of *spell #7* (1979)
where Shange explores individual creative fantasy as another liberating strategy for the oppressed. Sechita's story also connects the
mystic powers of womanhood with women's past and present lives.
Sechita's retreat to ancient African female rituals—conjuring and
dance—empowers her to transcend both temporal and physical boundaries.[37] That Sechita images herself as an empowered Egyptian
goddess is Shange's celebration of Afrocentrism and an abandoning
of western ideals that particularly restrict African American women's
creative possibilities.

The Lady in Brown's narrative of her childhood attraction to
Haitian liberator Toussaint L'Ouverture illustrates Shange's belief
that females, like Sechita, have always used creative imagination to
liberate them from an immediately oppressive reality. In this childhood reminiscence, the Lady in Brown tells of her discovery of
Haitian liberator Toussaint L'Ouverture through reading, an avenue
that removes this youngster from her socially restrictive environment.
In "toussaint" (26), the Lady in Brown explains the childhood
impact he had on her life:

TOUSSAINT L'OUVERTURE
became my secret lover at the age of 8
i entertained him in my bedroom
widda flashlight under my covers
way inta the night/ we discussed strategies
how to remove white girls from my hopscotch games
& etc. (28)

Even as a child, Shange was keenly aware of racial injustices and the upheaval of school integration in St. Louis in the fifties; this awareness is a major issue in both *spell #7* and her closely autobiographical novel *Betsey Brown* (1985). In meeting a boy who alleges that his name is Toussaint Jones and that his ideas about resisting racial oppression parallel L'Ouverture's and her own, she willingly parts with her imaginary hero. Indeed, even Shange's younger females can separate fantasy and reality. Whether this young boy's name is or is not Toussaint is not Shange's focus here. Instead, it is on this young girl's conscious decision to abandon a sustaining fantasy for a new and exciting reality.

The complex personal and political realities surrounding female sexuality as a liability form a second thematic and structural movement of *for colored girls* and is founded upon a basic feminist issue: a girl's coming of age is simultaneously a time for celebration and fear. Protesting against the reality that a woman's sexuality is often a self-endangering asset, Shange bitterly acknowledges that any woman can fall prey to the brute force of any male "fulla his power" (39) at any time. In such a simple statement of fact, Shange captures what is at the heart of a rapist's motives: a desire to control his environment. The power to control a woman's life, her livelihood, then becomes a test of his alleged manhood. As Marie M. Fortune clarifies, "Rape is only pseudosexual because it is committed in order to fulfill non-sexual needs related to power, anger, and aggression. . . . Anger and the desire to dominate and control the victim are the primary motivations of the rapist."[38] From celebrating the female body through sexuality and dance, Shange explores the complexities of rape most straightforwardly. Like "dark phrases" (1), "latent rapists'"[39] (17) is not an account of one woman's personal experience. While it is both a personal and political statement of the injustices suffered specifically by females because of their gender, all of the women join in this redefinition of the rapist and the nature of rape; they become the threatened voice of any female who has or might at any moment become any male's victim.[40]

In simplest terms, a rapist is redefined: "a friend is hard to press charges against" (17). Shange's use of "hard," "press," and "against" conjures the image of the erect penis "hardened" for penetration "against" the victim's body and "against" the victim's will. The use of "charge" also reiterates the aggressive physical force of the act. This redefinition highlights an irony that has only recently attracted social and critical attention—acquaintance or confidence rape. A rapist, Marie Fortune confirms,

> may be a neighbor, date, friend, classmate, co-worker, family member, etc. The rapist has some kind of prior relationship with the victim, which he uses as a way of establishing trust and then *betrays*. . . . The victim of this rapist in particular may be hesitant to seek assistance or report the assault because she . . . feels that no one will believe it was rape since she . . . had a relationship with the person. (emphasis mine)[41]

For Shange, rape is the ultimate treachery of a male against the source of his own life—a woman. That same betrayal is rendered in Shange's use of "friend" as the newly defined rapist.[42] The women explain that any male—boyfriend, lover, employer, co-worker, husband, brother, and even father or son—is subject to "latent rapists' bravado" (19). Sarcastically, the Lady in Red suggests that "the nature of rape has changed" (21). Indeed, the nature of the violent act itself has not changed; the perceived change is the recognition that rapists do not conform to a stereotype. Shange warns females against this myth of the stereotypical rapist; he need no longer

> . . . be a stranger
> . . . .
> someone you never saw
> a man wit obvious problems
> pin-ups attached to the insides of his lapels
> ticket stubs from porno flicks in his pockets
> a lil dick
> or a strong mother
> or just a brutal virgin. (17-18)

A rapist need no longer be the outwardly recognized social deviant as outdated notions would define him. As Shange reveals, he need simply be a male who feels violent and powerless. The women assert that "women relinquish all personal rights // in the presence of a man // who apparently *cd* be considered a rapist" (20, emphasis mine). Contrary to what many males hear in such a statement, Shange does not say that every man *is* a rapist. Nor is this issue held up for public acknowledgement and discussion meant to thrust women into a state of constant paranoia. Rather, she stresses the urgency of women's and men's awareness of the everpresent possibility of sexual violence with which women everywhere live at all times.

That "a rapist is always to be a stranger // to be legitimate" (17) is Shange's assault on a legal system and a prevailing social attitude that further victimizes female rape victims. While "women who have been raped by strangers develop fears of the unfamiliar," the woman in acquaintance rape suffers "a triple-barreled assault. . . . Not only is the woman assaulted physically and emotionally . . . her sense of trust and integrity in friendship is also destroyed"[43] as well as her confidence in her own judgement—all as a result of an act which a patriarchal legal system does not consider a "legitimate" violation. And while a man who suffers from "latent rapists' bravado" may or may not be caught, convicted, and sentenced, the assaulted female is "left wit the scars [physical and emotional]" (19) and multiple reasons to consider suicide—physically, socially, and psychologically.

Through role-playing, these women voice the absurdities that an unsympathetic, condemning legal system uses to legitimize males' aggressive sexual behavior, to suggest that victims are in some way responsible for provoking such attacks, and to undermine a woman's authority and credibility:

> lady in red
> if you know him
> you must have wanted it
> lady in purple
> a misunderstanding
> lady in red
> you know
> these things happen
> lady in blue
> are you sure

> you didn't suggest
>   lady in purple
> had you been drinkin. (17)

Those in control—presumably and usually male—of the justice system
fail to realize that "no woman asks to be raped by the way she
dresses or talks, or by the places she goes."[44] Feminist Susan
Brownmiller clarifies: "All rape is an exercise in power, but some
rapists have an edge that is more than physical. They operate within
an institutionalized society that works to their advantage and in
which a victim has little chance to redress her grievance."[45] As does
Brownmiller, Shange objects to the notions of the predominantly
male disciples of Freud—and not a few females—who apologize for
male sexual aggression and inadvertently justify rape.[46] In "i usedta
live in the world" (39), the Lady in Blue shows the physical and
social restrictions placed on women who, because of their gender,
are forced to "come in at dusk // [and] stay close to the curb" in a
"universe of six blocks" (39). Indeed, rape is far more than a
"misunderstanding," as the courts would often have it; it

> is a form of mass terrorism, for the victims of rape
> are chosen indiscriminately, but the propagandists
> for male supremacy broadcast that it is women who
> cause rape by being unchaste or in the wrong place
> at the wrong time—in essence, by behaving as
> though they were free. . . . The fear of rape keeps
> women off the streets at night. Keeps women at
> home. Keeps women passive and modest for fear
> that they be thought provocative.[47]

Being born female in patriarchal societies means being born with
limitations, a feminist issue Shange expands in *boogie woogie landscapes* and in *From Okra to Greens*. And beneath this feminist issue
is the added dimension of racism that makes realities for black
women and other women of color doubly oppressive when the voices
of authority are usually white males'.

From physical, psychological, and social sufferings inflicted
upon female victims of rape, the choreopoem moves to still another

distinctly female suffering also related to female sexuality—abortion. Whether a pregnancy results from a consensual or coerced sexual encounter, abortion itself is a metaphoric rape that can also leave deep and lasting scars. "abortion cycle #1" (22) details the violent procedural invasion of a female's body:

> tubes tables white washed windows
> grime from age wiped over once
> legs spread
> anxious
> eyes crawling up on me
> eyes rollin in my thighs
> metal horses gnawin my womb
> . . . .
> & i didnt say a thing
> not a sign
> or a fast scream
> to get those eyes offa me
> get them steel rods outta me
> this hurts
> this hurts
> & nobody came. (22-23)

This account of an abortion experience works imagistically on a number of levels. Images of "legs spread," "anxious," "crawling up on me," "rollin in my thighs," "tween my legs," and "gnawin my womb" recapture the action and atmosphere of both forced and consensual sexual intercourse. The language of the poem, however, clarifies this experience as one of great physical and psychological torture and discomfort. Images of blood and shattered bones reinforce not only the physical violence of the surgery itself but also the effect on a victim of sexual assault. That rape victims are often silenced by fear for their lives parallels the silent terror of this gender-specific experience. Adrienne Rich highlights this trauma:

> A man may beget a child in passion or by rape,
> and then disappear; he need never see or consider
> child or mother again. Under such circumstances,

> the mother faces a range of painful, socially
> weighted choices: abortion, suicide, abandonment
> of the child, infanticide, the rearing of a child
> branded "illegitimate," usually in poverty, always
> outside the law. . . . Whatever her choice, her body
> has undergone irreversible changes, her mind will
> never be the same, her future as a woman has been
> shaped by the event.[48]

The Lady in Blue's greatest suffering occurs inwardly because of
social expectation. While she admits that becoming pregnant was a
mistake, her greatest burden is shame,[49] a kind of social and psychological suicide. The invasion of her body—becoming pregnant acci-
dentally—leaves her empty and in pain:

> i really didnt mean to
> i really didnt think i cd
> just one day off . . .
> . . . .
> i cdnt have people
> lookin at me
> pregnant
> i cdnt have my friends see this
> dyin dangling tween my legs
> . . . .
> once i waz pregnant & ashamed of myself. (22-23)

As in the Lady in Yellow's experience with Bobby in the back seat of
the Buick, there is no emphasis here on the male as one who has
abandoned this pregnant female. Instead, this female shares the same
sexual freedom but is "penalized" by biology. Pregnancy, abortion,
rape, and the isolation and alienation—"afterlife"—of each of these
physical traumas are sufferings that a female experiences alone,
despite the fact that a male actively participated in the sexual encounter.[50]

On another level, this abortion poem acknowledges a broader,
more metaphoric rape of the female again because of her biology.
The scenario recreates the physical and psychological invasion of a

female's body during any "routine" gynecological examination with the phallic imagery of "steel rods" probing internally. With this physical invasion and the vulnerability of the stirruped reclining position of a female during such an examination is the fact that "most gynecologists are males, . . . a colossal comment on 'our' [patriarchal] society"[51] where males are in yet another authorial position over women's bodies.

The story of the Passion Flower chronicles the revenge of all women who have been psychologically or physically abused by men. As if responding to the issue of women's sexuality being a liability, this woman plays a game of sexual seduction to avenge herself and her tortured sisters. Unlike Sechita's, however, the Passion Flower's game is not one of survival but one of shouldering the burdens of all women who have been made powerless by a man. The Passion Flower experiences a fleeting physical and psychological power over men who predictably fall prey to her "feminine charms":

> . . . she wanted to be unforgettable
> she wanted to be a memory
> a wound   to every man
> arragant enough to want her. (34)

Her attractiveness even threatens other women fearful of losing their male companions to her. Making herself physically attractive for men in much the same way that Sechita dresses and arranges herself for her male audience, the Passion Flower calculates her every move in the presence of potential male prey:

> she glittered in heat
> & seemed to be lookin for rides
> when she waznt & absolutely
> eyed every man who waznt lame white or noddin out
> she let her thigh slip from her skirt
> crossin the street
> she slowed to be examined
> & never looked back to smile
> or acknowledge a sincere 'hey mama'
> or meet the eyes of someone

purposely findin sometin to do in
her direction. (32-33)

Reversing gender-roles of a stereotypical one-night stand scenario,[52]
this woman lures men to her bed, drains them of their sexual energies, then orders them from her bed, her house, and her life without
warning or explanation. The Passion Flower, who is not "in heat"
sexually but "in heat" for revenge, ostensibly wants such a setup
though it only temporarily insulates her from the realities of male
sexual and social domination:

> . . . she glittered honestly
> delighted she waz desired
> & allowed those especially
> schemin/ tactful suitors
> to experience her body & spirit
> tearin/ so easily blendin with theirs/
> & they were so happy
> & lay on her lime sheets full & wet
> from her tongue   she kissed
> them reverently   even ankles
> edges of beards. . . . (34)

The language of the passage reiterates the multilayered ironies in the
scene. First, the Passion Flower is not glittering "honestly." She
glitters purposely to attract and devour. And while the men may
think themselves the schemers to have their way with her, it is she
who is the ultimate schemer. Although the men experience the
Passion Flower's body, they do not experience her fullness spiritually. There is deliberately no meshing of the spirit here on the Passion Flower's part; her only goal is power and revenge. The narrator's authorial position is evident in her depiction of the shallowness
of men who "were so happy" (34) just to experience this woman's
sexuality. While these males' lust is the source of their alleged
manhood, it is also the source of their vulnerability. For the Passion
Flower, the sex act is not one of physical pleasure but of an aggressive assertion of power over men. Consequently, her empty triumph
in the end is as shallow as the men "who fell prey to the // dazzle of

[her] hips painted with // orange blossoms & magnolia scented wrists" (36). Once the game has ended and the men have been forced to leave, she washes away her body decorations and becomes a "reglar colored girl // [still] fulla the same malice" (37). Such a physically dangerous and psychologically and emotionally stagnant life offers only an immediate and deceptive satisfaction in this avenging of her sisters. That she cries herself to sleep—her metaphorical withering as a flower—indicates the Passion[less] Flower's confusion and despair at being compelled to play this avenging game—her "night's work" (36)—to prove a woman's power over men. This woman is ultimately trapped in a game that is spiritually and physically unsatisfying. So while she momentarily controls men physically, she does not control her own life. In contrast to her male victims who "were so happy" experiencing her sexual passion, she is detached and saddened by her compulsions, by doing without "what she really wanted"—a spiritually honest connection with a sincere man.

The Passion Flower's story is one of contradictions. First, that Shange identifies the female as a "passion flower" is ambiguous. The Passion Flower's encounters with men are filled not with the passion of love but with the passion of anger and resentment at men's ritual mistreatment of women. The poem, densely packed with references to plants (ivy, orange blossoms, magnolia scent, roses, lilies), colors (orange, aqua, iridescent, pastel, lime), and butterflies creates an Edenic setting that contrasts with the sterility of the Passion Flower's orchestrated life of self-destruction. The seduction game itself, with its glittering jewels and alluring fragrances, camouflages her own despair and loneliness, and she is anything but "delighted" that men only want her sexually.

Turning from the physical and psychological assaults on black women by men who rape and scheme, the choreopoem moves toward a woman's spiritual betrayal in a romantic relationship. The Lady in Blue's "now i love somebody more than" (11) first sounded the betrayal of women by men in matters of romance. That betrayal takes the form of a one-sided romance in the Lady in Red's "no assistance (13). Still moving toward more realized sisterhood—realized especially through shared sufferings—"pyramid" (41) is an account of three women whose friendship is first ended then made stronger because of their inadvertent involvement with the same man. A complicated poem, it shows the intricate networks and boundaries of friendship and romance:

> we all saw him at the same time
> & he saw us
> i felt a quick thump in each one of us
> didnt know what to do
> we all wanted what waz comin our way
> so we split
> but he found one
> & she loved him
>
> the other two were tickled
> & spurned his advances. (42)

The friendship between these women is based on trust and loyalty. They "split" to allow each one equal opportunity to have the male initiate a romance. In the detail of "he found one," there is no evidence that this man was searching for anything special in a female companion. That each woman desires a fulfilling romance is evidenced in the narrator's acknowledgment that the woman whom he pursued "loved him." Pleased that their friend found romance, the other two "spurned his advances," an overt indication of his insincerity to the first woman, their friend. The second woman falls prey to his deception as well, primarily out of her own need for love, not out of deliberate betrayal of her friend. That the man "waz what they were lookin for" (42) provided the test of their loyalties. The second woman is torn between her loyalty to her friend and her need to love and be loved:

> . . . i dont wanna hurt you
> but you know i need someone now
> & you know
> how wonderful he is
> her friend cdnt speak or cry
> they hugged & went to where he waz
> wit another woman. (43)

Irony resounds in the detail that the women initially thought this man was "wonderful" and "what they were lookin for." The poem also reiterates the implicit role of sexuality in providing a foundation for fuller romance. That each woman "felt a quick thump" suggests the physical attraction these women have to this man, a physical attraction that leads them to consider further romantic possibilities despite their reservations. The man's involvement with the third friend proves his triple infidelity. Hence, when confronted by the three women, he can only "smile a lot" (44), revealing his own shallowness or their naivete. This final scene of "pyramid" foreshadows the culminating moment of the choreopoem—one of shared sisterhood and of self-love:

> she [friend three] held her head on . . .
> the lap of her sisters soakin up tears
> each understandin how much love stood between
>   them
> how much love between them
> love between them
> love like sisters (44).

The women's shared betrayals by the same man move them toward renewed sisterhood and renewed personal strength through that sisterhood, just as the sufferings the women have met with at the hands of some men move them toward self-discovery.

    The "no more love poems" (44) series defines the identity of a black woman in her newfound selfhood. Her first step toward self-actualization is realizing and accepting that she is not "symmetrical & // impervious to pain." Her efforts to conform to social expectation and to deny instinctive responses to her particular experiences and circumstances have meant pain, betrayal, rejection, and self-destruction—scars hitherto camouflaged "wit smiles & good fuckin" (46). The Lady in Orange clarifies:

>   . . . this is not a love poem/
> . . . .
> . . . this is a requium for myself/ cuz i have died in a
> real way/ . . . .

. . . .
real dead lovin is here for you now/ cuz i dont know
anymore/ how to avoid my own face wet wit my
tears/ cuz i had convinced myself colored girls had no
right to sorrow/ & i lived & loved that way & kept
sorrow on the curb/ allegedly for you/ but i know I did
it for myself/. (45)

Although this black woman has been the target of some men's abuse
physically and emotionally, the metaphoric "death," or suicide,
results from social conformity and personal self-neglect. The pain
from forced pretensions and internalized negative self-images has left
her even more battered, an image that opens the choreopoem. Significantly, this black woman does accept partial responsibility for her
own self-destruction. Her self-acknowledgment becomes a major step
toward her independence and self-definition:

. . . i dont know any more tricks
i am really colored & really sad sometimes and you hurt
me more than i ever danced outta/ into oblivion isnt far
enuf to get outta this/ i am ready to die like a lily in the
desert/ & i cdnt let you in on it cuz i didnt know. (46)

Having experienced rejection, infidelity, rape, abortion, and disappointment, and having worked to camouflage or escape that hurt
through seduction games, dance, and imagination, the collective
black woman is finally able to articulate her need to love and to be
loved spiritually; she is finally able to abandon prescribed social
roles and to admit her own vulnerabilities. The Lady in Yellow
articulates this self-discovery:

i've lost it
touch wit reality/ i dont know who's doin it
i thot i waz but i waz so stupid i waz able to be hurt
& that's not real/ not anymore/ i shd be immune/ if
i'm still alive & that's what i waz discussin/ how i am
still alive & my dependency on other livin beins for
love i survive on intimacy & tomorrow/ that's all i've

> got goin & the music waz like smack & you knew abt
> that & still refused my dance waz not enuf/ & it waz
> all I had but bein alive & bein a woman & bein
> colored is a metaphysical dilemma/ i havent conquered
> yet. (47-48)

Shange uses "metaphysical" in her assessment of black female experience as one that, while based on the physicalities of race and
gender, creates suffering far beyond the physical. She also demonstrates the physical manifestations of self-perceived spiritual barrenness. At this moment, the women realize collectively that the love
they have given some men has been consistently abused. Their love,
they then see, is "too delicate, too beautiful, too sanctified, too
saturday night, too complicated, too music, and too magic" (49) to
be trampled upon by an insensitive man. Not only have the women
moved toward self-redefinition, even their language—making nouns
adjectives—becomes a black cultural move toward self-empowerment. And not only do these women acknowledge their unique
position in the social and political order, but their knowledge is a
declaration that they are no longer spiritually or socially dead, no
longer "clothed in silence"; they now hear and recognize "the
sounds of their own voices."

Appropriately, such a self-realization leads into the Lady in
Green's rendition of "stuff" (52), wherein she accuses a man of
stealing part of her identity. What the black male left behind and
could not steal from her continues to define her black femaleness—
her "big thighs/ [and] lil tits" (46), her shapely rear, her laugh, her
allegedly "unladylike" manner of sitting, her toes, her unmanicured
fingernails, her scarred arm, her irregular rhythms, and her imperfect
voice. These details highlight Shange's belief that much of a black
woman's identity lies in her ethnic physicalities.[53] The Lady in
Green, in her celebration of a new freedom to be herself with no
concern for impressing anyone with verbal and behavioral politeness
or emotional indifference, signifies the voice of a self-actualized
black girl initiated into womanhood. The Lady in Green reveals:

> somebody almost walked off wid alla *my* stuff
> not *my* poems or a dance *i* gave up in the street

. . . .
                            . . . somebody
almost run off wit alla *my* stuff/ & *i* didnt bring anythin
but the kick & sway of it the perfect ass for *my* man &
none of it is theirs this is *mine*/ ntozake 'her own
things'/ that's *my* name/ now give me *my* stuff/ *i* see
ya hidin *my* laugh/ & how *i* sit wif *my* legs open
sometimes/ to give *my* crotch some sunlight/ & there
goes *my* love *my* toes *my* chewed up finger nails/
. . . .
. . . *i* wants *my*
things/ *i* want *my* arm wit the hot iron scar/ & *my*
leg wit the flea bite/ *i* want *my* calloused feet & quik
language back in *my* mouth. . . . (52-53; emphasis
mine)

Shange's use of the word "stuff" makes clear the connections she
realizes between a woman's spiritual and sexual identity. To men
who objectify women, a woman's sexuality is her "stuff," something
he feels he "takes" or "gets" during any intimate encounter.
Shange further particularizes "stuff" as it relates to the historical
objectification and devaluing of black women as black and white
men's sexual pawns and as the antithesis of the white female ideal.
Black female identity is "stuff" in the sense of "worthless objects or
junk"[54] only to an unthinking "man whose ego walked // round like
Rodan's shadow" (54). To the victim of this metaphoric theft, her
identity—dance, sexuality, laughter, pain, and "quick language"—is
much more than "stuff," and she knows fully well that "someone"
is a man with whom she has been romantically and/or sexually
involved. She also realizes that this man does not "almost" walk
away with her identity by force; she accepts responsibility for allowing a man—or anyone—so dangerously close to changing her identity.
This narrator's repetition of first person nominative, objective, and
possessive pronouns adds to the dramatic effectiveness of the poem
and stresses emphasis on self-possession, on possessing without full
awareness of what one possesses, on giving away and repossessing.
Shange expands this idea of the colored girl coming to accept her
physical body in Layla's story in *boogie woogie landscapes*. Robin

Lakoff summarizes the unique pain of women of color who fall short of an alleged beauty ideal:

> As painful as is the ordeal of women of the dominant culture who spend so much of their money, their time, and their emotions trying to live up to the modern ideal of beauty, how much deeper is the agony of the woman who—whatever she does —inevitably must find in the mirror that her hair is too kinky, or too straight, or too black, that her nose is too broad, that her lips are too full, that her eyes are too narrow, or slanted, or too dark, and if this is not enough, that her skin is irrevocably the wrong color. . . . In her quest for assimilation, for acceptance, she might try to forget her language, her culture, even her whole behavioral style. But the color of her skin, the shape of her eyes, the texture of her hair, the form of her body, will speak more clearly than her perfectly shaped words.[55]

Lakoff suggests here the creative, intellectual, and spiritual limitations others automatically prescribe for and ascribe to any black girl based on what meets their eyes. Redefining female beauty, Shange's colored girls abandon the dominant culture's standards: their speech is quick, their attitudes belligerent, their actions and behavior unpretentious. In short, these "black women are [stereotypically] everything the lady is not."[56] Shange's colored girls are more than society allows them to be. They are free and honest, and have survived challenges that the traditional "lady" would never have to face.

Considering a rather conventional structure of the play and the overall ordering of poems, it seems that the climax or turning point in *for colored girls* occurs in the Beau Willie Brown-Crystal episode. And while the women have moved toward greater self-awareness in episodes before this moment, the gender-specific nature of the loss here seems the most complex and tragic. Not surprisingly, it is this episode that critics use to allege that Shange presents all black men as insensitive brutes with violent tempers, ready to destroy.[57] This scene represents an ultimate feeling of powerlessness for a woman in the spectrum of female loss and suffering presented throughout the choreopoem. Perhaps greater than infidelity, rejection, rape, and abortion is the suffering Crystal, a mother, experiences as she witnesses her two children being dropped from a fifth-story apartment window by their father, the man she loves. While it is Beau Willie who actually drops the children, particular attention to character motives during the episode reveals that both Crystal and Beau Willie sacrifice their children because of their own selfishness and their inability to communicate true feelings to one another. The Lady in Red's simultaneous intertwining of both Crystal and Beau Willie's perspectives in the story is Shange's means of seducing the audience into this intensely emotional and contradictory moment. This blending of voice further dramatizes the complexity of the couple's circumstances and highlights their overall victimization.

Over a three-day period of extreme physical and verbal violence, Beau Willie Brown and Crystal torture each other to the breaking point. Since it is Beau Willie who drops the children, all attention generally falls upon him as a destructive maniac and less attention is paid to Crystal. While Shange does not excuse Beau Willie's final act of control over Crystal, she does not present him without sympathy or his life without complexity. He is addicted to drugs and alcohol and is a Vietnam veteran betrayed by a country and a social and legal system for which he has fought. Having failed at efforts to get an education and to hold a job, Beau Willie, frustrated by his situation, becomes destructive even toward that which he loves most—his girlfriend (and intended wife) and his own children. "There waz no air" (58) describes Beau Willie's life alone, without Crystal and his children, as well as the tense atmosphere of this "family" dynamic preceding the tragedy. Sandra Hollin Flowers offers insight into Beau Willie's complex character:

> Beau Willie Brown is the quintessential black man
> of his generation [Vietnam era]. By this, I do not
> mean, nor does Shange intend to imply, that Beau
> Willie Brown is all there is to black manhood. Conversely, I am not suggesting that the political realities embodied in Beau Willie justify his treatment or
> his attitude toward Crystal. Instead, I believe that

> Shange's compassion for black men surfaces most
> noticeably in this poem and that her characteriza-
> tion of Beau Willie recognizes some of the external
> factors which influence relationships between black
> men and women.[58]

Shange does show that Beau Willie is a victim of a racist and capitalist society that defines manhood as the ability to be economically,
physically, and psychologically able to care for oneself and one's
family. And while Beau Willie and Crystal wish to embrace traditional values of family and marriage, they represent the antithesis of
a social ideal.[59] There is no real evidence that these two do not love
each other. Yet their love is not able to overcome the economic and
social powerlessness of their circumstances. Beau Willie, recognizing
his own destruction, sees marrying Crystal and living with his children as salvation. However, as Flowers adds, Beau Willie's dropping
his children to their death—an unpremeditated display of his authority
over Crystal—symbolizes his own ultimate self-destruction.[60]

Yet Crystal is not without responsibility for her own suffering in
this episode, just as the Lady in Green is partially responsible for
allowing someone to "almost" steal her identity. Shange insists that
socially conditioned responses to males' realities as a primary focus
do not allow for the recognition and full consideration of the complexities of Crystal's circumstances and actions. Hence, Shange
argues, too much attention is given to Beau Willie with the faulty
assumption that he represents all black men. Certainly Crystal's story
is one of ultimate vulnerability; Shange explains:

> The pain I've had about people responding to Beau
> Willie Brown is that they so very often don't under-
> stand that Crystal had no more idea of what she was
> doing than he did. And [she is] just as pitiful and
> just as in need of love and respect as Beau was
> since the day he was born. It's unfortunate and it's
> another indication to me that we always shift our
> attention to the male character no matter what hap-
> pens. No one ever discusses Crystal. She's not
> important; she's a woman—which is really stupid to

me. For her to have endured all these things that
she endured with him and really think that's all she
could ever expect or have—a marriage proposal
from a jackass is better than anything she's ever
known—indicates to me that we're in an awful lot of
trouble emotionally as people and that as long as we
don't care about Crystal and other women like her
and like me who have known moments of great
powerlessness—and for that reason just to go across
the street becomes a great attack on the world—we
have an awful lot of work to do.[61]

Despite the fact that Beau Willie, given the particular circumstances
of his existence, gains our sympathies, perhaps it is Crystal who
experiences the greater loss: she loses control over her environment,
her life, and her children's lives. The tragic irony of such a relationship is that Crystal has, throughout their "romance," remained
implicitly content in this abusive relationship. That she has kept Beau
Willie in her life at all after his repeated physical and psychological
abuse is an indication of her emotional vulnerabilities and social
misdirection. Like the Passion Flower whose "waist ache[d] to be
held," Crystal's love for Beau Willie exists despite having "known
so lil [kindness]" (63) from him or perhaps any other male in her
past. Confused about what she can expect from life, a man, and
herself at age twenty-two, she is a single parent of two who gives up
her chance to marry and create an "ideal" family because of a rumor
of Beau Willie's infidelity. Crystal's pain at the possibility of his
infidelity and her subsequent desire for revenge compel her to get a
court order barring Beau Willie from visiting their children. No
evidence reveals that Beau Willie means direct physical harm to the
children. When he beats a pregnant Crystal and later attacks her with
Kwame's high chair, with Kwame in it, Beau is not directing his
anger toward the children as objects. In fact, the children become
objects toward controlling Crystal just as they do for Crystal in her
efforts to control Beau. Likewise, when he dangles them out the
window, he, like Crystal—and many other disputing and divorced
parents—uses the children as pawns in this adult dispute.

The dramatic and intensely emotional impact of Crystal's help-lessness is simply but poignantly expressed in her final words: "but i cd only whisper/ & he dropped em" (63). Shange's use of the words, "only whisper," emphasizes Crystal's powerlessness. Such words also reiterate the inadequacy of verbal language to describe or control this situation and these circumstances. Purposefully, Shange veils even this action of "dropping" the children in ambiguity. It is possible that the high energy of the moment causes Beau to drop the children quite by accident. Perhaps his sweaty hands led to his dropping them. Perhaps their clothes ripped from their bodies as the children were being dangled. Such possibilities further complicate our perceptions of this action and of Beau's character.[62] Even in this final act of violence, it is Beau Willie who seems to act and Crystal who reacts. The image of a mother's lover dangling their two screaming children outside a fifth-floor window with her arms out-stretched in helpless desperation is meant to be emotionally over-whelming. With the death of her children, an emotional death occurs in Crystal, out of which new life develops—new life for the black woman that is not based on her socially prescribed role as lover, wife, or mother.

Crystal's loss is emblematic of an ultimate powerlessness of a black female who has been battered, raped, debased, and lied to. The socioeconomic conditions of this relationship add to its racial and social specificity; this is not necessarily any male-female relation-ship. The final loss of her children demands the recovery of a new sense of power over her own emotional and psychological destiny. In the play's denouement, all of the women agree that their lives were missing something spiritual. As the Lady in Red explains,

> i sat up one nite walkin a boardin house
> screamin/ cryin/ the ghost of another woman
> who waz missin what i waz missin
> i wanted to jump up outta my bones
> & be done wit myself
> leave me alone
> & go on in the wind
> it waz too much
> i fell into a numbness. (66)

Shange's use of "ghost" and "numbness" reiterates the social, emotional, and psychological deaths that these black women have experienced. Such images also connect with those in the opening monologue of the choreopoem. Although these women's powerlessness is induced mostly from external sources, their pain is inward and self-destructive—hence suicidal—and simply expressed imagistically: "i wanted to jump outta my bones // & be done wit myself." Internalized negativity, shame, and an inability to accept oneself as she is lead to these variant deathwishes.

Perhaps too ideally, these women experience a rejuvenation of individual selfhood, of collective black womanhood. Understanding that physical love with a man will not overcome powerlessness that results from their race and gender oppressions, the women find salvation as in a religious conversion. Appropriately, the "layin on of hands" (64) recalls an intense emotional release and conversion at faith healing sessions and celebrates renewed strength and hope. In this philosophical move, Shange reiterates the possibilities of women who realize the fullness of their inner beings. The Lady in Blue speaks of "all the gods comin into me // layin me open to myself" (65), and the Lady in Purple tells of "the holiness of myself released" (66) in each black woman as a result of surviving painful experiences individually and collectively. In the women's final proclamation of "i found god in myself // & i loved her/ i loved her fiercely" (67) comes a song of joy—"a righteous gospel" (3)—and a hope that will lead them "to the ends of their own/ rainbows" (67). This final scene indeed takes on a religious aura as the women, now one voice, are reborn into a kind of holy selfhood just as the Lady in Brown's opening plea foreshadowed: "let her be born // let her be born // & handled warmly" (3). Their tears are tears of celebration rather than tears from pain and abuse shed at various other moments in the choreopoem. Shange's final stage direction affords brighter days for these black women both on stage and in the audience: "The ladies sing first to each other, then gradually to the audience. After the song peaks, the ladies enter into a closed tight circle" (67), the circle symbolizing continuity and renewed strength. As T.E. Kalem agrees, the women's rebirth after their personal and collective storms has a "revivalist fervor that might have inspired Shadrach, Meshach, and Abednego in the fiery furnace."[63] Yet the choreopoem is not about women finding the Christian "God." Instead, it is about women who find "god," not as an externally sought-after force, but within themselves, a force which asserts their own beauty and self-worth.[64] Shange adamantly rejects any traditional Christian reading of the religiosity of the final moment, insisting that

> "i found god in myself" is feminist ritual. It's feminist hedonist awakening. . . . It's hedonist in the generic sense of hedonist as feminist self-realization that allegedly occurs. . . . [The black woman] finds it [god] in herself; she does not find it [God] outside [herself].[65]

While poet and playwright Amiri Baraka defined revolutionary theater of the 1960s as "the holiness of life[,] . . . the constant possibility of widening consciousness,"[66] Shange's colored girls find a "holiness of [themselves] released" in this revolutionary black feminist celebration.

* * * * *

In *for colored girls*, Shange manages to transform personal pains associated with race and gender into a public celebration of black women's potential for selfhood and self-determination in a racist and sexist society. While the experiences are not necessarily autobiographical and while there is a distinct focus on black female realities, the experiences connect with a larger womanist and feminist community. About the autobiographical and fictional threads in *for colored girls*, Shange explains:

> To me, anything that [I] imagine is just as immedi-
> ate and personally felt as the physical. If I felt
> someone had torn my insides out emotionally, I'd
> still feel that I had experienced a certain kind of
> death. If I was mutilated verbally, I'd feel mutilated
> physically. So while everything in the play hasn't
> happened to me, I've endured everything men-
> tally—and that can be even more painful.[67]

That Shange's own upper-middle-class background may not parallel the exact circumstances of the women she has presented in no way invalidates the message or the effectiveness of this presentation. As a movement from the particular experiences of a single black girl to the realm of possible experiences for any female of any race, *for colored girls* shows the female realities of rape, abortion, pregnancy, and tortured motherhood. At the same time, the choreopoem transcends gender boundaries: from loss of virginity; the pains of rejection and infidelity in romance; the discovery of fraternal love or sororal love through a common suffering; the transformation of physical, psychological, and verbal abuse to a final celebration of an individual's personhood and self-reliance. Granted, these experiences can transcend racial and gender boundaries, but these same experiences are remarkably different from the perspectives of race and gender. As for Shange's attitude toward black men, those who maintain that she is anti-black male have not recognized the traumatic emotional impact of Crystal's willing physical and spiritual involvement with a man who abuses her. Nor have they fully acknowledged and accepted the professed joy of the Lady in Yellow's sexual awakening in "graduation nite" (5). Even the Toussaint story reveals a black girl's discovery of and satisfaction with unthreatening male companionship.

While the women's pain in "no assistance" (13), "one" (32), and "a nite with beau willie brown" (58) derives from a general sense of powerlessness, their greatest pain results from finding an inadequate response to their need to love and to be loved by a black man. Shange's portrayal of black men is based on the reality that men abuse women, and that "in a crunch, they [men] can always rely on their brute force"[68] to overcome their female victims. As an adamant feminist, Shange admits: "[my] target [in for colored girls] is not Black men per se, but the patriarchy in general, which [I] view as universal in its oppression of women."[69] That Shange's colored girls emerge from double oppressions makes their final triumph more resounding, their song uniquely their own.

NOTES

1. Judy Grahn's slender volume of seven narrative poems describes seven "common" women's individual experiences as collectively they create a final statement of the "not-so-common" existence of the "common woman." Grahn concludes that "The common woman is as common / as the common crow; . . . as common / as a rattlesnake; . . . as common as / a nail; . . . as common / as a thunderstorm; . . . as common / as the reddest wine; . . . as solemn as a monkey / or a new moon; . . . as common as the best of bread." With drawings by Wendy Cadden, the volume was printed by the Women's Press Collective, Oakland, Calif.

2. Shange clarifies that the bars were not necessarily lesbian bars but gender-segregated bars where women were not threatened by the sexual politics of a male-dominated society.

Shange reads some of the poems that became *for colored girls* at San Francisco State University (November 17, 1976): "consorting with latent rapists," "sorry," "one," "my name means my own [things] & this is for me." Dancer Rosalee Alfonso performs to "one," "consorting with latent rapists," and "the woman don't stand up straight," the opening monologues for the choreopoem, *From Okra to Greens*.

3. Allen Woll, *Dictionary of the Black Theater: Broadway, Off-Broadway, and Selected Harlem Theater* (Westport, Connecticut: Greenwood, 1983), 65.

4. Linda Winer, "Theater: On Broadway . . . ," *Chicago Tribune/Arts and Fun*, 23 January 1977, 3.

5. Alan Rich, "Theater: For Audiences of Any Color When *Rex* Is Not Enuf," *New York*, 14 June 1976, 62.

6. Clive Barnes, "Stage: Black Sisterhood," *New York Times*, 2 June 1976, 4. While Shange was flattered by Barnes' response to her play, her regret is that she had to be the medium to get a white male in touch with a black woman's realities. See "Ntozake Shange: *for colored girls who have considered suicide/ when the rainbow is enuf*" (audiocassette), Los Angeles: Pacifica Tape Library, 1978, Side A.

7. Jessica B. Harris, "*For Colored Girls* . . . from Ntozake to

Broadway," *New York Amsterdam News/Arts and Entertainment*, 9 October 1976, D11.

8. John Simon, "On Stage: *Enuf* Is Not Enough," *The New Leader* 59 (5 July 1976): 21.

9. "Ntozake Shange Talks with Marcia Ann Gillespie," *Essence*, May 1985, 122-23. Shange discusses her life after *for colored girls* and identifies herself as primarily a "noncommercial artist."

10. "Ntozake Shange," *New Yorker*, 2 August 1976, 19.

11. "Ntozake Shange Interviews Herself," 70.

12. Carol P. Christ, *Diving Deep and Surfacing: Women Writers on Spiritual Quest* (Boston: Beacon, 1980), 99.

13. "Ntozake Shange," *Current Biography* (New York: H.W. Wilson, 1978), 381.

14. Mark Ribowsky, "A Poetess Scores a Hit with Play on 'What's Wrong with Black Men,'" *Sepia* 25 (December 1976): 46. Shange revises the Other-defined beauty principles outlined in E. Azalia Hackley's *The Colored Girl Beautiful* (Kansas City: Burton, 1916).

15. Christ, 99.

16. Tate, 162.

17. Personal interview. Portions of this interview, formally titled, "At the Heart of Shange's Feminism: An Interview," appear in *Black American Literature Forum* 24 (Winter 1990): 717-30.

18. Tate, 162.

19. Jacqueline Trescott, "Ntozake Shange: Searching for Respect and Identity," *Washington Post*, 29 June 1976, B1.

20. Shaun Considine, "British Theater Had Its Angry Young Men—Off-Broadway Savors Its First Furious Woman, Ntozake Shange," *People Weekly*, 5 July 1976, 68.

21. For the sake of clarity, and because of Shange's careful attention to the typography of her poems, I am adopting throughout this text Carol Christ's *Diving Deep and Surfacing: Women Writers on Spiritual Quest* use of the double slash (//) to represent the end lines of poetry. The single slashes (/) are Shange's own marks of punctuation. No double slashes appear in Shange's text.

22. Tate, 163. Shange here follows the lead of such revolutionary poets as Sonia Sanchez, Nikki Giovanni, and Amiri Baraka.

23. See Robin Lakoff, *Language and Woman's Place* (New

York: Octagon, 1976), 20. Lakoff offers an excellent account of how "standard" English reflects the subjugation and oppression of females. She maintains that "linguistic and social change go hand in hand." Shange's use of "lady" is not in opposition to Lakoff's assertions but rather a modifying of a sexist ideal to make it real and just as ennobling. Yet Lakoff's commentary in this instance does not consider the racist implications of "lady" as white. Hence, according to racist thought, a black woman who is lady-like is one who is acting as white ladies do. The slave narratives bear out this distinction when the mistress is always the virtuous woman ideal (i.e., lady) and the female slave is the exact opposite. Barbara Christian, in her commentary on the mammy figure and images of black women historically, asserts: "The Mammy is presented almost as an antithesis of the white lady, [as] the person who does not have the qualities of fragility and beauty which would make her valued in the society" [*Ethnic Notions: Black People in White Minds* (a video documentary), produced and directed by Marlon Riggs, 1987].

24. *Oxford English Dictionary* (Oxford: Clarendon, 1933), 6:22.

25. In recent years, Shange has been part of a musical group, "Syllable," which consists of Shange and two other musicians, jazz woodwind player, John Purcell, and guitarist, Jean-Paul Bourelly. In performances, Shange and the musicians become three distinct and blending voices that accent and complement one another. See performance by Syllable in a videorecording at San Francisco State University Poetry Center (5 May 1989). The group performs the following Shange pieces: "You Fill Me Up So Much When You Touch Me," "Even Though Yr Sampler Broke Down on You," "With No Immediate Cause," "These Kisses," "Mood Indigo," "I Live in Music," and "Crack Annie." The group also performs on an American Audio Prose Library production, "Beneath the Necessity of Talking," (1989). Working with live musicians, as opposed to recorded music, emphasizes the performative jazz-like improvisational element of Shange's poetry.

26. Tate, 163-64.

27. Ntozake Shange, *Nappy Edges* (Great Britain: Methuen, 1987), 126.

28. William Morris, ed., *The American Heritage Dictionary of the English Language* (Boston: Houghton-Mifflin, 1978), 988.

29. The television production does not accurately render Shange's piece and loses the emphatic intimacy of the performance before a live audience. In the Public Broadcasting Service's American Playhouse production (14 June 1983) of *for colored girls*, Patti LaBelle, whose distinctly traditional black gospel voice characterizes her songs, sings the opening and closing scores. The opening theme is a moderately fast, lively, and upbeat rendition of the Lady in Brown's opening lines—from "dark phrases of womanhood" (1) through "don't tell nobody" (2). The televised version of the choreopoem technically ends as does the play version with the a cappella rendition of "i found god in myself/ . . . & I loved her fiercely" (67); the uneven and untrained voices at the choreopoem's end reinforce the unadorned "ordinariness" of these black women. The song is a resounding proclamation of their newfound communal faith. The televised version ends with a slower black gospel rendition by LaBelle that completes the Lady in Brown's opening poem. The credits continue with LaBelle's opening upbeat tune. The musical themes are arranged by composer Baikida Carroll. Shange discusses the transformation of *for colored girls* from stage play to television adaptation in *"for colored girls who have considered suicide/ when the rainbow is enuf," TV Guide*, 20 February 1982, 14-15.

30. In offering the uniqueness of a black woman's song, Shange follows a black feminist literary tradition of Zora Neale Hurston, Maya Angelou, and Toni Morrison. Hurston, in *Their Eyes Were Watching God* (1937), voices this unique position: ". . . de white man is de ruler of everything as fur as Ah been able tuh find out. . . . So de white man throw down de load and tell de nigger man tuh pick it up. He hand it to his women folks. De nigger woman is de mule uh de world so fur as Ah can see" (29). Shange's lady/woman revision parallels Hurston's redefinition of the patriarchy's negative mule stereotype to represent endurance, strength, and power. Maya Angelou, in her autobiographical *I Know Why the Caged Bird Sings* (1969), explores this uniqueness of black femalehood when she asserts notably with murder/suicide imagery: "If growing up is painful for the Southern Black girl, being aware of her displacement is rust on the razor that threatens the throat" (3). Offering structural and thematic parallels to Shange, Angelou, in the closing moments of the novel, offers:

The Black female is assaulted in her tender years by
all those common forces of nature at the same time
that she is caught in the tripartite crossfire of masculine prejudice, white illogical hate, and Black
lack of power.

The fact that the adult American Negro female
emerges a formidable character is often met with
amazement, distaste, and even belligerence. It is
seldom accepted as an inevitable outcome of the
struggle won by survivors and deserves respect if
not enthusiastic acceptance (231).

31. Lawrence W. Levine, in *Black Culture and Black Consciousness: Afro-American Folk Thought from Slavery to Freedom* (New
York: Oxford UP, 1977) reports that this black children's playsong is
a revision of the 1890's white playsong, "Sally Water":

Little Sally Water
Sitting in a saucer
Weeping and crying for some one to love her.
Rise, Sally, rise,
Wipe off your eyes;
Turn to the east,
Turn to the west,
Turn to the one that you love the best. (198)

While both songs are female-centered, clearly the black version
accentuates a more defiant attitude towards Sally's weeping and
wailing. Hands on hips, slipping backbones, and shaking emphasize
the black cultural connection with dance and rhythm even in this
generally female child ritual.

32. Harriet E. Wilson's *Our Nig* (1859), acknowledged as the
first African American novel and the first published novel by an
African American woman, considers this gender issue in the opening
moments of the novel. Wilson attacks the imbalance between social
and sexual mores based solely on gender. Mag Smith's realities as a
woman are significantly more complicated and more limiting than

those of the males in her life.

This gender liability is also part of Nanny's determination to get Janie married off to Logan Killicks in Zora Neale Hurston's *Their Eyes Were Watching God*. For Nanny, marriage equals social security for a sexually curious Janie.

33. Ntozake Shange, *Sassafrass, Cypress & Indigo* (New York: St. Martin's, 1982), 166-68. Shange explains that this poem was a review of a dance festival she was once asked to cover. Her poetic response to the dancers and the dances established legitimate connections between African Americans' creative responses to historical racial oppression.

34. Morris, 176.

35. Shange, while stressing the role of dance in the piece, does not offer stage directions concerning what actors should be doing as poems are being rendered. The improvisational nature of the piece lends itself to improvisational dance by the actors. Definitively, dance, music, and poetry must come together as one unified expression. Breaking the boundaries of traditional theater is the improvisational angle that means each performance during any run of the play and with different actors will yield variations. This aspect of theater makes Shange more comfortable in identifying herself as a writer of performance pieces.

36. This moment recalls the many instances in Jean Toomer's *Cane* (1929) when women unconsciously cast "spells" over judgmental, condescending, and ultimately powerless men. See especially the stories of Karintha, Fern, Aver, and Carma.

37. This same imagery of a woman's magic opens Shange's first novel, *Sassafrass, Cypress & Indigo*:

> Where there is a woman there is a magic. If there is a moon falling from her mouth, she is a woman who knows her magic, who can share or not share her powers. A woman with a moon falling from her mouth, roses between her legs and tiaras of Spanish moss, this woman is a consort of the spirits. (3)

This idea is also not far removed from the imagery presented in Zora Neale Hurston's *Their Eyes Were Watching God*, wherein the narrator opens with a message of gender-empowerment for women whose realities and dealings in and with the world are allegedly and decidedly different from men's:

> . . . women forget all those things they don't want
> to remember, and remember everything they don't
> want to forget. The dream is the truth. Then they
> act and do things accordingly. (1)

38. Marie Marshall Fortune, *Sexual Violence: The Unmentionable Sin* (New York: Pilgrim, 1983), 8.

39. In the original Broadway sound recording of *for colored girls* (Buddah Records, BDS 95007-OC), "latent rapists'" is not included in the presentation. There are also no comments on the poem in the notes and background materials included with the album, nor is it part of the PBS televised version. Perhaps the forwardness and the frankness of the language and the very idea of presenting acquaintance rape as an issue for women were thought too graphic for a sensitive Broadway and television audience.

40. In my interview, "At the Heart of Shange's Feminism: An Interview," *Black American Literature Forum*, 24 (Winter 1990): 717-30, Shange discusses manhood, males' physical abuse of women, and other issues which ground and explain her feminist foundations and perspective.

41. Ibid., 142.

42. Date rape and acquaintance rape are not new phenomena. According to *Newsweek*, they account "for about 60 percent of all reported rapes. And the true percentage may be far higher, since only an estimated 10 percent of all rapes are ever reported" ("The Date Who Rapes," 9 April 1984, 91). Such assaults are grossly underreported for several reasons: (1) it is difficult for a victim to prove coercion, (2) myths of male sexual aggression and definitions of masculinity justify such behavior, and (3) victims feel guilty and responsible for giving off "the wrong signs." Efforts not to give off the "wrong signs" automatically limit the freedoms of any female who does not want to seem responsible for provoking a man's behavior.

43. Ibid.

44. "Surviving Rape: Facts and Feelings," a pamphlet published by Rape Response, 3600 Eighth Avenue South, Birmingham, Alabama 35222.

45. Susan Brownmiller, *Against Our Will: Men, Women and Rape* (New York: Simon and Schuster, 1975), 256. Brownmiller's text is fundamental to Shange's perspective on sexual assault. This text traces the history and definitions of rape from the early existence of human life to the present, recognizing the reality that rape is a violent extension of a patriarchal view of females as property to be controlled and possessed by males.

46. According to Freud, "The sexuality of most men shows an admixture of aggression, of propensity to subdue, the biological significance which lies in the necessity for overcoming the resistance of the sexual object by actions other than mere courting" [Sigmund Freud, *Three Contributions to the Theory of Sex* (New York: E.P. Dutton, 1962), 22. Quoted in Fortune, *Sexual Violence: The Unmentionable Sin*, 114]. Chapter Five, "Rape Is an Unnatural Act," discusses psychological theories which endeavor to "normalize" male sexual aggression. Brownmiller's *Against Our Will* attacks "the legacy of Freudian psychology for fostering a totally inaccurate popular conception of rape," a perception that acknowledges the "primacy of the penis." See especially pages 177-78.

47. Susan Griffin, "Rape: The All-American Crime," in Jo Freeman, ed., *Women: A Feminist Perspective* (Palo Alto, California: Mayfield, 1975), 39.

48. Adrienne Rich, *Of Woman Born: Motherhood as Experience and Institution* (New York: W.W. Norton, 1976), 12.

49. Parallels exist here with Mag Smith's gender and social realities in Harriet E. Wilson's *Our Nig; or, Sketches from the Life of a Free Black* (1859).

50. Alice Walker's short story, "The Abortion," from her collection, *You Can't Keep a Good Woman Down* (1980) details the complex social, psychological, physical, and emotional realities associated with abortion from a distinctly female perspective. Walker also presents a male's responses to this female reality.

51. Mary Daly, *Gyn/Ecology: The Metaethics of Radical Feminism* (Boston: Beacon, 1978), 9. A fundamental theoretical text underlying Shange's feminist beliefs, this book examines historically

and culturally female experiences in patriarchal societies toward positive and sustaining redefinitions of being female. Daly implements her feminist attack through language. Calling *Gyn/Ecology* "a way of wrenching back some wordpower" (9) for women from the patriarchy, Daly says her book is "about the journey of women becoming . . ." (1), and is about "radical feminist consciousness spiral[ing] in all directions, discovering the past, creating/disclosing the present/future" (1). Both Daly and Adrienne Rich assert that so many of the "fatal" female diseases are in fact iatrogenic diseases created by male gynecological specialists as a form of controlling females' bodies.

52. Shange further attacks those men who use women as sex toys then cast them aside in her poem "some men," in *From Okra to Greens*.

53. Maya Angelou's poem, "Phenomenal Woman," celebrates, among other things, black femaleness physically and spiritually.

54. Morris, 1279.

55. Robin Lakoff, *Face Value: The Politics of Beauty* (Boston: Routledge and Kegan Paul, 1984), 246-47. See especially Chapter Five, "Beauty and Ethnicity."

56. Ibid., 250.

57. Shange's attitude toward black men is still much-debated when discussing *for colored girls*, most critics asserting that Shange, as a feminist, hates the black man. Erskine Peters in "Some Tragic Propensities of Ourselves: The Occasion of Ntozake Shange's *for colored girls who have considered suicide/ when the rainbow is enuf*" [*Journal of Ethnic Studies* 6 (Spring 1978): 79-85] avers that "in rightly trying to reveal other dimensions of Black womanhood besides the strong, hard, enduring, and surviving ones, Shange conversely portrays Black men basically as pasteboards or beasts." Curtis E. Rodgers in "Black Men View *For Colored Girls/* Good Theatre but Poor Sociological Statement," (*New York Amsterdam News/Arts and Entertainment*, 9 October 1976, D11) writes that "in her unrelenting stereotyping of Black men as always 'shucking' and 'jiving' . . . [Shange], without realizing it, just as insistently caricatures Black women as being easily duped, and as emotionally frivolous. This is so because Ms. Shange's 'colored girls' invariably take up with those Black men whom she damns as mean and trifling."

T.E. Kalem, in "He Done Her Wrong" (*Time*, 14 June 1976, 74), writes: "If they see themselves through Shange's eyes, black men are going to wince. They are portrayed as brutal con men and amorous double-dealers." Robert Staples in "The Myth of Black Macho: A Response to Angry Black Feminists" [*Black Scholar* 10 (March-April 1979): 24-33] argues adamantly that "[in] watching a performance [of *for colored girls*], one sees a collective appetite for black male blood." And in his efforts to justify the black men's vicious behaviors, he argues: "Ms. Shange does not care to tell us the story of why so many black men feel their manhood, more accurately their feeling of self-respect, is threatened by black women. We are never told that many of these men are acting out because, of all groups in this society, they have no basis for any sense of self-actualization, or somebodiness." Staples seems to excuse black men's destructive displays of brute force: "There is a curious rage festering inside black men because, like it or not, they have not been allowed to fulfill the roles (i.e., breadwinner, protector) society ascribes to them." Jacqueline Trescott in "Ntozake Shange: Searching for Respect and Identity" (*Washington Post*, 29 June 1976, B1, B5) insists that Shange's men "are scheming, lying, childish, and brutal baby-killers. They are part of the unconquerable cruelty of the environment, obstacles insensitive to the black woman's double oppression. Shange's men are beasts humiliated for the message of sisterly love." In defense of Shange's portrayal of black men, Sandra Hollin Flowers in "*Colored Girls*: Textbook for the Eighties" [*Black American Literature Forum* 15 (1981): 51-54], insists that "Shange demonstrates a compassionate vision of black men—compassionate because though the work is not without anger, it has a certain integrity which could not exist if the author lacked a perceptive understanding of the crisis between black men and women."

I examine this issue in "Shange's Men: *for colored girls* Revisited, and Movement Beyond," *African American Review* 26 (Summer 1992): 319-29. The article considers Shange's sympathies for males in their often futile efforts to define manhood in *for colored girls*; the poem sequence, "some men"; *a photograph: lovers in motion*; and *From Okra to Greens*. I argue that Shange does not hold men solely responsible for women's oppression. The article also offers that Shange defines manhood by detailing what it is not.

A "creative" response to Shange's alleged insensitivity toward all black men is *For Colored Guys Who Have Gone Beyond Suicide and Found No Rainbow: A Choreopoem/Drama* (1986) by James Able, Harrison Bennett, Harry McClelland, John Mingo, Roland Robertson, and Baari Shabazz. These male prisoners constitute the Writers Club at the Maryland House of Correction for Men (Jessup, Maryland). While the piece works aesthetically as an imitation of Shange's style, it falls short in coherence and logic. In essence, the work seeks to justify black men's abuse of Shange's colored girls. Philosophically, the piece is an extreme example of male chauvinism, bordering on misogyny. All of black men's problems—hence, the reason these men are behind bars (they allege)—result from black women's failure to understand black men's struggles with "the system." And while the piece grew out of a formal discussion of Shange's text led by Clarinda Harriss Lott, their exercise shows absolutely no indepth understanding of the complexities Shange has presented concerning the lives of African American women. Unlike Shange's text, this one bashes black women in order to elevate and draw sympathies for the black man, whom they see as "a rare specimen of the past warrior spirit, long extinct in the African American race."

George C. Wolfe's play, *The Colored Museum* (1985) is not quite as vicious as the above presentation, though Wolfe does parody Shange's colored girls in the segment, "The Last Mama-on-the-Couch Play." Mocking both Lorraine Hansberry's *A Raisin in the Sun* (1959) and Shange's *for colored girls* in the segment as sacred cows that need to be put out to pasture, Wolfe presents Walter-Lee-Beau-Willie and his wife, The Lady in Plaid.

58. Sandra Hollin Flowers, "Colored Girls: Textbook for the Eighties," *Black American Literature Forum* 15 (1981): 52.

59. In much the same way, Toni Morrison's *The Bluest Eye* (1970) presents a black family's reality as the complete reverse of the American ideal of family. The Breedloves, whose experiences are complex and legitimized in the novel, are the exact opposite of the Dick, Jane, father and mother nuclear family established as a social and cultural ideal. As does Shange, Morrison offers domestic violence, both physical and verbal, as a cultural reality within black families. Both authors offer that violence is not something innate for

blacks but may be an expression of powerlessness against the multi-layered oppressions of classism, racism, capitalism, and sexism.

60. Ibid.

61. Shange, *for colored girls*, audiocassette, side A.

62. This same ambiguity surrounds the death of Clare in Nella Larsen's *Passing* (1929). Does Clare fall out of the window? Does she jump? Is she pushed? If pushed, who pushes her? Is the pushing intentional or accidental? Does Clare faint as a result of the hysteria of the moment and then fall out of the window? Certainly, Irene, as narrator, is not a reliable or credible witness in the aftermath of the fall.

63. T.E. Kalem, "He Done Her Wrong," *Time*, 14 June 1976, 74.

64. Nikki Giovanni's poem, "Ego Tripping (There May Be a Reason Why)" (1970), in *The Norton Anthology of Modern Poetry*, eds. Richard Ellman and Robert O'Clair (New York: W.W. Norton, 1973), expresses this same idea of inner spirituality and celebration of positive black womanhood:

> I turned myself into myself as was
>   jesus
>   . . .
> All praises All praises
> I am the one who would save. (1385)

65. Personal interview, unpublished, August 1986.

66. Amiri Baraka/LeRoi Jones, "The Revolutionary Theatre" (1966), in *Selected Plays and Prose of Amiri Baraka/LeRoi Jones* (New York: William Morrow, 1979), 130.

67. Ribowsky, 43.

68. Personal interview, unpublished, August 1986..

69. Yvonne Smith, "Ntozake Shange: A 'Colored Girl' Considers Success," *Essence* (February 1982): 12.

CHAPTER III

"colored & love it/ love it/ bein colored": *spell #7*

While *for colored girls* played before sell-out audiences at home
and abroad, Shange's second published "theater piece" (as she
subtitles it), *spell #7* (1979)—originally produced by Joseph Papp's
New York Shakespeare Festival in New York City for nine months in
1979-80—met with less commercial success perhaps because a stri-
dent feminist perspective is more socially and politically palatable
than a racially conscious one, particularly given America's history of
strained black-white race relations.[1] Although critics recognized
parallels in form between *spell #7* and *for colored girls*, their assessments registered skepticism about Shange's theatrical unconventionality. Indeed, much of the same criticism leveled at *for colored girls*
echoed in critical assessments of *spell #7*, the first play in Shange's
three pieces volume. After seeing a performance, Christopher Sharp
insisted that *spell #7* "is a workshop production, and it looks it, . . .
a fecund garden that badly needs trimming,"[2] contending that it was
not a play at all but merely unconnected monologues. Close attention
to the structure and thematic issues of the piece, however, reveals
that Shange has broadened the range of the choreopoem as a theatrical expression. While *for colored girls* consciously emphasizes a
black feminist voice, *spell #7* focuses on the subtle and overt manifestations of racism in America.

spell #7 is generally about the socially prescribed limitations of
being black, particularly the problems of being a black artist. While
sexism is always an issue in Shange's work as a feminist, attention to
sexism and gender roles might seem secondary to race in this piece;
in fact, Shange's direct treatment of sexism is mostly relegated to Act

II of *spell #7*. Racism and white America's associations of blackness with negativity, ugliness, and shame are centrally focused in this piece. Shange's text echoes one of the strongest tenets in O'Neill's *Long Day's Journey into Night* (1955): "[T]he past is the present, isn't it? It's the future, too. We all try to lie out of that but life won't let us."[3] *spell #7* shows that attention to the past is fundamental to understanding the nature of present-day racism, both outwardly manifested and individually internalized. Shange argues—and film, movie, and theater history document[4]—that a legacy of mockery and self-mockery continues to confront contemporary black artists. Thus, Shange incorporates a minstrel show as the prologue to *spell #7* and has a large minstrel mask suspended above the stage, creating visual reminders of the play's theme of black misrepresentation and self-deception.

A minstrel mask is foregrounded at three significant moments during *spell #7*. Already suspended at center stage when an audience arrives, the huge blackface encourages an immediate emotional involvement from an audience, even before the play proper begins. The mere presence of this grotesque figure hovering in clear view above an audience commands attention, provokes comment, and more importantly engages an audience emotionally, intellectually, historically, and psychologically. Karen Cronacher suggests that the centralized symbol commands very different responses from white males and black males, and from white females and black females.[5] In her stage direction, Shange describes the mask as "a larger than life misrepresentation of [black] life" (7). To correct this racist image, Shange explores and explodes stereotypes, dismantling their "wholeness," rejecting some while perpetuating others. Exploring the complexities of stereotyping, Shange recognizes their function as performatives that keep people in their prescribed places, particularly according to race and gender. Additionally, the mask underscores a dialectic between creative dream and unproductive fantasy necessary for a black person's psychological survival in any racist environment. While Shange does not abandon all stereotypes associated with black experience, she works to redefine them in ways that are more psychologically productive for blacks. In embracing some aspects of racist stereotypes, Shange shows that the status of a description is not as significant as how it functions and what it does socially and psychologically within an individual. Once these characters' minstrel masks are literally removed and the actors and artists become black people dressed in street clothes, the mask ascends and attention turns to what these professionals have experienced because of "bigger than life" stereotypes and misconceptions. At the end of Act I when an audience's emotional involvement peaks in the narrative of Sue-Jean, who murders her infant and experiences an emotional breakdown, the mask descends and remains during intermission, underscoring the self-destructiveness of those images to blacks who allow themselves to be defined by a dominant white culture.[6] Literally, the mask serves as a kind of punctuation, marking the end of the scene and this first portion of the magic spell of controlling one's own self-image(s). Presenting potential psychological problems of being black and negative myths surrounding the existence of blacks, Shange shows, in the prologue and Act I, how power over one's physical environment does not necessarily confer the ability to control one's level of self-esteem. Removed from audience view during Act II, the mask makes its final descent at the production's end to warn blacks of the self-destructiveness of internalizing racist stereotypes. It also affirms that individuals can liberate themselves from oppression by intellectually and psychologically transforming what is socially and personally negative into something positive and spiritually satisfying. It further reiterates visually Lou's initial challenge to the characters and their own conclusions after fantasizing about and acting out what they allege is the sterility of white people's lives: "we gonna // be colored & love it" (52). Shange legitimizes the presence and the experiences of black people in a society that would render them invisible or insignificant.

    In reassessing African American experience and accentuating those positively sustaining aspects of racial identity, Shange creates a parody of the traditional American minstrel shows popular in the mid- and late-nineteenth century. Rather than present the conventional white male actors with burnt-corked faces to portray Negroes as buffoons and idiots, sources of entertainment and amusement for white audiences,[7] Shange modifies this racist form of American entertainment. Edith J.R. Isaacs recognizes black minstrelsy as "[black people's] first authentic American theater form,"[8] and historical data show that black slaves, in mastering the master for basic survival, metaphorically blackened their own faces in self-caricature as "happy slaves" to please and entertain their masters. Shange suggests that modern attitudes of whites toward blacks and of some blacks toward themselves and other blacks emerge from these earlier unflattering ethnic notions. Renouncing any validity in the minstrel presentations, even when in the 1850's blacks, such as Bert Williams, blackened their own faces for work on the stage, Shange insists: "'Coon shows' [whether the face under the black paint was white or black] were somebody else's idea"[9] of black existence. Minstrel shows, Shange reminds us, made no efforts to arrive at truth of experience but rather a contrived mockery of degradation, dehumanization, and humiliation.

One major difference between Shange's minstrel show and traditional shows is that Shange's black minstrels do not effect stereotypical comic relief through their portrayals; rather, they recall the pain of black people's history of subservience to whites. They also contradict negative stereotyping by showing blacks' contributions artistically and creatively, highlighting particularly blacks' enduring contributions in dance and music—two vital elements of the choreopoem form: "with a rhythm set on a washboard . . ., [the minstrels] begin a series of steps that identify every period of afro-american entertainment: . . . acrobats, comedians, tap-dancers, calindy dancers, cotton club choruses, [and] apollo theater du-wop groups" (9). Through these references, Shange validates blacks' creative contributions to an American history and culture that deem these experiences insignificant. And since racism is not gender-specific, Shange's minstrel show includes both males and females who, initially masked and in tattered slave attire, eventually shed their costumes to contend with racial and social injustice personally and professionally. Having the audience witness the blackfaced minstrels' transformation into the unmasked actors reiterates contextually the inseparability of art from life, of past from present regarding racism and racist perceptions. And Shange targets this inseparability also through the actors' parallel dance movements in the minstrel show and as they move into the Manhattan bar: "members of the company enter the bar in their street clothes, & doing steps reminiscent of their solos during the minstrel sequence. As each enters, the audience is made aware that these ordinary people are the minstrels" (12). While the historical moments of slavery and minstrels have passed, the resultant stereotypes have been sustained and perpetuated over generations. Consequently, blacks have continued to define themselves through the contemptuous and pitying eyes of oppressors. In this gesture of shedding masks, Shange offers *spell #7* as a kind of self-help book particularly for an audience of color. The subtitle of *spell #7*, "geechee jibara quik magic trance manual for technologically stressed third world people," connects black people with an historical association with African conjuring and voodoo or "black magic." It recaptures an African association between dream and reality, spirituality and communal empowerment, and blurs these lines in the African psyche. While Geechee speech is a dialect of Gullah Creole,[10] colloquially, the term "geechee" is also used by African Americans as a kind of insult associated with unsophistication and condescension within black communities. The "quickness" of this magic involves the ready accessibility of an individual's psychological control over and rethinking about oppressive and potentially limiting aspects of an individual's environment or self-perceptions. The frustrations of these characters derive largely from the failure of society to rid itself of racial and gender biases. Such outdated modes of thought have not advanced with alleged technological gains. Cultural illiteracy and its resulting bigotry create a kind of stereotypical, unsophisticated "third world" for these black professionals in the minds of a dominant white culture. The title also clarifies the play's purpose(s) and structure—movements from cultural misrepresentations to cultural self-definition and clarity. Thematically, structurally, and philosophically, this play parallels *for colored girls* although the political emphasis has shifted.

Shange's opening minstrel show also announces the play-within-a-play dramatic structure. As various actors describe the social barriers interfering or threatening to interfere with their artistic and professional pursuits, they incorporate improvisation, role-playing, and creative fantasy; they become each other's audience as an off-stage audience experiences their end-of-the-day rap session. Once again, as black performers, each of their professional plights is the same; whether male or female, each shares an understanding derived from perceived social limitation and expectation. With interest in and

concern for each other, they listen, contribute, and console. And as
Richard Eder recognized in a production of *spell #7*, "the performers
are genuinely listening to each other, reacting and encouraging. It is
like a jam session among musicians who tense up when the soloist
reaches a difficult moment; and relax when it has come off well."[11]
In the manner of *for colored girls*, individuals bring their own particular experiences via song, dance, and poetry (dramatic and narrative)
to another segregated group, and their individual and personal experiences ultimately emerge as one collective voice. As in *for colored
girls* where black women do not bemoan being black and female,
Shange does not assemble these actors to wallow in self-pity. Rather,
they are empowered by Shange, by each other, and are self-
empowered to vent their anger and to work through their disappointments and disillusionments collectively and individually.

Just as traditional minstrel shows incorporated an Interlocutor or
"straight man" who served as master of ceremonies for the vaude-
ville entertainment, Shange introduces Lou as that figure who nar-
rates the action, summons the actors to perform, and provides transitions between scenes. Unlike the traditional shows, however, Lou is
not detached from the action he commands. In fact, the play is Lou's
own personal magic show, a show in which he actively participates
and controls. It is by way of his personal experiences with his black
third-grade friend, his magician father, and his own bouts with the
woes of integration that this show is created and performed under his
direction. As Shange makes clear in a stage direction, "[Lou]
reminds us that it is thru him that we are able to know these people
without the 'masks'/ the lies/" (27). As a professional black magician personally affected by issues of race, Lou makes no effort to
remain objective during the conversations between the performers.
He takes part, observes, and challenges. Karen Cronacher posits that
Shange's revision of the Interlocutor's role is the play's most blatant
move away from the traditional minstrel presentation:

> The interlocutor [traditionally] plays the "straight
> man" to two "end men," who speak in an imita-
> tion of African-American dialect and play the bones
> and tamborine. The interlocutor feigns a dignified
> air and is responsible for setting up jokes and regu-

> lating the pace. Shange's interlocutor, Lou, . . . is
> not a straight man, but a trickster figure who fools
> whites in the audience with the trope of the minstrel
> show. . . . Lou intervenes between the audience's
> complicit acceptance of the minstrel show by con-
> fronting them with the implications of racism and
> citing African-American history. (Cronacher 185)

Lou, sometimes duplicitous, sometimes bitter and angry, makes no effort to "feign dignity" or react with indifference to the stories he allows to unfold. Indeed, it is through his own past, his own personal feelings of powerlessness that he has found his magical gift of self-empowerment. This same self-empowerment or magical gift has been transferred at least two generations and is being offered and transferred to this racially familial theater audience. And while Lou's father retires early as a result of his son's friend's desire to be white, Lou is determined to re-cast a spell that elevates and celebrates blackness over whiteness racially.

As in *for colored girls*, a song motif structures *spell #7* dramatically and thematically, opening with Lou's rendition of what Shange calls "a traditional . . . black play song" (7) about pickaninnies. In the same way that the word "colored" takes on different connotations when used by blacks and whites, here, the word "pickaninny" is simultaneously endearing and condescending. Shange's use of the word "colored" in the minstrel show sequence recalls her use of that word in *for colored girls*. While the song about pickaninnies expresses a playful mockery of black children toward each other, it also represents a condescending white person's negative image of black children and even the intraracist attitudes of some blacks. The song itself recaptures childhood pleasantries for Lou, but the image of pickaninnies is one that has been primarily unflattering in its association with blacks since slavery. Thus, Lou's official greeting to his theater audience is intentionally ambiguous: "yes/ yes/ yes isnt life wonderful" (7). On a superficial level, life for and as a black child can be wonderful—being well housed, well fed, and well cared for by a nurturing family. Yet after re-examining his childhood days in the integrated south, Lou concludes: "i didnt want certain moments at all // i'd give them to anybody" (11). Despite painful memories associ-

ated with racism, which he and the other characters share collectively, Lou celebrates blackness and expects to coerce his black
theater audience members to do the same.

In introducing himself to the theater audience, Lou announces
Shange's immediate reason for assembling these characters at this
moment in time: Lou's magician father chose early retirement "cuz
this friend a mine // from the 3rd grade/ asked to be made white // on
the spot" (7). While Shange's magician-narrator claims abilities to
remedy problems in romance, to banish nightmares, even to cure
sexual problems, he is immobilized by this child's request. That the
magician cannot change the youth's skin color is not as important as
the black child's request. And while "[s]uch an outlandish re-
quest/ . . . // waz . . . politically dangerous for the race" (7-8),[12] it
nevertheless reminds Lou of the complexities associated with the
formation of positive black identity in a racist society.[13] The choreopoem, then, explores the potential reasons that any black person
would want to be white.[14] Because of this black child's desire to be
white, Lou creates before the audience a different kind of magic, not
a deceptive magic of "razzamatazz hocus pocus zippity-doo-dah" (7)
full of lies and crippling deception, but a magic that invokes new
ways of honest thinking and feeling for and about themselves for the
black professionals.

Shange acknowledges and attacks those difficulties blacks
encounter in achieving positive self-esteem in a society that bom-
bards them with racist ideals—of beauty, of intelligence, of success,
of education—in language, the media, politics, and literature. She
thus creates on the stage a kind of ideal: a segregated territory,
segregated for the very specific purpose of delving into the minds of
black folks—black actors, black audience members—and those whites
in the audience who themselves consciously or unconsciously hold or
perpetuate racist notions about blacks.[15] In this racially segregated
moment, blacks as individuals and as artists can freely vent their
frustrations about racism and admit their fears and vulnerabilities.
Like the individual worlds created in *for colored girls* and *boogie
woogie landscapes*, worlds that exclude intruders, Lou's magic
kingdom demands from its inhabitants a harnessing of creative
fantasy to overcome societal restrictions. Lou explains that with his
kind of magic,

all things are possible
but aint no colored magician in his right mind
gonna make you   white
i mean
        this is blk magic
you lookin at
& i'm fixin you up good/ fixin you up good & colored
& you gonna be colored all yr life
& you gonna love it/ bein colored/ all yr life/ colored &
        love it
love it/ bein colored. (8)

Hence, the Interlocutor summons the other actors to shed their minstrel masks[16] and to experience their full potential as black individuals, their full creative potential as black artists. The magician's brand of magic is a kind of "black magic," not the racist image associated with voodoo, evil, and the Devil, but the magic of changing their mental perceptions. The hortatory tone of Lou's final speech challenges an audience to follow him on a journey toward positive selfhood. The words of Lou's last speech in the minstrel prologue are repeated at the play's end, offering not the challenge they present at the outset but a final celebration of race- consciousness, self-satisfaction, and racial contentment.

Before identifying and then basking in the positive energy of blackness, Shange introduces racist stereotypes and attitudes that mock blacks and lead black children early on to social frustration and self-alienation. Notably, Shange continues with the childhood motif announced in the opening play song, for it is this early experience that makes a third-grade black child[17] resent his blackness. Embittered by the fact that external forces can undermine a black child's self-image, Lou asserts:

why dont you go on & integrate a german-american
school in st. louis mo./ 1955/ better yet why dont
ya go on & be a red niggah in a blk school in 1954/
i got it/ try & make one friend at camp in the ozarks
in 1957/ crawl thru one a jesse james' caves wit a
class of white kids waitin outside to see the whites

of yr eyes/ . . . be a lil too dark/ lips a lil too full/
hair entirely too nappy to be beautiful/ be a smart
child trying to be dumb/ you go meet somebody
who wants/ always/ a lil less/ be cool when yr body
says hot/ & more/ be a mistake in racial integrity/
an error in white folks' most absurd fantasies/ be a
blk kid in 1954/ who's not blk enuf to lovingly
ignore/ not beautiful enuf to leave alone/ not smart
enuf to move outta the way/ not bitter enuf to die at
an early age. (9)[18]

Within Lou's recounting are racist myths that still dictate modern
treatment of and attitudes toward and about blacks.[19] In offering
these stereotypes, Shange questions and redefines the standards from
which these negative images emerge. More devastating than negative
perceptions of blacks by whites is the unconscious internalization of
those negative perceptions by blacks. Shange qualifies these racist
stereotypes as "white folks' most absurd fantasies." She submits that
whites' "absurd" fantasies directly contrast the necessary creative
fantasies of blacks struggling against racial oppression.

Lou's open hostility results from Shange's own impressionable
encounters with southern racism, for it was during her childhood
years in St. Louis—from about age seven to thirteen—that her attitudes toward segregation, integration, and racism were molded.
Having been selected as one of the "gifted" black children bused to
a white school, Shange recalls with deep resentment the trauma of
that experience:

When I was eight, I was put into a school where
everyone else was white. With kids there are no
pretensions and they can be very hurtful. They
wouldn't play with me. They took my cookies and
said I'd have to prove I wasn't "colored" before I
got them back. I asked my mother one day if I was
colored and she said I was "Negro" but the same
as everyone else. I never could understand why I
wasn't colored when I was with her but was with
everyone else. You just can't tell a child she's nor-

mal, then send her out into the world where she
isn't normal and expect her to accept the difference
easily. I couldn't.[20]

Her years in St. Louis[21] helped solidify her attitudes about race
relations; she continues:

I think it is unfortunate that we [blacks] buffaloed
ourselves into thinking that the black children who
were integrated had a good time because that was
the worst period of my life. The problem was that
nobody asked us. . . . I had decided long before
Stokely Carmichael ever said anything that I would
not make my child do anything "for the race."
Everything I did for her would be about her. She,
being part of the race, I didn't have to take it much
further than that. . . . I think that in major social
movements, the first people to be tended after and
nurtured [should be] the ones being experimented
on. . . .[22]

While Shange recalls bitterly her childhood experiences with racism,
she admits:

I don't feel sorry for the child I was. I'm finally developing great respect for her because I
think I did a good job. I'm able to teach very well
now; I can teach white kids and black kids. I can
confront them about stuff they don't know about or
that they're not willing to admit. I'm able to write
with some clarity about things that we don't discuss
because we're allegedly so integrated.[23]

By the end of Alec and Lou's account of St. Louis life for black
children in the 1950s with its physical and psychological dangers, it
becomes clear that the play's purpose is to show that "surviving the
impossible [—the historical oppression of blacks physically, socially,
psychologically, politically, and economically—] is *sposed* to accen-

tuate the positive aspects of a people" (51; emphasis mine). Shange
recognizes that celebration of positive black identity is possible and
necessary though not an automatic occurrence in the evolution of
collective and individual black selfhood. With masks shed physically
and metaphorically, the characters claim the stage as their personal
terrain for revealing their dreams and disillusionments. In such a
place, Alec can boldly stake his claim in the black-white, external-
internal "territorial dispute" (10):

> we will stand here
> our shoulders embrace an enormous spirit
> . . . .
> our dreams draw blood from old sores
> this is our space
> we are not movin. (11)[24]

With courage, anger, and pride in the resilience of his black ances-
tors who shed blood just to exist freely in America, Alec makes his
racial territorial claim in light of African peoples' diaspora and a
dominant white power structure. Highlighting racial segregation as
positive and necessary for blacks' psychological survival, Shange
offers an alternative meaning to "segregation" and "integration"
that is free of its civil rights connotations.[25] "Our space" becomes a
racially segregated territorial claim, integrated only by gender.
Hence, through shared experiences, these characters gain healthier
attitudes about themselves and their race.

To create a setting for the "magic" Lou proposes to work on the
characters and the audience, Shange defines her territory literally as
the stage, metaphorically as individuals' minds. In such a place,
inhabited solely by those who share frustrations, dreams, and disappointments, Shange creates a haven for her racial pep talk. Eli, the
owner of the bar and appropriately the poet in the group becomes
Shange's mouthpiece when describing this place in which black
magic reigns:

> *MY* kingdom.
> there shall be no trespassers/ no marauders
> no tourists in *my* land

you nurture these gardens   or   be shot on sight
carelessness & other priorities
are not permitted within these walls
i am mantling an array of strength & beauty
no one shall interfere with this
the construction of *my*self
my city   *my* theater
my bar   come to *my* poems
. . . .
come to *my* kitchen *my* parlor even *my* bed
i sleep on satin   surrounded by hand made
infants who bring me good luck & warmth
. . . .
you are welcome
to *my* kingdom   *my* city   *my* self
but yr presence must not disturb these inhabitants
leave nothing out of place/ push no dust under *my* rugs
leave not a crack in *my* wine glasses
no finger prints
clean up after yrself in the bathroom
there are no maids here   no days off
for healing   no insurance policies
for dislocation of the psyche
. . . .
i sustain no intrusions/ no double-entendre romance
no soliciting of sadness   in *my* life
are those who love me well. (12-13; emphasis mine)

Eli's monologue is first a territorial claim.[26] The repetition of first-person possessive pronouns underscores Shange's belief that while black people characteristically do not own a lot of land in the States, they were instrumental in building this country through their toils on and with the land. The monologue affirms that blacks have the power to reconfigure their own individual and collective psychic land-scapes. This "kingdom" is void of whites' stereotypes of blacks: black people are not aliens; they are not careless about matters of personal hygiene; they appreciate theater, poetry, and wine.[27] In short, they are culturally rich, physically and spiritually beautiful.

And if given complete social, political, and economic autonomy, blacks would have no desire to assimilate into the dominant white culture. Eli's kingdom is then one of "strength & beauty," of positive self-identity, of sensuality and sexuality, of "good luck & warmth," of joy—all those qualities that work against white culture's conscious or unconscious conspiracy to "dislocat[e] . . . the psyche" of a black person. Eli's use of the word "kingdom" as opposed to "world," "realm," "space," or "place," yields richly fantastic connotations. While the tone of the monologue is that of blunt imperative, Shange's choice of "kingdom" affords a fairy-tale quality where dreams imaginative powers prevail. Finally, Eli's "kingdom" is not a place singularly ruled. Instead, it is an ideal place where each black person is his or her own ruler and all inhabitants ideally work responsibly to re-order a collective cultural and racial consciousness. For Shange, such a racial ideal does not always prove ideal for black women whose gender realities are as relevant and potentially limiting as their race realities.

This Manhattan bar, the immediate stage, Shange's play, and the minds of black people all become a place where blacks' dreams are explored and nourished. Shange urges that black people stake a territorial claim in some realm of their psychic existence, recognizing the forced social and psychological displacement of African Americans by a dominant culture. She settles for herself and encourages minorities to settle for themselves the "territorial dispute" (10) introduced early in the play when the minstrels reenact a racial riot in St. Louis. She further recognizes the unique displacement of African Americans in the States—being neither native Africans nor native North Americans—brought by force to the New World. And before blacks can celebrate who they are and where they belong, they must create for themselves a sense of place both socially and spatially. Entertaining questions about this territorial imperative in her work at the "Conference on Common Differences: Third World Women," held at the University of Illinois at Champaign (April 1983), Shange explains:

> As a people in exile, land or territory becomes
> terribly important. For me, I have to make up
> things all the time about where I live. That's why I

erable effort generally for black males and females alike, Shange celebrates the cultural richness surrounding this ritual of a black person's life.[31] With the frequency of the word "dream" when Lily begins to discuss characteristically black hair or "nappy" (26) hair[32] oiled to avoid scalp dryness and subsequent flaking, Shange elevates a mundane hygiene to a necessary art. Such an image connects experientially with black people but is an image foreign to whites and embarrassing to blacks when considered in the context of whites' hair grooming rituals. The differences between characteristically white and black hair and even hair care—for example, whites shampoo their hair to get the grease out—further accentuate this conscious celebration of difference, defined outside black culture as negative. In this segregated kingdom "where magic is/ [and] // . . . where magic is involved in // undoin our masks/" (27), physical traits of blackness are revered, not sources of·shame.

The image of a black Rapunzel extends to another fantasy exercise about white females. In "being a white girl for a day," Natalie furthers Lily's ideas to white females who lead empty and ineffectual lives. This monologue also recalls the choreopoem's opening premise: that Lou's father retired from life as a professional magician because a black friend of Lou's wanted to become white. In Natalie's creative fantasy, however, there are no limits:[33]

> . . . today i'm gonna be a white girl/ i'll retroactively wake myself up/ ah low & behold/ a white girl in my bed/ but first i'll haveta call a white girl i know to have some more accurate information/ what's the first thing white girls think in the morning/ do they get up being glad they aint niggahs/ do they remember mama/ or worry abt gettin to work/ do they work?/ do they play isadora & wrap themselves in sheets & go tip toeing to the kitchen to make maxwell house coffee/ oh i know/ the first thing a white girl does in the morning is fling her hair. (47)

Several parallels exist between Lily's dream and Natalie's fantasy as each actor offers what she perceives as the stereotypical white girl's

existence. Since images of white girls bombard her at virtually every
turn, she has ready access to her own observations and imagination.
From television images, the white girl, Natalie alleges, first flings
her hair, then tiptoes "to the kitchen to make maxwell house coffee," an image, however mythical, of white middle-class existence.
According to Natalie's fantasy, a white girl is mindless. Too preoc-
cupied with her perceived physical beauty, the "typical" white
female is "a sophisticated & protestant suburbanite" (47) who takes
valium to get through the day, spends her time absorbed in soap
operas, and internalizes the racist myth that she is the desire of all
men, the envy of women of color. Aloof and pretentious, a white
girl, according to this improvisation, is actually threatened by the
sensuality and spirituality of a woman of color.

In a play that centers primarily on racial consciousness, Shange
does establish a community between black and white females. However vicious and comical the attack upon them, white women are not
without Shange's compassion since she finds their ineffectuality "the
fault of white man's sexism" (48). The monologue then, in its
attacks on white females inherently attacks the patriarchy's calculated luring of white females into lives of social and cultural sterility.
The attack on white men specifically is heightened by Natalie's
celebration of black male virility, which, according to myth, is
attractive to white women and threatening to white men.[34] Natalie
adds: "oh how i loathe tight-assed thin-lipped pink white men/ even
the football players lack a/ certain relaxed virility" (48). In Alec's
description of the "proverbial white person who is usually a man who
just/ turns yr body around/ looks at yr teeth & yr ass/ who feels yr
calves & back/ & agrees on a price" (46), Shange attacks the past
reality of slave valuations where white males most often attached
monetary values to slaves' physical attributes. Metaphorically, white
directors seeking black actors for stereotypical roles might participate
in a kind of valuation also, using actors' physicalities to determine
their appropriateness for roles. This same process is not far removed
from white team owners' bidding for black athletes. Shange inverts
this emphasis on black peoples' physicality and their alleged social
and self-worth to attack white males' other physical shortcomings as
compared to characteristically negroid features: wide nose, thick
lips, and full buttocks. In Shange's celebration of black virility and

negroid physical features, she again transforms negative racist stereotypes into positive ones. On at least two occasions, Shange refers to whites as having "pink" skin (16, 48), imagistically attacking the "manliness" of white men. The description also comically contrasts her description of black people as "colored," a word she endows with passion and integrity. Whiteness or being white then becomes passionless, empty, and inconsequential—at least in the context of this reconfigured psychological landscape.

This stereotyped description of a white girl's behavior ends with Natalie's recognition that as a black woman she can think for herself, experience emotional ranges that define and validate her humanness, and refuse absolutely to play prescribed roles for social survival:

> being a white girl by dint of my will/ is much more complicated than i thought ,it wd be/ but i wanted to try it cuz so many men like white girls/ white men/ black men/ latin men/ jewish men/ asians/ everybody. so i thought if i waz a white girl for a day i might understand this better/ . . .
>
> oh/ i'm still not being fair/ all the white women in the world dont wake up being glad they aint niggahs/ only some of them/ the ones who dont/ wake up thinking how can i survive another day of this culturally condoned incompetence. . . .
>
> i'm still in my house/ having flung my hair-do for the last time/ what with having to take 20 valium a day/ to consider the ERA/ & all the men in the world/ & my ignorance of the world/ it is overwhelming. i'm so glad i'm colored. boy i cd wake up in the morning & think abt anything. i can remember emmett till & not haveta smile at anybody. (48-49)

Natalie, sarcastically calling a white girl's life "complicated," portrays a white girl as having no significant political thoughts, no social awareness, and no concerns beyond her own celebrated physical appearance and attractiveness to men. As Shange portrays them, black women, on the other hand, do not have the luxury of political and social passivity; life for black women is a struggle to remain physically and psychologically intact in the face of both racism and sexism. This passion for life, a necessity for and legacy of survival, according to Shange, defines black spirituality, a spirituality of resilience and strength significantly different from whites' cultural realities.[35] Recall from *for colored girls* the Lady in Blue's description of whites as intellectuals void of emotional responses to being alive.[36] Natalie, however, celebrates being a black woman with freedoms and choices that white women forfeit to their white men. She joins the women of *for colored girls* who admit that the black woman is not "symmetrical & // impervious to pain" (*for colored girls* 47). Natalie's response to the mythic black Superwoman is a simple declaration: "the colored woman of the world . . . [is not] a strange sort of neutered workhorse" (49). White women, in contrast, at least according to Shange, are forever trapped in the white patriarchy's myth of white female perfection, especially physical perfection. The white woman as the patriarchy's cherished ideal is a constant source of pain and of racial injustice for any black person who "can remember emmett till"—"a fourteen-year-old Chicagoan . . . [who] while visiting relatives in Money, Mississippi [in 1955], allegedly whistled at a white woman. A mob of whites kidnapped the youth and lynched him. The case was highly publicized, even abroad. The lynchers were, however, cleared of all charges"—[37]"& not haveta smile at anybody."[38] Natalie's game of being a white girl soon bores her. Through the process of fantasizing, she realizes the fullness of her own existence as a black female. Natalie's conclusion is Shange's message in *spell #7*: take pride in being black for being black means "laughin', . . . lovin' . . . [and] . . . livin"[39]—honest and instinctive emotional responses to being alive. According to Shange, it also means acknowledging psychological pains that do not have to muffle out spiritual vibrance of black identity.

While Shange offers creative fantasy to combat racial stereotypes, she warns against unproductive fantasy or the fantasy of controlling the world around us in the sequence about Sue-Jean, narrated by Alec and dramatized by Natalie. An "ordinary colored girl" (28) with neither satisfying social nor personal identity, nor social attachments, Sue-Jean desires an identity she defines as power over her environment. Her longing for control in her life is imaged specifically and importantly in her intense desire to bear a son:

> she had always wanted a baby/ never a family/ never a
>   man/
> she had always wanted a baby/ who wd suckle &
>   sleep
> a baby boy who wd wet/ & cry/ & smile
> suckle & sleep. (28)

Sue-Jean's life and story break with tradition, her unconventional dream of motherhood without a husband and without a father for the child. The baby's infantile dependence on her physically is what she considers most fulfilling about motherhood. With "no claims to anything/ or anyone" (28), Sue-Jean seeks identity and self-affirmation through motherhood and aggressively manipulates and abuses a friendship toward her own selfish end:

> when she sat in bars/ on the stool/ near the door/ &
> cross from the jukebox/ with her legs straddled &
> revealin red lace pants/ & lil hair smashed under
> the stockings/ she wd think how she wanted this
> baby & how she wd call the baby/ "myself" . . .
> the men in the bar never imagined her as someone's
> mother/ she rarely tended her own self carefully/
> just enough to exude a languid sexuality that teased
> the men off work/ & the bartender/ ray who waz
> her only friend. . . . (28)

On the one hand, Sue-Jean's power over Ray represents a stereotyped concept of female sexuality as a trap for males. While Sue-Jean does seduce Ray, her motive is clearly not to gain sexual pleasure from him but to become pregnant with a child she thinks she wants. In a voice ringing with condescension, she describes her accomplishment, presenting her male counterpart as naive and easily gulled into thinking that his sexual performance is remarkable:[40]

> & there waz nothin special there/ only a hot rough
> bangin/ a brusque barrelin throwin of torso/ legs &

sweat/ ray wanted to kiss me/ but i screamed/ cuz i
didnt like kissin/ only fuckin/ & we rolled round/ i
waz a peculiar sorta woman/ wantin no kisses/ no
caresses/ just power/ heat & no eaziness of thrust/
ray pulled himself outa me/ with no particular
exclamation/ he smacked me on my behind/ i waz
grinnin/ & he took that as a indication of his skill/
he believed he waz a good lover/ & a woman like
me/ didnt never want nothin but a hard dick/ . . . &
i lay in the corner laughin/ with my drawers/
twisted round my ankles & my hair standin every
which way/ i waz laughin/ knowin i wd have this
child/ myself/ & no one wd ever claim him/ cept
me cuz i waz a low- down thing/ layin in sawdust &
whiskey stains/ i laughed & had a good time mast-
urbatin in the shadows. (28-29)

Sue-Jean's use of motherhood to fashion an identity for herself as
well as her deliberate misuse of a friend is anything but "ordinary,"
as she describes herself. Masturbation is an appropriate metaphor for
Sue-Jean's narcissistic love since all of her actions of manipulation
are toward her own end. Her "grinnin" and "laughin" take on dimensions of the grotesque, and Ray is never the wiser regarding his
role in Sue-Jean's fantasy and ultimate self-destruction.

Once pregnant, Sue-Jean changes dramatically her attitudes
toward life and herself: "now with the boy achin & dancin in her
belly/ sue-jean waz a gay & gracious woman/ . . . she waz someone
she had never known/ she waz herself with child/ & she waz a
wonderful bulbous thing" (30). Her behavior resembles a rebirth
since she is now spiritually exploding with her prospects as a mother.
As a "traditional" mother, Sue-Jean wants to protect her newborn
from the social abuse and criticism she has experienced. She vows:
"myself waz gonna be safe from all that his mama/ waz prey to"
(29). More interestingly, the male "myself" would have a power
afforded by his gender that his mother lacks.

Despite Sue-Jean's seeming rebirth through motherhood, when
the baby physically separates from her body and develops his own
sense of self, she realizes that she can not control another indepen-

dent creature. Hence, her last act of power is to destroy the child she
has desperately wanted:

> *natalie*
> everythin waz going awright till/ myself wanted to
> crawl
> > *alec (moving closer to natalie)*
> & discover a world of his own/ then you became
> despondent/ & yr tits began to dry & you lost the
> fullness of yr womb/ where myself had lived. (31)

Because she is unable to exact total dependence from or exert absolute control over another, not even her child, Sue-Jean kills him and
sucks his blood in a final attempt to incorporate the child into herself;
she is left psychologically traumatized and paralyzed by the incident.
Not only does Sue-Jean lose power over her environment, but she
loses control of her own rational faculties. Hence, madness becomes
an ultimate tragedy for Sue-Jean, whose portrait serves to distinguish
creative fantasy from unproductive dreaming.[41] Entrapment in
fantasy, as opposed to liberation through creative fantasy, leads Sue-
Jean to destruction rather than the long-awaited birth into positive
selfhood. Sue-Jean's experience is far more tragic than the Passion
Flower's (*for colored girls* 32-37) because while the Passion
Flower—fully aware of her purpose throughout the seduction
routine—can separate fantasy from reality, Sue-Jean cannot. For
Shange, the ultimate power for any oppressed individual comes in
controlling one's own mind, not through futile efforts to control
others—their actions, attitudes, or values.[42]

In terms of emotional intensity, Sue-Jean's story parallels the
Beau Willie Brown-Crystal episode in *for colored girls*. Both present
a woman's desire for power in her life, and both present tragic loss in
mother-child relationships. Yet each mother's end is distinctly different. Crystal's loss ideally moves her toward self-discovery and an
identity not based on a female's role as wife, lover, or mother. Sue-
Jean's emotional devastation has a different message. Sue-Jean's act
of infanticide and the motivation behind it is perhaps more psychologically paralyzing for an audience.[43] Unlike *for colored girls*, this
climactic moment in *spell #7* is the culmination of a gradual aware-

ness of how to combat stereotypes with an existentialist goal of re-constructing black peoples' psychological landscapes.

Appropriately following Sue-Jean's story is Maxine's final monologue celebrating black racial identity rather than wishing it away. Recalling the child motif that opens the choreopoem, Maxine's improvisation continues Natalie's celebration of blackness as freedom to choose, to think independently, and to feel. While the monologue attacks racism in the media—portraying white people as the only victims of polio, muscular dystrophy, mental illness, and multiple sclerosis—it simultaneously and just as importantly examines an adolescent female's confusion about the physical dangers of her own gender. An initiation story, Maxine's recognizes that demeaning behavior is not the sole province of any single race:

> the pain i succumbed to each time a colored
> person did something that i believed only white
> people did waz staggering. my entire life seems to
> be worthless/ if my own folks arent better than
> white folks/ then surely the sagas of slavery & the
> jim crow hadnt convinced anyone that we were
> better than them. (51)

Again, to counter racist stereotypes of blacks by whites, Shange drives home the fact that white people behave in ways that are just as immoral, unjust, and shameful as those whites attribute to blacks. Her point is made more forceful when she is reminded of the documented atrocities of slavery and the irrationality of Jim Crow. And just as the seven women in *for colored girls* emerge triumphant after their sufferings, Maxine challenges black people collectively to feel racial pride from surviving the white patriarchy's historical oppression. Thus, Shange prescribes that black people's triumph from "a past [and present] rooted in pain"[44] be the source of self-satisfaction. Maxine explains her way of atoning for blacks who fail to realize their worth from a past and present of unyielding racial strife:

> i commenced to buying pieces of gold/ 14 carat/ 24
> carat/ 18 carat gold/ every time some black person
> did something that waz beneath him as a black

person & more like a white person. i bought gold
cuz it came from the earth/ & more than likely it
came from south africa/ where the black people are
humiliated & oppressed like in slavery. i wear all
these things at once/ to remind the black people that
it cost a lot for us to be here/ our value/ can be
known instinctively/ but since so many black people
are having a hard time not being like white folks/ i
wear these gold pieces to protest their ignorance/
their disconnect from history. (51)

Shange recognizes a collective identity of black people rooted in
Africa, a fact in which she personally takes great pride.[45] While
Shange does not suggest that the life of blacks is one without
self-inflicted sufferings, she admonishes that "surviving the impossible is sposed to accentuate the positive aspects of a people" (51).
Emphasizing the word "sposed" in this statement recalls the note of
expectation in Lou's final lines of the choreopoem. His monologue,
repeated exactly as in the opening moments of the play, gives *spell
#7* a circular structure. While there have been no distinct develop-
ments in the actions or the characters, at least in a conventional or
linear sense—only examples of why wanting to be white is counter-
productive for black people—the technique has a cumulative effect of
prodding blacks' reassessments of their own attitudes about their
identity. Lou's final assertion at the play's end is a collective statement for these black actors and black audience members:

crackers are born with the right to be
alive/ i'm making ours up right here
in yr face/ & we gonna be
colored & love it. (52)

Lou's deliberately racist identification of white people as
"crackers"—perhaps the closest black counterpart to whites' use of
"nigger"—diminishes white people and their attitudes toward blacks.
And having demonstrated black legitimacy on the stage through
fantasy and dream or "black magic," Lou affords blackness a source
of pride rather than shame. Shange reports the emotional effect that

such a celebration reversing negative racial stereotypes had on white technicians working with a production of *spell #7*, at once reiterating the focus on emotion over intellect in her theater pieces:

> I . . . want to create situations that unavoidedly involve us in some way or another where we have to say: "Oh God, I can't deal with this!" or "I can deal with this!"—something where the response is unavoidable, and not to whether we like this material but to the emotional impact of the imagery. We had two white technicians quit work on *spell #7*. That was important. They couldn't handle what was going on [didactically] in the show. Emotionally, that's fine. That meant it worked. They never discussed the ideas. It just upset them. That's fine. That's incontrovertible evidence that it [the play] does something to human beings. That's all I needed to know. If they had been bored, that would have been different. That's not working if people are bored.[46]

Redefining aspects of black experience in much the same way she redefines aspects of black female experience in *for colored girls*, Shange attacks racist stereotypes that blacks have internalized. With characters who are actors, dancers, and poets—all performance artists—Shange addresses the external, socially imposed barriers that black people confront daily. In their opening exchange, the actors acknowledge typecasting as a genuine personal and professional problem in American theater:

> *lily*
> i wish i cd get just one decent part
> *lou*
> say as lady macbeth or mother courage
> *eli*
> how the hell is she gonna play lady macbeth and macbeth's a white dude?
> . . . .

> *bettina . . .*
> . . . if that director asks me to play it any blacker/
> i'm gonna have to do it in a mammy dress. (13-14)

Such an exchange accurately depicts a common plight of black actors in America. Since the majority of productions on New York stages, for example, are overwhelmingly white—written by whites, for white actors, and for predominately white audiences—black actors are generally sought for roles that often reinforce racist stereotypes of blacks as comedians, mammies, butlers, whores, or pimps. Even commercially successful theater, if one accepts America's measure of theatrical success as reaching Broadway, perpetuates myths about the talents of black people—that blacks sing and dance, that their lives lack complexity and fullness, that their main function in the theater is to entertain whites. Such stereotypical castings reinforce notions that blacks' lives are inconsequential and uncomplicated as compared to whites'. Indeed, a clear connection exists between the multitude of successful black musicals such as *The Wiz, Bubbling Brown Sugar, Ain't Misbehavin', Dreamgirls, Sing Mahalia, Sing!,* and most recently *Jelly's Last Jam,* and the 1830's minstrel shows that ill-defined experience for the purpose of keeping blacks subservient to whites.[47] Yet neither entertainment enhances race relations between blacks and whites nor intraracial relations among blacks; they merely perpetuate a racist social order. After a lighthearted and comical improvisation about a black female character who is not a whore, and whom Maxine creates, she confesses:

> when am i gonna get a chance to feel somethin like
> that/ i got into this business [acting] cuz i wanted to
> feel things all the time/ & all they [white directors]
> want me to do is put my leg in my face & smile.
> (23)[48]

Shange's strategy of attacking stereotypical roles for blacks (not coincidentally in this particular case, for black women) involves stereotyping the attitudes of white directors. In this role reversal to raise blacks' consciousness, Shange makes no excuses for presenting the complexities of black people at the expense of stereotyping whites.

The characters are aware of the tight job market for actors of any color. Still, as creative artists, their skills remain only partly realized because skin color and stereotypes continue to dictate roles.[49] Shange attacks stereotyping of black actors and offers imagination, fantasy, and self-definition as ways of combatting these stereotypes. The actors continue to voice their frustrations:

> *bettina (to alec)*
> . . . i'm tired of having to take any & every old job
> to support us/ & you get to have artistic integrity &
> refuse parts that are beneath you
> > *alec*
> thats right/ i'm not playing the fool or the black
> buck pimp circus/ i'm an actor not a stereotype/
> i've been trained. you know I'm a classically
> trained actor
> > *bettina*
> & just what do you think we are?
> > *maxine*
> well/ i got offered another whore part downtown
> > *eli*
> you gonna take it?
> > *maxine*
> yeah
> > *lily*
> if you dont/ i know someone who will
> > *alec (to bettina)*
> i told you/ we arent gonna get anyplace/ by doin
> every bit part for a niggah that someone waves in
> fronta my face
> > *bettina*
> & we arent gonna live long on nothin/ either. . . .
> (44-45)

As a feminist, Shange reminds us that sexism exists even within this group of oppressed black professionals, a reality explored more directly in Act II. Alec represents the black actor who refuses to audition for roles that have little to do with his "classical training" as an actor; he seems relatively unmoved by the plight of black female actors. In his allusion to his "classical training," one wonders if he means his training as an actor for white European classics. Shange makes clear that black men's sensitivity to racism does not necessarily mean that they are equally aware of and concerned about black women's additional struggles with sexism.[50] As the more militant spokesperson of the group, Alec boasts that he would rather not work than "stay in these 'hate whitey' shows/ [that] arent true" (45), possibly referring to black politically militant theater of the 1960s[51]—such as the plays of Ben Caldwell, LeRoi Jones, Ed Bullins, and Ron Milner—wherein blacks' energy was spent attacking an oblivious white racist majority with very little focus on blacks themselves and their realities outside white society. This kind of "segregation" is not, according to Shange, an answer for the non-politicized black who wants only to play Shakespeare.[52] Filled with racial (in)dignity, Alec recognizes roles as darkies or fools as "an insult to my person" (45). Yet Shange sounds a note of economic reason and survival in Bettina's comment: "there is nothin niggardly abt a decent job. work is honorable/ work!" (46). What becomes problematic in Bettina's comment is how, who, and what defines "decent." Shange would offer that roles that do not allow for complexities of black experience are thereby "indecent." Even Lou has accepted and internalized what white culture has deemed "decent roles"—specifically those of Lady Macbeth and Mother Courage—since these are roles traditionally for white actors.[53] Not only are Lady Macbeth and Mother Courage conventionally "white" characters, they are also women who aggressively take control of their environments, another feminist touch Shange adds to this race issue.[54] Laurie Carlos highlights Shange's efforts to destroy racial stereotypes that plague black performers, insisting that "what Zake is bringing to the American stage—legitimate and complex black experience—is not new to black people, but new to the American stage."[55] Shange's decision to write almost exclusively about blacks and for black actors recalls the central political and artistic thrusts of the 1960's Black Arts Movement and even Langston Hughes' "Note on Commercial Theater," wherein he declares: "But someday somebody'll/ stand up and talk about me, And write about me—/ Black and beautiful—/ And sing about me,/ And put on plays about me!/ I reckon it'll be/ Me myself!/ Yes, it'll be me."[56] Reversing commercial discrimination, Shange writes about black characters to be played specifically by black actors; she submits: "I won't ever write a part for a white person. They already own the theaters, so let them do it. I'll do my writing for black actors. . . ."[57] In a National Public Radio interview discussion of her novel, *Betsey Brown*, Shange reiterates this firm stance: "I want to make sure that I have absolutely irresistible characters, all of whom are black. I will be giving no voice to white people. They have a lot of writers. They can write their own stor[ies]."[58]

In her foreword to *three pieces*, Shange labels commercially successful productions about blacks as monolithic and oversimplistic. Indeed, Shange offers all of her theater pieces toward complexity and legitimacy, insisting that "if the lives of our geniuses arent artfully rendered/ & the lives of our regular and precious are ignored/ we have a double loss to reckon with" (ix). A potential contradiction exists in Shange's choice of characters throughout her theater pieces since her characters are mostly creative artists—poets, photographers, actors, and dancers—rather than blue collar or uneducated blacks. While Shange's characters challenge the stereotype of blacks as solely capable of filling blue collar jobs, she also does not write about black characters who are presidents of corporations. Her characters reveal Shange's bias and sensitivity toward middle-class artistic blacks—those most likely to be theater-goers or readers of her plays. Still, Shange manages to communicate with blacks at large by using a common language and cultural and spiritual realities that blacks potentially share experientially, not necessarily intellectually or even economically. Indeed the common connector between blacks of various intellectual abilities and economic levels is the reality that "[r]acism lives in other people and is not something from which one can be insulated"[59] except through their own minds. Black bank president Ronald A. Homer asserts: "To be black and to believe that you will not be affected by racial stereotypes is to be extremely naive about human behavior. To not prepare yourself to deal with them is to be inadequately prepared to accept the challenges of making a dream a reality."[60]

spell #7 not only lashes out against stereotyped roles for black actors, but it redefines unflattering stereotyped behavioral patterns of blacks. Along this line, Shange considers the physical attributes that characterize and ultimately lead to racist stereotyping by whites. Black journalist Sylvester Monroe describes the frustrations and reality of racism for blacks: "To be sized up, categorized and dismissed all within the space of a . . . glance solely on the basis of race is more than annoying; it's demeaning and damaging to the psyche of an entire people."[61] Indeed, a fundamental part of racism derives from blacks' physical bodies, from whites' visual perceptions. The pain and anger from such negative assessments of blacks by whites lie beneath Shange's presentation. Here, characters combat their resentment through jest and reassessment of themselves in a supportive group context. Just as blacks in the play are coached to reject white America's minstrel images of blacks, Shange's characters challenge head-on the myth that blacks are illiterate, inarticulate, unintelligent, and unable to realize aesthetic beauty. As the actors joke about whites who want to give them beads and ribbons for their work or about beating a tambourine for subway fare, they revel in denouncing such primal images—the often customary wearing of rings in noses and porcupine quills in ears—whites and some blacks have of them by reversing those "primitive" images to whites at Madison Square Garden functions.[62] All of the characters join in this redefining exercise, becoming one shared voice. This moment structurally and performatively recalls the choreopoem technique demonstrated in *for colored girls*' commentary on acquaintance rape:[63]

> *lily*
> . . . when ringlin' bros. comes to madison square
> garden/ dontcha know the white people just go
>> *ross*
> in their cb radios
>> *dahlia*
> in their mcdonald's hats
>> *eli*
> with their save america t-shirts & those chirren who
> score higher on IQ tests for the white chirren who
> speak English

> *alec*
> when the hockey games absorb all america's atten-
> tion in winter/ they go with their fists clenched &
> their tongues battering their women who dont know
> a puck from a 3-yr-old harness racer
> > *bettina*
> they go & sweat in fierce anger
> > *ross*
> these factories
> > *natalie*
> these middle management positions
> > *ross*
> make madison square garden
> > *bettina*
> the temple of the primal scream
> > *lily*
> oh how they love blood
> > *natalie*
> & how they dont even dress for the occasion/ all
> inconspicuous & pink. (15-16)

Shange stereotypes what could just as easily be characterized as primitive animalistic behavior on the part of whites[64] at sporting events in Madison Square Garden. She specifically chooses hockey, rather than football or basketball for instance, as the sporting event because it is played predominantly by white athletes and has a pre-dominantly white following. The brutal assaults frequent among hockey players become a source of perverted glee for white fans who seem to crave graphic violence. In this stereotype, Shange also depicts an abusive relationship between white men and women, suggesting that domestic violence of men against women is not just a black reality. Interestingly, Shange implicitly characterizes white women as intellectually ignorant; this issue becomes the premise for the white girl fantasies in Act II. And finally, Shange derisively comments on whites' overly casual dress in a reversal of the stereo-type of blacks' allegedly misplaced values as revealed in their alleged overdressing for social events. Her technique of image reversal highlights the importance of individual and cultural perspectives of

those who define—those with power—and those who are defined—
those without power. Movement through this poem, other
monologues, in essence, and the whole choreopoem results in
conscious self-empowerment.

Contrasting whites' behavior at sporting events and general
outings, Shange describes blacks' behavior when they gather to see
important people of color: here, Willie Colon, Muhammad Ali,
Stevie Wonder, or Bob Marley. Her description of blacks transforms
a negative stereotype into something positive and celebratory:

> *eli*
> now if willie colon come there
> *bettina*
> if/ we say/ the fania all stars gonna be there
> in that nasty fantasy of the city council
> . . . .
> *ross*
> even in such a place where dance is an obscure notion
> . . . .
> *dahlia, lily, alec, natalie, & ross (in unison)*
> we dress up
> *bettina, eli, & lou (in unison)*
> we dress up
> *dahlia*
> cuz we got good manners
> *ross*
> cd you really ask dr. funkenstein to come all that way &
> greet him in the clothes you sweep yr kitchen in?
> *all*
> NO!
> . . .
> *natalie*
> we honor our guests/ if it costs us all we got
> *dahlia*
> when stevie wonder sings/ he don't want us lookin like
> we aint got no common sense/ he wants us to be as
> lovely as we really are/ so we strut & reggae
> . . . .

lily
we simply have good manners
    ross
& an addiction to joy
    female cast members (in unison)
WHEE . . .
    dahlia
we dress up
. . . .
    bettina
we gotta show the world/ we gotta corner on the color
    ross
happiness just jumped right outta us/ & we are lookin
good. (16-20)

Shange uses stereotyping of whites to denounce and reevaluate
whites' stereotyping of blacks. Dismantling the wholeness of some
racist stereotypes, Shange allows us to witness the process of becoming empowered by appropriating a stereotype and turning it against
its originators, the essence of the spell Shange casts in this play. For
instance, dressing in a way that is distinguished from day-to-day
casual dressing is, alleges Shange, one way that black people show
respect for significant occasions and guests as well as a way to
accentuate the loveliness about which Stevie Wonder sings. This
cultural reality has little to do with the stereotypic image of blacks
who spend money on status cars and designer clothes rather than
improve their living conditions. Shange's cultural documentations
offer positive images of accomplished persons of color with whom
audience members might readily identify. Indeed, Stevie Wonder's
pop song, "Isn't She Lovely," composed by Wonder on the birth of
his daughter, expresses Shange's celebration of blackness physically
and spiritually, and of black female beauty specifically. In the New
York Shakespeare Festival production (1979), characters dance the
entire poem while clapping their hands and improvising to jazz
rhythms. With the movement and music, the poem sequence itself
becomes a microcosm of what the entire choreopoem celebrates with
the revelry of music and dance: the cultural and physical beauty of
blackness. The collective shout of "WHEE . . ." leads immediately

and effectively into Dahlia's "we dress up." Shange's word play on "WHEE . . ." as an exclamation of joy reiterates the actors' cele-bration of their black "we-ness," their collective black conscious-ness, that can be grandly celebrated in this racially segregated mo-ment and place.

Shange also utilizes negative cataloguing or simple denial[65]—here, the repetition of words such as "no," "it's not," and "we don't"—to combat negative stereotypes of black people. In the Madison Square Garden poem, she argues that blacks do not neces-sarily become violent and disorderly whenever they gather publicly. Recognizing that such can be the case when whites gather as well, particularly for sporting events, the actors continue:

> *lily*
> we fill up where we at
> *bettina*
> no police
> *natalie*
> no cheap beer
> *dahlia*
> no nasty smellin baño
> *ross*
> no hallways fulla derelicts & hustlers
> *natalie*
> gonna interfere wit alla this beauty. (18-19)

While Shange makes no efforts to deny realities of unpleasant black experience—police, cheap beer, smelly bathrooms, derelicts, and hustlers—these realities do not overwhelm the "filled up" spiritual beauty of black community and celebration. Bob Marley in concert can remove black people from immediate unpleasant realities as Willie Colon's music removes the Lady in Blue from her immediate disappointment in his dance marathon cancellation. Shange might also be magnifying a stereotype that some blacks have of whites being careless about personal hygiene and of whites being "cheap beer" guzzlers.[66]

Despite the subservient roles that blacks have repeatedly played on the commercial stage as well as the alleged primitive behavior and

unaffordably lavish lifestyles whites commonly associate with blacks,
Shange's characters acknowledge that blacks are neither stupid nor
ignorant. The issue of intelligence and learning informs Shange's
emphasis on spoken and written language, particularly for blacks
who are devalued and negatively stereotyped when they do not
communicate according to the grammatical rules of the King's
English.[67] In Act II, blacks' learning and language are discussed with
the same sarcasm as the myths associated with blacks' behavioral
patterns. Note the actors' playfulness in addressing the potentially
painful stereotype of black people's intellect, more specifically their
alleged inadequacy with standard English and foreign languages:

> *natalie*
> i swear we went to that audition in good faith/ & that
> man asked us where we learned to speak english so
> well/ i swear this foreigner [the English director] asked
> us/ from the city of new york/ where we learned to
> speak english.
>   *lily*
> all i did was say "bom dia/ como vai"/ and the english-
> man got red in the face
>   *lou (as the englishman)*
> yr from the states/ aren't you?
>   *lily*
> "sim"/ i said/ in good portuguese
> . . . .
>   *lou*
> how did you pick that up?
>   *lily*
> i hadda answer so simple/ i cdnt say i learned it/ cuz
> niggahs cant learn & that wda been too hard on the
> man/ so i said/ in good english: i held my ear to the
> ground & listened to the samba from belim
> . . . .
> when the japanese red army invaded san juan/ they
> poisoned the papaya with portuguese. i eat a lotta pa-
> paya. last week/ i developed a strange schizophrenic
> condition/ with 4 manifest personalities: one spoke

> english & understood nothing/ one spoke french & had
> access to the world/ one spoke spanish & voted against
> statehood for puerto rico/ one spoke portuguese. "eu
> naõ falo ingles entao y voce"/ i dont speak english
> anymore/ & you? (33-34)

Natalie and Lily go to an audition because they are qualified actors. Yet this casting director reveals his racist misconceptions in his surprise that they are in full command of standard English and Portuguese. That this director is white is implicit in the nature of his reactions. While standard English is taught and exclusively accepted in American public schools, and while the language of minority children is often denied, these actors recognize the necessity of speaking standard English as professionals competing in white theater. Yet the bias they confront from this condescending director goes beyond whether or not blacks speak standard English properly; the broader implication is that blacks are incapable of learning and mastering standard English, let alone foreign languages. In this instance, a racist stereotype of blacks' intellectual and linguistic limitations has transcended American boundaries. Lily's knowledge of Portuguese, Spanish, French, and English represents for Shange blacks' challenge of white hegemony and a kind of linguistic appropriation turned against the perpetrators of a stereotype. A staunch supporter of multilingual education for blacks, Shange explains:

> One of the things that was a freeing instinct for me
> as a child was not speaking English around white
> people when I didn't have to. If they bothered me, I
> could just not speak English and then there was
> nothing they could do. Of course, there was some-
> thing they could do, but I had some power to con-
> trol their influence on what was going on in my
> life. And then, of course, most of the other black
> people in the world, who are intellectuals, don't
> necessarily speak English. And so it was another
> way to be involved in a greater community.
>   It's also important to assist those of us who live
> in North America to understand that it is not our

right to be monolingual; it is not a good state of
affairs. The identification with Anglo culture *solely*
is not intelligent if we are not to feel totally isolated
and in our isolation therefore feel less powerful and
less capable of doing things about how we live and
who we are and what total impact we're going to
have on the world.[68]

Shange recognizes language as a political tool and multilingualism as
a wedge in the stronghold of white patriarchy. This attitude in part
explains her seemingly arbitrary use of Spanish terms and phrases in
for colored girls also. Not only are these languages the languages of
other people of color in the world—hence a connection with a global
community—but multiculturalism also represents a culturally liberating force, to move freely and at will between languages.

Shange's second tool for blacks' survival is creative fantasy,
which sometimes takes the form of linguistic games. In this episode,
fantasy combats this frustration caused by the director's ignorance.
Lily transforms her reactions to his condescension into a game of
creative fantasy to highlight the absurdity of his racist attitudes.
Since racist stereotyping controls this director's perceptions, neither
acting experience nor training seems an issue for this director. Not
coincidentally, Shange, as a feminist, uses black females to highlight
this discrimination though gender is not a primary focus at this point.

Not only does Shange attack the subtle and overt manifestations
of racism in *spell #7*, but as a feminist, she also considers gender
stereotypes within but not limited to black experience. In Act II, the
actors engage in lighthearted improvisations that comment on male-
female relations. The satiric thrust of their role-playing exercise is at
first directed at the shallowness of some black males who objectify
black women and think them naive. In contrast, she presents the
women in the scenario as cunning and witty. Shange suggests that too
many men are attracted only to women's physical attributes and
offers a playful yet telling pseudo-courting improvisation:

> *ross*
> aw babee/ you so pretty
> . . . .

> *lou*
> aw babee/ you so pretty
> . . . .
> *alec (to natalie)*
> aw babee/ you so pretty
> . . . .
> *natalie*
> i know. thank you
> . . . .
> *eli (stroking bettina's thigh)*
> what nice legs you have
> . . . .
> *bettina (removing his hand)*
> yes. they run in the family
> *maxine*
> oh! whatta universe of beautiful & well traveled women!
> *male cast members (in unison)*
> aw babee/ i've never met anyone like you
> *female cast members (in unison, pulling away from
> men to stage edges)*
> that's strange/ there are millions of us! (40-41)[69]

With clever retorts, these women prove they have beauty and intellectual substance and that they are not easily duped by single-minded males.

While Shange uses women's situations in Act I to highlight race issues, Act II presents a clearer feminist dimension. In fact, perhaps more evident in *spell #7* than in *for colored girls* is Shange's attack on black men. While the women in *for colored girls* are drawn to men romantically despite the abuse they receive from them, here, the actors dramatize males' aggressive insincerities toward women who quickly discern their true motives, be they sexual or economic. Just as Shange creates stereotypes of whites to renounce negative stereotypes of blacks, she here stereotypes black men while redefining black females as shrewd critics of black males' behavior. This image of black women's strength and intelligence perpetuates the myth that all black men are manipulative and self-centered. While she continues to attack male insincerities in *boogie woogie landscapes*, Shange qualifies these assertions about male behavior toward women in *From Okra to Greens*. Assessing non-American black males since sexism—like racism—transcends national boundaries, Maxine's character summarizes Shange's opinion of male-female relationships: "i noticed this yng man waz so much like the other yng men from here/ who use their bodies as bait & their smiles as passport alternatives" (39).[70] This presentation of male behavior seems one-sided, especially considering the actors' discussion of stereotyped acting roles earlier in the choreopoem and since the male characters are willing participants in this improvisation. Perhaps these male artists are sensitive to feminist realities, as is Greens, who becomes sensitive to Okra's complex realities in *From Okra to Greens*. Shange idealizes the female, particularly the black female—African Americans and others—as perceptive, sharp-witted, clever, and intelligent to counter traditional negative stereotypes of black females. The myth of black female intellectual inferiority is further challenged in the detail that Maxine's character reads Nietzsche. Here Shange modifies Nietzsche's philosophy of life as struggling forces against ideals and conventions to include black women's struggles against both sexism and racism. Ross' comment echoes the Englishman's surprise at Lily's knowledge of Portuguese: "i never saw a black woman reading nietzsche" (39). Perhaps Ross is equally startled that a "woman" reads Nietzsche and that a "black" woman comprehends the philosopher's ideas.

Male chauvinism transcends racial boundaries, and Shange's presentation here scolds black males who take black women's physical and intellectual beauty for granted. Nevertheless, it is unfair to say that Shange rebukes black men. What she attacks are prevailing patriarchal attitudes toward black women. Allusions to Farrah Fawcett and Marilyn Monroe also reiterate the stereotype of the white female ideal as the blond bombshell.[71] Structurally, this switch of focus in Act II to the stereotyping of black males seems to have little to do with the play's power to dispel false and psychologically paralyzing images of blacks by the dominant white culture, aside from the fact that Shange recognizes the intertwining of sexism and racism in patriarchal (dis)order.

spell #7 ends structurally as does *for colored girls*; the actor's song of "colored & love it/ love it bein colored" becomes a communal experience among the actors and is sung "as [the] audience exits" (52), recalling the women's song of finding god in themselves in *for colored girls*. Clearly, Shange might well have been in the Reverend Purlie Victorious Judson's audience when he preached in the final moments of Davis' play:

> Tonight, my friends—I find, in being black, a thing of beauty: a joy, a strength; a secret cup of gladness; a native land in neither time nor place—a native land in every Negro face! Be loyal to yourselves: your skin; your hair; your lips, your southern speech, your laughing kindness—are Negro Kingdoms, vast as any other! Accept in full the sweetness of your blackness—not wishing to be red, nor white, nor yellow: nor any other race, or face, but this.[72]

Shange reiterates the Reverend Purlie's message and transforms James Brown's 1960's sentiment—"Say it loud, I'm Black and I'm proud"—into a theatrical voice that includes a clearly feminist dimension. In such a presentation, she posits the necessity for an agenda for women and women's realities even within the politics of racism.

NOTES

1. In March-April 1985, *spell # 7* was presented in London (England), by the Womens Playhouse Trust (Donmar Warehouse). A predominantly white British audience did not receive the play particularly well, primarily—according to various reviews of the productions—because of alleged cultural barriers: "For [the play] is nothing if not heavy with irony and American allusions to the idea and experience of being black. Much of the humour therefore sweeps clean over this ageing, white Cockney head" (Eric Shorter, "At Sea with Racial Satire," *The Daily Telegraph*, 3 April 1985). Interestingly, Shorter also complained that he missed jokes because "the language is often too native . . . to be intelligible." Others found offense in the fact that Shange does not present whites collectively very positively: "*Spell Number 7* demands and fully expects sympathy for the various characters depicted by a group of actors and artists gathered in a Manhattan bar, but conveys no compassion itself for those beyond black society. . . . Ms. Shange insults us all: suggesting no promotion of racial harmony herself, she expects the same attitude from others" (Lynda Murdin, "The Colours of Bitterness," *The Standard*, n.d.). Murdin seems unable or unwilling to accept the play on its own segregated terms; racial harmony seems less an issue than a black person's psychological harmony amid racist [and sexist] turmoil. Asking for a white audience's compassion does not seem a dimension of the play either. Suzie Mackenzie, of *Time Out*, wondered: "Can't you celebrate being black without denigrating being white?" and added about its structure: "[T]he whole production lacked movement and interaction—more painting by numbers than a spontaneous, creative whole." Concerning its alleged lack of structure, Ros Asquith joined Mackenzie: "[The play] is marred by an absence of structure that makes it more of a revue than a play" ("Black Magic," *The Observer*, 14 April 1985). Another reviewer described the play as "too much of a theatrical jumble" ("It's That Old Black Magic," *London Week*, 19 April 1985). Of the reviews obtained from Womens Playhouse Trust General Manager, Rosemary Squire, only one seemed positive or receptive to Shange's presentation and interestingly comes from one of the black cast members,

Brick Ray Evans: "For once [*spell #7*] is a play in which, for a lot of the time, we define ourselves [black men and black women] in relation to each other, as opposed strictly in terms of our relations with the white world at large" ("Spell Bound!" *The Voice*, 6 April 1985).

2. Christopher Sharp, "*Spell #7: A Geechee Quik Magic Trance Manual*," *Women's Wear Daily*, 4 June 1979. Found in *New York Theater Critics' Reviews* 40 (1979): 109.

3. Eugene O'Neill, *Long Day's Journey into Night* (New Haven: Yale UP, 1955), 87.

4. *Ethnic Notions: Images of Blacks in White Minds* (1987), directed and produced by Marlon Riggs, is an excellent historical documentary of the racist images of African Americans today and in the past. It considers stereotypical presentations of blacks in popular culture, music, cartoons, advertisements, and folk art, ultimately questioning whether these images and the portrayals of African Americans in the public eye have changed considerably since their inception.

See also Marlon Riggs' documentary, *Color Adjustment* (1991), which traces the images of blacks in American television. Part I of the program, "Color Blind TV?," considers the years 1948-68, and Part II, "Coloring the Dream," addresses the years from 1968 to the present. Additionally, see documentaries, *A History of Racist Animation* (1988) and *Just Shuffling Along: The Black Stereotype in Motion Pictures* (1988), produced by Ray Atherton (Wavelength Video).

Also of interest is producer Woody King, Jr.'s, documentary, *Black Theatre: The Making of a Movement* (1978), which examines black theater during the 1950s, the 1960s, and the 1970s. Shange appears on this videotape, and a segment from *for colored girls* is shown.

5. See Karen Cronacher's article, "Unmasking the Minstrel Mask's Black Magic in Ntozake Shange's *spell # 7*," *Theater Journal* 44 (1992): 177-93. Cronacher examines the social and political history of American minstrelsy, offering theories regarding Shange's feminist appropriation of a traditional male form: "Shange's play addresses this absence of a subject position for African-American women by reclaiming and rewriting the legacy of minstrelsy, writing herself back into a history in which she was excluded by virtue of her

sex and implicated by virtue of her race" (178). Cronacher also looks at reasons that white males particularly seemed to popularize minstrels as entertainment and as "a discourse of desire" (179).

6. African American literature abounds with examples showing white as advantageous and black as undesirable. And such issues as assimilation, "passing," and intraracism pervade the African American experience in America. Ossie Davis' exercise, "The English Language Is My Enemy!" [*Negro History Bulletin* 30 (April 1967): 18], presents racist implications of language, revealing quite simply black as the opposite of the white ideal. Also, the American Broadcasting Company News documentary, "Black in White America" (29 August 1989, produced by Ray Nunn), examines conflicts between dominant white cultural ideals and African American realities. Particularly important is the opening segment which examines black children's ideals of beauty and desirability that render them absent or marginal.

7. These blatantly racist images arrived on the American stage with T.D. Rice's 1820's creation of the fictitious character, Jim Crow. Minstrels were amazingly popular to white audiences throughout the 1890's. Al Jolson also popularized the form in the film, *The Jazz Singer* (1929). For detailed background on this entertainment, see Hans Nathan's *Dan Emmett and the Rise of Early Negro Minstrelsy* (Norman, Oklahoma: U of Oklahoma P, 1962) and Robert C. Toll's *Blacking Up: The Minstrel Show in Nineteenth-Century America* (New York: Oxford UP, 1974). See also Yvonne Smith's video documentary, *Mo' Funny: Black Comedy in America* (1992).

8. Edith J.R. Isaacs, *The Negro in the American Theater* (New York: Theater Arts, 1947), 27. Quoted in Doris E. Abramson, *Negro Playwrights in the American Theater 1925-1959* (New York: Columbia UP, 1969), 7.

9. Shange, foreword to *three pieces*, x.

10. Geneva Smitherman, in *Talkin and Testifyin: The Language of Black America* (Boston: Houghton Mifflin, 1977), notes that "Geechee . . . is spoken by rural and urban blacks who live in the areas along the Atlantic coastal region of South Carolina and Georgia. . . . Even the names Gullah and Geechee are African in origin—they refer to languages and tribes in Liberia" (14). Clarence Major (ed.) in *Juba to Jive: A Dictionary of African-American Slang*

(New York: Penguin, 1994), adds the following definitions of "geechee": "1. a language derived from a mix of Mandingo, Bantu, Fante, Wolof, Ewe, Twi, Yoruba, Ibo, and other West African languages; a language of the coast of Guinea; also of Kissi County, Liberia. It has its own well-focused grammar and syntax. This term has also been used by whites in a derogatory way to refer to any 'very black' Southern Negro; 2. any black (and sometimes non-black) person from the coastal area of Georgia or North Carolina; 3. a derogatory term for a southern person whose speech is not easily understood; unable to speak clearly; to speak with a heavy accent" (194). Shange inverts the image of the inarticulate "geechee" of the above to be the articulate, well-spoken, and frustrated black person. Their communications, verbal and nonverbal, may seem like gibberish to an outside world but is clearly presented within this safe bar.

11. Richard Eder, "Dramatic Poetry," *New York Times*, 4 June 1979, C13.

12. Lou's entire opening monologue, excluding his black play song, appears in *Nappy Edges* as the poem "my father is a retired magician," dedicated to Shange's siblings "ifa, p.t., & bisa" (136-37). Actually, much of the material in *spell #7*, a celebration of collective black consciousness, comes from Shange's earlier poetry collection *Nappy Edges*, the title of the volume itself referring to a texture characteristic of black people's hair as it grows without chemical treatments. She clarifies her reference contextually on the title page:

> "the roots of your hair/ what
> turns back when we sweat, run,
> make love, dance, get afraid, get
> happy: the tell-tale sign of living."

To wish away one's blackness is the same as wishing away a black person's "nappy edges."

13. Shange obviously pays homage to W.E.B. DuBois who in *The Souls of Black Folk* (1903) [In *Three Negro Classics*, New York: Avon, 1965] eloquently articulates the psychological confusion and negative self-images of blacks in America:

> After the Egyptian and Indian, the Greek and
> Roman, the Teuton and Mongolian, the Negro is a
> sort of seventh son, born with a veil, and gifted
> with second-sight in this American world,—a world
> which yields him no true self-consciousness, but
> only lets him see himself through the revelation of
> the other world. It is a peculiar sensation, this dou-
> ble-consciousness, this sense of always looking at
> one's self through the eyes of others, of measuring
> one's soul by the tape of a world that looks on in
> amused contempt and pity. (214-15)

Through a multitude of different experiences and approaches, DuBois argues for total exorcism of self-contempt and self-pity from the black psyche.

14. Toni Morrison's *The Bluest Eye* (1970) details a whole community of blacks trapped by their futile efforts to be part of a perceived white ideal. Characteristic of fiction about passing is the passing character's sacrificing of spiritual peace for material and social gains. See James Weldon Johnson's *The Autobiography of an Ex-Coloured Man* (1927), Nella Larsen's *Passing*, and Langston Hughes' short story, "Passing," in his collection, *The Ways of White Folks* (1933).

15. Langston Hughes' play *Simply Heavenly* (1956), though a comedy, presents a similar segregated bar in Harlem where blacks take refuge from a white racist society and find strength in their freedom to discuss, criticize, and celebrate their own culture. This idea of freedom in segregation emerged earlier in Shange's original readings of the poems that become *for colored girls* in segregated women's bars.

16. Paul Laurence Dunbar's poem, "We Wear the Mask" (1892), obviously connects metaphorically and historically with this masking motif as both Dunbar and Shange recognize the necessity of mask-wearing for basic physical survival. Shange goes beyond Dunbar to offer continuous means of ridding blacks of the masks and the need for masking.

17. Note that Pecola Breedlove in Toni Morrison's *The Bluest Eye* literally prays to God for blue/bluest eyes. She feels that having

the bluest eyes will make her and her family's life less complicated and less painful socially. When God does not answer her prayers, she, as does Shange's third-grader, turns to a sorcerer of sorts, Soaphead Church, who allows her to obtain her blue eyes through her own psychological powers. Morrison does not glorify Pecola's ultimate desires; neither does she try to exorcise this self-alienation from Pecola as Shange here does. Both authors attack racist ideals that foster feelings of failure, inadequacy, and inferiority culminating in self-destructive tendencies among many African Americans.

18. Lou's opening monologue after the minstrel show appears in *Nappy Edges* as "on becomin successful: 'she dont seem afrikan enuf to know bt . . .'/ 'seems she's dabblin in ghetto-life . . .'" (102).

19. According to a recent General Social Survey by the National Opinion Research Center at the University of Chicago, most whites believe that "blacks are more likely to be lazy, violence-prone, less intelligent, and less patriotic" ("Archie Bunker, Alive and Well," *Newsweek*, 21 January 1991, 59).

20. Ribowsky, 46.

21. Shange's novel *Betsey Brown* (New York: St. Martin's, 1985) is her closely autobiographical account of growing up in St. Louis in the 1950s and is rendered from a thirteen-year-old black girl's perspective. *Betsey Brown* was transformed into a musical, produced in 1989 at the Forum Theater (Philadelphia, Pennsylvania) by the American Music Theater Festival.

22. Jo Ann Levine, "'Bein' a Woman, Bein' Colored'," *Christian Science Monitor*, 9 September 1978, 23.

23. Shange, "A Colored Girl: Ntozake Shange," video-recording.

24. Alec's opening speeches, with interjections by "Voices," constitute Shange's title poem in *Nappy Edges* (86-88); it is subtitled "a cross country sojourn." Shange changes the individual's first-person experience to the speaker's first-person plural experience. Langston Hughes' poem "Still Here" connects with this validation of black presence in racist North America despite forces which endeavor to render that presence insignificant or illegitimate as does Maya Angelou's "Still I Rise" which celebrates human survival in the face of racism and sexism.

25. Shange argues that forced integration was not necessarily

physically, psychologically, intellectually, or emotionally healthy for
black Americans. In fact, such a move may well have contributed to
many blacks' self-doubts and low self-esteem. Shange questions the
appropriateness of such a government move for blacks asked to "feel
at home" and function "normally" in often hostile and physically
threatening white environments.

26. See Nikki Giovanni's volume, *My House* (New York: William Morrow, 1972), and its title poem, "My House." Giovanni
stakes these same territorial claims and sounds her authorial voice
also as a poet:

> . . . it's my house
> and i want to fry pork chops
> and bake sweet potatoes
> and call them yams
> cause i run the kitchen
> and i can stand the heat
> . . . .
> and my windows might be dirty
> but it's my house
> and if i can't see out sometimes
> they can't see in either. (68)

Giovanni's poem also parallels Shange's ideas about the English
language and the psychological limitations involved in restricting
one's emotional expressions solely in a language that seeks to define
and to limit black Americans' possibilities for full livelihood:

> english isn't a good language
> to express emotion through
> mostly i imagine because people
> try to speak english instead
> of trying to speak through it[.] (68)

27. Notice that Shange associates blacks here with the drinking
of wine while she uses beer to associate a stereotype of whites in the
Madison Square Garden poem sequence.

28. Ntozake Shange, "Conference on Common Differences:

Third World Women," University of Illinois at Champaign, April 1983, audiocassette, side B. The poem "i live in music" from *Nappy Edges* (126) is cited in Chapter II.

29. Shange may also be attacking Eurocentric children's "classics" which render women passive as compared to men who act and rescue, and minorities absent altogether. FOX Network comedy show, "In Living Color," offers a parody of the Rapunzel tale, presenting a black Rapunzel with a hair weave (1990). When the Prince tries to climb the weave, it breaks off. Additionally, Fred Crump, Jr., a revisionist of Eurocentric fairytales with an Afrocentric emphasis, has created a black Rapunzel with extremely long African braids and characteristically Negroid facial features. See *Rapunzel* (Nashville: Winston-Derek, 1991).

30. This section appears as a separate short story in *The Black Scholar* 10 (November/December 1978): 13-14.

31. Similarly, bell hooks examines the ritual of hair straightening among African American women in her article, "Straightening Our Hair," *Z Magazine* (September 1988), in *Reading Culture: Contexts for Critical Reading and Writing*, eds. Diana George and John Trimbur (New York: HarperCollins, 1992): 290-98. See also Alice Walker's short story, "Olive Oil" [*Black Erotica*, eds. Miriam DeCosta-Willis, Reginald Martin, and Roseann P. Bell (New York: Doubleday, 1992)], which connects eroticism with a black man's scalp-oiling by a black woman.

32. Head hair and its racist and sexist implications as associated with aesthetics of beauty has been documented in both literature and popular culture from plantation and minstrel songs and Malcolm X's *Autobiography* (1964) to Spike Lee's film *School Daze* (1988). See also the documentary, *The Question of Color* (1992), produced and directed by Kathe Sandler. While this documentary explains the dynamics of and offers testimonials of those who have experienced intraracism based on their skin tones, it also shows that hair—alleged "good" and "bad" hair—is connected with this issue of intraracism.

33. Wanting to be white as compared to wanting acting jobs that are not skin-color dictated is the essential difference here between destructive fantasy and creative imagination.

34. See James Baldwin's play, *Blues for Mister Charlie* (1964), wherein Baldwin explores and explodes stereotypes that connect

race, gender, and sexuality. See also Lawrence R. Tenzer's theories concerning the origins of the black-white penis size myths in *A Completely New Look at Interracial Sexuality: Public Opinion and Social Commentaries* (Manahawkin, New Jersey: Scholars' Publishing House, 1990), especially chapter six, "Is There Really a Sexual Difference?" (90-105).

35. See Maya Angelou's poems, "And Still I Rise" and "Phenomenal Woman."

36. Notably, Shange does not in her examples here report simple stereotyping so much as acknowledge different cultural traditions, celebrating an Afrocentric tradition of emotional freedom, improvisation, and spontaneity over a Eurocentric one of emotional control, strict adherence to order, and logic.

37. *Ebony Pictorial History of Black America (Volume II): Reconstruction to Supreme Court Decision 1954* (Nashville: Southwestern, 1971), 307-08. According to another source, rather than whistling at the white woman, Till merely told her "Bye, Baby" as he left the woman's store. See Chapter Two, "Standing for Justice: Mississippi and the Till Case," in Juan Williams' *Eyes on the Prize: America's Civil Rights Years, 1954-1965* (New York: Blackside, 1987), 37-57. This was the least historically documented of the two incidents that sparked the Civil Rights Movement, the other being the Montgomery Bus Boycott.

38. Note the emotional implications of Shange's allusion to an incident in the history of black people's existence in racist North America. That an adolescent black male would be murdered for allegedly "whistling" at a white woman strikes at least two chords. First is the irony of the white man's historical sexual access to black women. There is no historical evidence that black men lynched white men for sexually assaulting black women. Secondly, the incident reiterates the white patriarchy's attitude toward white and black women as property. If a black man's attentions to a white woman are anything but subservient, it becomes the white man's duty to assert his ownership status. See also Beah Richards' monologue play, *A Black Woman Speaks* (1975), in *Nine Plays by Black Women*, ed. Margaret B. Wilkerson (New York: Penguin, 1986, 27-39), which offers a message of unity among black and white women against patriarchal oppression.

In addition, the implications behind smiling are complicated as well. Not only did slaves generally smile and wear "masks" for physical survival, but slave women particularly groomed masks for their white male superiors who often perceived them as objects for their own personal sexual enjoyment. This same necessity of smiling or masking for survival characterized the lives of blacks during the days of Jim Crow. See Richard Wright's autobiographical story, "The Ethics of Living Jim Crow" (1938), from his collection, *Uncle Tom's Children* (New York: Harper and Row, 1940).

39. Langston Hughes, "Still Here," in *Selected Poems of Langston Hughes* (New York: Alfred A. Knopf, 1959), 123.

40. Such a situation of an aggressive female's sexual behavior toward her identity-clarification occurs in Maya Angelou's *I Know Why the Caged Bird Sings*, when Maya naively has sex with an unsuspecting male to determine whether or not she is a lesbian. This type of sexual aggression contrasts Hurston's presentation of Janie in *Their Eyes Were Watching God* when she discovers her sexuality, and Johnny Taylor somehow seems more attractive than before.

41. Interestingly, Toni Morrison's Pecola in *The Bluest Eye* experiences a similar end, plunging into madness. Unlike Sue-Jean, whose fantasy is unfulfilling, Pecola experiences an existential redefinition of her self. Her new version of a blue-eyed reality sustains her but is limited by the perpetual uncertainty of her possessing the bluest eyes. Additionally, both Shange and Morrison present female characters who, through fantasy and imagination, seek to mold their own realities.

42. Sue-Jean's tragedy, her inability to realize that her own empowerment does not come through her controlling others, is not far removed from the nameless narrator's experience of powerlessness and insanity in Ralph Ellison's short story, "King of the Bingo Game" (1944), in *Dark Symphony: Negro Literature in America*, eds. James A. Emanuel and Theodore L. Gross (New York: Free P, 1968), 271-79.

43. Sue-Jean's murderous act is in no way self-sacrificial as Sethe's murdering of her infant daughter in Toni Morrison's *Beloved* (1987). And Sue-Jean's ideal of remaining pregnant with a child that is perpetually a part of her is physically impossible and psychologically self-destructive.

44. Maya Angelou's "Still I Rise" offers this same lesson of resilience in black existence.

45. Recall the political statement Shange made when she changed her name in the 1970s. Her dress of brightly colored scarves, numerous chains dangling around her neck, and an earring in her right nostril also suggested her strong racial and political ties with an African ancestry.

46. Personal interview, *Studies in American Drama.*

47. Henry Louis Gates, Jr., in "TV's Black World Turns—But Stays Unreal," summarizes the history of African American presence in American television. In that article, reprinted from the "Lifestyle" section of the *New York Times*, Gates posits that images of blacks in television, even in "politically correct" 1992 American society, seem to fall into what poet and critic Sterling A. Brown, in his article, "Negro Character as Seen by White Authors" [*Journal of Negro Education* 2 (April 1933): 179-203], deemed the seven categories of black character types in American literature: the contented slave; the wretched freeman; the comic Negro; the brute Negro; the tragic mulatto; the local color Negro; and the exotic primitive. Gates' article appears in *Reading Culture: Contexts for Critical Reading and Writing* (New York: HarperCollins, 1992), Diana George and John Trimbur, eds., 463-70. See also Barbara Ann Teer's article, "The Great White Way Is Not Our Way—Not Yet," *Negro Digest* (April 1968): 21-29.

48. Actor and singer Leslie Uggams highlights the reality of racism as a fundamental barrier in the careers of black actors. She explains: "Dramatic series about black families are not being made. . . . It's hard to get a black television show—period. Here we are talking about this, here in 1990. They want us to make them laugh all the time. That's the brainwashing—that nobody wants to see a serious show about blacks" (*Birmingham News*, 18 October 89, A2). While Uggams' comments are specifically about television, they apply just as appropriately to circumstances in American theater.

49. See Robert Townsend's movie "Hollywood Shuffle" (1987) about a black actor's conflicts in deciding whether or not to compromise his professional integrity for a stereotypical role.

50. Langston Hughes' Jesse B. Semple is an example of a racially and politically aware black male with clearly sexist attitudes

about women. See any of Hughes' "tales" of Semple: *Simple Speaks His Mind* (1950), *Simple Takes a Wife* (1953), *Simple Stakes a Claim* (1957), *Best of Simple* (1961), and *Simple's Uncle Sam* (1965).

51. While a number of these plays attacked white racism, many also attacked blacks who assimilated into white culture, abandoning or belittling their own values and ideals as African Americans. See Amiri Baraka's essay, "In Search of Revolutionary Theater" (1966); Ed Bullins' revolutionary Commercials, especially "The American Flag Ritual: A Short Play or Film Scenario" (1969) and "A Short Play for a Small Theater" (1970), from Bullins' *The Theme Is Blackness: The Corner and Other Plays* (New York: William Morrow, 1973); Baraka's *Madheart* (1967); and Ron Milner's essay, "Black Theater—Go Home!" (1968).

52. In addition to attacking Alec's sexist attitudes, Shange here frowns upon his boasting of being classically trained. She launches a political and cultural attack on the alleged "classics" and on those black individuals who accept Eurocentric values and ideals as measures of their self-worth. See the Julliard-trained black female character, Medea Jones, in the segment, "The Last Mama-on-the-Couch Play," from George C. Wolfe's *The Colored Museum* (1985). In "African American Renderings of Traditional Texts," in *Global Perspectives on Teaching Literature: Shared Visions and Distinctive Visions* (Urbana: National Council of Teachers of English, 1993, 239-53), I examine this issue of the "classics" and their reflection of Eurocentric ideals and experiences that potentially alienate or render absent people of color. I also examine Shange's purposes and experiences with her black cultural revisions of Bertolt Brecht's *Mother Courage and Her Children* and Willy Russell's *Educating Rita*.

53. My NCTE article "African American Renderings of Traditional Texts" also considers the political and social impact of nontraditional castings, castings not dictated by actors' race.

54. Shange's dismay that the literary "classics" are Eurocentric resulted in her own adaptation and demystification of Bertolt Brecht's *Mother Courage and Her Children*. While reviews of this adaptation were mixed, it fulfilled a purpose for Shange: making a dramatic experience more meaningful and culturally accessible for black people. In essence, Shange changes Brecht's German Thirty Years War to the post-Civil War era of fighting between the American

cavalry and the American Indians for the Southwest Territory; she also makes the title character an emancipated slave. *Mother Courage and Her Children* was performed at Joseph Papp's New York Shakespeare Festival during April-June 1980; it ran for 22 previews and 40 performances. Shange details the genesis of the adaptation in her essay, "How I Moved Anna Fierling to the Southwest Territories, or my personal victory over the armies of western civilization," which appears in *See No Evil: Prefaces, Essays & Accounts, 1976-1983* (San Francisco: Momo's, 1984):

> i had & still grapple with the idea of classics in the lives & arts of third world people. we have so much to do, so much to unearth abt our varied realities/ on what grounds do we spend our talents, hundreds of thousands of dollars, unknown quantities of time, to recreate experiences that are not our own? does a colonial relationship to a culture/ in this case Anglo-Saxon imperialism/ produce a symbiotic relationship or a parasitic one? if we perform the classics/ giving our culture some leeway in an adaptation/ which is the parasite? why aren't the talents & perspectives of contemporary third world artists touted in the same grand fashion successful rivals of dead white artists are? . . . Mother Courage gave me the opportunity to ground myself in the history of my people in this land. i can offer this version of Brecht's masterpiece as the adventures & trials of people of color of the last century in a language of my own. . . . i am settling my lands with my characters, my language, my sense of right & wrong, my sense of time & rhythm.

55. Telephone interview with Laurie Carlos, actress and author, New York City, 27 August 1986.

56. Langston Hughes, "Note on Commercial Theater," in *Selected Poems of Langston Hughes* (New York: Alfred A. Knopf, 1959), 190.

57. Tom Buckley, "The Three Stages of Ntozake Shange," *New*

York Times, 16 December 1977, C6.

58. "Ntozake Shange Interview," *All Things Considered*, National Public Radio, 6 June 1985.

59. "Black in White America: A Documentary," ABC News, producer Ray Nunn, August 1991.

60. Ronald A. Homer, "Combatting Racism on the Job," *Business Week Careers*, November 1986, 55. Homer is the president and chief executive of the Boston Bank of Commerce in Boston, Massachusetts. Homer's article considers the reality of racism in the business setting and offers the same advice to blacks that Shange offers in *spell #7*; he writes:

> Develop an attitude towards race that is not self-defeating or demoralizing, but rather is uplifting and inspiring to you as well as to others. Feelings of self-worth and self-esteem are vital ingredients to mental health and are essential to projecting confidence and self-assurance, while maintaining a sense of humor. . . . To believe that being black is all negative is to accept the racist attitudes in our society. . . . [And] finally, remember that racism is but one inequity and evil that exists in our society. Your ultimate success in whatever you attempt will be defined by your character, confidence, commitment, and competence[,] . . . characteristics on which no group has a monopoly. (56)

61. Sylvester Monroe, "Brothers," *Newsweek*, 23 March 1987, 57.

62. About her inspiration for the Madison Square Garden piece, Shange explains:

> I wrote it because Bob Marley had just been to town in Madison Square Garden and Madison Square Garden was sold out and all *The New York Times* could say was that "only 20,000 West Indians were there" which amazed me because I said "well would he [the reporter] have said only 20,000 white

people were there?" The rest of the sentence went
on to say that it wasn't really the breakthrough Bob
Marley needed because "only 20,000 West Indians
were there. . . ." I guess you don't "breakthrough" unless you bring white people with you.
[Ntozake Shange, "She Who Comes from Herself," audiocassette, Iowa State University
Women's Week (8 October 1984), side A.]

63. See "latent rapists'" in *for colored girls*, 17-21.
64. Writers of slave narratives, such as Frederick Douglass in
Narrative of the Life of Frederick Douglass, an American Slave
(1845), also reverse this stereotype of blacks as animals to show the
owners of human flesh and their treatment of slaves as the ultimate
behavior of brutes, savages—animals.
65. Recall this technique of negative cataloguing in "Journal
Entry #692" from Shange's novel *Sassafrass, Cypress & Indigo*
wherein she redefines the role of dance and song for black people
displaced and oppressed in racist North America.
66. The black myth concerning white people's careless hygiene
probably comes from traditional experiences of black maids in white
households. Whites as beer drinkers can be verified in television
commercials where athletes and actors, mostly white, endorse Miller
Lite and Budweiser. Shange addresses this broader issue of the
media's reflecting values of the dominant white culture in Maxine's
final fantasy sequence at the end of the play.
67. See Claude Lewis' "Too Many Blacks Don't Speak English
Correctly," *Birmingham News* (30 June 1989), A9; and Wayne
Lionel Aponte's "'Talkin' White,'" *Essence* (January 1989), 11.
68. Personal interview, *Studies in American Drama*.
69. "aw, babee, you so pretty" is published as a short story in
Essence (April 1979), 87, 145-46.
70. Shange's novel in progress, *Liliane or the Resurrection of a
Daughter*, considers the issue of sexism internationally. It treats one
woman of color's adventures with several international lovers as
rendered primarily from the male lovers' perspectives. Shange
explains the basic premise of the novel:

> [Sexism is] not [just] in our particular society.
> That's one of the big issues in *Liliane.* . . . [T]hat's
> one of the reasons I have her [the hero] go all over
> the world—so that the critics wouldn't be able to
> say, "Oh, here she is—attacking black men again."
> That's not the issue for me. I was raised in a segre-
> gated society where black men were the world. So
> that is all the world I knew. So for me, they were
> the world. That didn't apparently get through to
> people, that we could be the universal symbol of
> humanity. *Liliane* . . . is much more explicit. She
> goes all over the world and all over the world she is
> confronted with sexism. One of the neat things
> about books like *When God Was a Woman* and *Of
> Woman Born* and Shere Hite's research is that we
> can document sexism for 10,000 years in virtually
> every culture known to humankind. Therefore,
> being a woman who has a passport certainly doesn't
> give one entry into communities where sexism does
> not exist. It's entry into a community where sexism
> is manifested in different kinds of ways. (Personal
> interview)

71. Toni Morrison, in *The Bluest Eye*, uses Ginger Rogers, Mary
Jane (candy wrapper), Greta Garbo, and Shirley Temple as icons of
American female beauty ideals. Showing that minorities, even
children, are bombarded by these images at every turn helps to
demonstrate how blacks in the novel internalize black inferiority
early on in the face of American ideals of beauty, success, intelligence, and self-worth.

72. Ossie Davis, *Purlie Victorious: A Comedy in Three Acts*
(New York: Samuel French, 1961), 81. Ossie Davis' *Purlie Victorious* comically treats black and white stereotypes in the south. Allen
Woll, in *Dictionary of the Black Theater: Broadway, Off-Broadway,
and Selected Harlem Theater* (Westport, Connecticut: Greenwood,
1983), cites *New York Times* critic Howard Taubman's comment that
"while *Purlie Victorious* keeps you laughing, chuckling, and guf-
fawing, it unrelentingly forces you to feel how it is to inhabit a dark

skin in a hostile, or at best, grudgingly benevolent world" (130). Although Davis recommends a harmonious integration of blacks and whites and Shange condones segregation for blacks, both profess a message of positive racial identity for black people. Davis' comedy was successfully musicalized on the Broadway stage as *Purlie* (1970).

CHAPTER IV

"the contours of life unnoticed":
a photograph: lovers in motion

"Aside from music," Shange argues, "photography is the medium closest to poetry. Poetry is not about the whole world, but about the density of a moment. Photography also gives you the density of the truth. Poems are not novels and photographs are not films."[1] Using photography both as a subject and as a metaphor, Shange offers images of male and female sexual identity in *a photograph: lovers in motion* (1979). Shange's third published theater piece (the second play in the *three pieces* volume) was termed a "poemplay" by Shange when it was originally presented at the New York Shakespeare Festival in 1977 with the title, *A Photograph: A Still Life With Shadows/ A Photograph: A Study in Cruelty*. In 1979, the published text was performed at the Equinox Theater in Houston (Texas), under Shange's direction. Again, because of its unconventional dramatic form, critics questioned Shange's talents as a "real dramatist." While Edith Oliver praised *a photograph*, insisting that Shange's "own poetic talent and passion carry the show, and her characters are . . . flesh and blood . . . ,"[2] John Simon lashed out:

> *A Photograph* . . . calls itself a "poemplay." What is a poemplay? Something, evidently, that is neither poem nor play, but hopes that the poetry experts will let it pass as a play, while the drama critics will assume it to be poetry. Actually it is neither. It is exactly the same drivel as Miss Shange's previ-

> ous *For Colored Girls* . . . (which, with a similar
> strategy, called itself a "choreopoem"), so hailed
> by our gullible reviewers. . . . *A Photograph* is
> more of a play (albeit a rotten one) than [*For Col-
> ored Girls*] . . . , which was just a bunch of self-
> indulgent monologues and paltry dancing thrown
> together pell-mell.[3]

Simon's comments raise a number of relevant issues. Although he recognizes Shange's blending of the poetic and the dramatic—in an African American poetic tradition the two mediums are nearly inseparable—he seems unwilling or unable to accept this expression on Shange's own artistic and aesthetic terms. That critics like Simon insist upon artificial separations of art forms is not a particularly central concern for Shange as she consciously works to expand the boundaries of what we have come to know and accept as legitimate theater. That poetry and drama coexist simultaneously is especially evidenced in the performative nature of the revolutionary poetry of LeRoi Jones/Amiri Baraka, Sonia Sanchez, Nikki Giovanni, as well as the poetic language, rhythms, and imagery of Adrienne Kennedy's plays. Simon's commentary once again reveals more about his own personal and cultural biases than about the Shange piece itself.

Martin Gottfried echoes Simon, insisting that "*A Photograph* is a play and a series of poems, but unfortunately, it is never both. . . . Shange is a wonderful poet, but she is not yet a playwright and does not create playable characters. . . . [*A Photograph*] does not cohere as drama. . . . Shange is an inspired and original poet with a flair for the theatrical, but she is still a stage amateur."[4] That Gottfried would cite more traditional plays and playwrights as "real" coherent drama, except Samuel Beckett, for instance, is not at all surprising, given Western influences on American theater. Perhaps Dean Valentine's assessment accounts for some of the critics' intensely negative reception to *a photograph*: ". . . intelligibility stops. I have not the faintest notion how the multitudinous vignettes that comprise the play are related."[5] Valentine's statement resounds with criticism associated with much of Shange's dramatic work. Her response to Valentine would undoubtedly be that the choreopoem is appropriate for a specific audience and for particular cultural realities, that it is a genre that rejects artificial dramatic conventions as a reflection of Eurocentric thought and experience. Hence, the seeming incoherence among the pieces within a work does not indicate Shange's lack of skill as a playwright. And part of her craft is to present an order in what seems to have none. As poet-educator Quandra Prettyman expresses about the nature of a photograph,

> The picture is not real.
> Still, neither is the word.
> But the eye makes pictures,
> The mouth words,
> Pressing order
> Where none is.[6]

Such critics' comments reveal a consistent effort to fit Shange's theater pieces into more traditional dramatic categories. Whether it was the critics' reactions to the first versions[7] of *a photograph* or Shange's own dissatisfaction with the piece or a combination of both, the published Samuel French edition (1981) is subtitled "A Drama." Identifying the revision as drama, Shange does employ more conventional techniques of characterization and plot than in previous choreopoems. As in previous choreopoems, however, there is little effort to present characters with a linear narrative. As a blend of music, dance, and poetry, this piece presents the "density of a moment" that intertwines five characters whose lives are complicated, often contradictory, and whose identities are heaped with ambiguities. With minimal attention to traditional plot development, Shange focuses instead on the discussions, attitudes, and behaviors of these black individuals, particularly as they recognize and acknowledge their sexuality as essential parts of their identities. Shange presents a particular moment in these characters' lives, a moment gravely influenced by their ancestral and historical pasts. Tensions in the play might arise from the contradictions in the characters' behaviors and words, in the absence of a hero with which an audience might identify, and in Shange's unwillingness to resolve identity issues she raises. With multifaceted black characters, Shange extends this choreopoem form to present a tract on self-exploitation and the deliberate exploitation of others.

The title itself, *a photograph: lovers in motion*, announces not only the play's thematic tensions and ambiguities but its structural framework. A photograph presumes to capture a reality at a particular moment. Yet no matter how precisely a photograph seems to capture the subject and the moment, a photograph is not reality but an image or signifier of that reality. Photography, moreover, works as a metaphor for theater in particular since it is a means by which to manipulate time and movement simultaneously. In addition, a photograph presents stasis, not motion; once motion is illusively captured, movement ceases. Sean, the photographer of the play, insists that he is able to capture life in process: winds blowing, bread being kneaded, stars falling, and loving. Yet, a photographer can record only images of bread, stars, and people in love, frozen in time. As Timothy Murray further distinguishes, "the photographic process allows Sean to objectify the world around him, to stabilize the fluid and changeable referents around, and to arrange the world. . ." (112).[8] Shange's *a photograph* is about people who share anxieties, frustrations, and fears. It is less about their daily existence as about a particular moment—the time of the play's running on the stage during a performance—in the lives of those in quest. Episodic in structure, the piece is like a slide show presentation, each of the twelve scenes being a frame or slide. The play ends with an ambiguous alliance between Michael and Sean, two characters who enjoy the most dependable relationship in the play. Exposed to an intricate network of human relationships, the audience witnesses Shange's manipulation of various emotional responses to the same characters at different moments during the play. We also recognize the tentativeness of human interactions, the uncertain and fleeting nature of life as process that dies when captured on film.

Defying both her stereotype as a black feminist who allegedly hates black men and critic John Simon's assessment of *a photograph* as her attempt to "sleazily bad-mouth black men,"[9] Shange does in fact sympathize with black men whose abuse and exploitation of black women she sees as growing out of black men's own personal and private conflicts.[10] Just as Beau Willie Brown is presented compassionately, so too is Sean, an aspiring photographer, who wrestles with the meaning of success and manhood while trying to resolve for himself the tensions of his past relationship with his father. Since

Sean is the photographer of the play's title and since he is the character around which the other characters revolve and become interconnected, he might appear to be the heroic center of the play. Yet Sean
is just as confused about his sexual identity and his personal and
professional goals as are the other characters. Indeed, all of the
characters are equally significant as representatives of a particular
aspect or dimension of black male-female identity. Their conflicts are
internal and intensified by social stereotypes and expectations.

Sean is the first male character to dominate a published play by
Shange and is perhaps one of Shange's most complex characters as
well; we witness the entire realm of his social, physical, and psychological existence during the course of *a photograph*, particularly
through his treatment of three female lovers. As a stereotype, Sean
represents a male, regardless of race, whose image of himself is
determined by his sexual performance with women.[11] Most confident
of his sexual skills, Sean prides himself in his ability to juggle a
number of female lovers while retaining complete control with each.
He admits to his "special" lover Michael—the female to whom he
feels closest of his three lovers—that he is not a one-woman man:
"there are a number of women in my life/ who i plan to keep in my
life/ & i'll never let any of them come between us/ between what we
have in our world/ you hear" (61). On the one hand, such a proclamation might seem hollow, for if Michael were as "special" to him
as he professes her to be, he might have no need for outside romantic
or sexual relationships. We learn later in the play that Michael's
relationship with Sean is very different from his other relationships.
Still, the statement reveals Sean's belief that his perceived manhood
derives from his ability to manage numerous lovers without conflict.
Throughout the play, however, Sean is unable to keep these relationships apart. And not only are the relationships awkwardly overlapping, but the women struggle against each other for his attentions.
His attempt to maintain discrete categories in his personal life is
reflected as well in his profession; he struggles to keep his raw
photographs of Vietnam separate from the contrived photographs he
intends to be his ticket to commercial success. In the early moments
of the play, Sean represents the black male as stud whose overwhelming sense of his own masculinity precludes a monogamous relationship with any female. Emotionally calloused in his treatment of

women, Sean abuses them verbally, physically, and psychologically—priding himself on the fact that they return for his attentions. His attitude toward women generally is highlighted in his failed attempt to arouse jealousy in Michael over his involvement with other women: "dont be getting all holy & above possession/ aint a bitch in the world cant get jealous & loud/ they been running me crazy" (69). This statement reveals Sean as one of contradictions. While he wants Michael to understand his need to have other lovers, he can not understand her "unbitch-like" behavior. Indeed, his manhood is affirmed only when women are fighting over him. Even language, for Sean, is a means of psychological power and until the final moments of the play, he defines his alleged male superiority through such phrases as "i dont take no orders from no bitch" (84), "stupid bitch" (85), and "you are sucha dumb bitch" (86).

Often going beyond verbal lashings, Sean is quick to assault and exploit his female companions physically. Not only does he convince Claire to pose nude under a shower of Jack Daniels and to parade around his apartment naked with feathers inserted vaginally, but he also forces whiskey into her mouth when she taunts him with her own alleged sexual escapades; in a fit of resentment and jealousy, Sean threatens to have Claire gang raped: "c'mere claire/ i got something for ya. if you ever so much as look at willie/ or come down with something [a venereal disease]/ i'm gonna take you down to the 500 club on fillmore/ & give everybody some of that magnolia . . ." (65). In the same moment of outrage at the perceived threat to his manhood, he turns to lovemaking and makes it part of this rather destructive game: [He] "picks claire up/ [and] tumbles onto the bed with her" (66), searching for the rhinestones, palm leaves, and magnolia petals she claims to have hidden in her vagina. Sean views sexuality not as passion and spirituality but as exertion of his physical and psychological control over his lovers. He also submits to the myth that violence (sexual or otherwise), here in his allusion to gang rape, is the means by which males maintain control over females. Yet Sean's sexual advances are not rejected by Claire; on the contrary, she eagerly awaits his physical passion, perhaps revealing a part of Claire's psyche that welcomes such abuse as foreplay to intimacy. Despite her seemingly independent and progressive attitudes, she clearly subscribes to mythic gender roles of aggressive male and passive female. With Michael, Sean at most grabs her arms or resorts to harsh name-calling, whereas with Claire, he is able to act out his sexual fantasies. In his treatment of Nevada, however, Sean gloats over her psychological dependence on him, preying on Nevada's emotional vulnerability and using her as a means of financial support; she pays his rent and buys his expensive camera equipment. Despite Nevada's own professional success, she craves attention which she has convinced herself only Sean provides. In the face of her hysteria, he revels in his control: "i dont want yr face/ nevada. i got what i want from you/ you love me dont you? well/ thats all i want/ i'm probably the only real thing in yr life & i can feel it/ how you love me/ . . ." (78). Sean wants Nevada's love because her love for him makes her vulnerable to his selfish demands.

At the heart of Sean's identity problem is a warped definition of manhood. As most of his actions evidence, to Sean manhood is simply power over women. And indeed, it seems that a violent temper, a sharp tongue, and brute force give Sean control in these relationships. Clearly, Shange attacks these mythical notions of manhood. At the same time, she offers mitigating factors that explain Sean's attitude toward and his treatment of women. She uses Michael as her mouthpiece in redefining manhood:

> *michael*
> i thot you were a man
> > *sean*
> i fuck you fool/ you still dont know i'ma man?
> > *michael*
> i mean somebody who loves in the world/ loves himself
> & his work & some people. (87)

Shange attacks this myth that sexual performance automatically grants manhood. Manhood, she prescribes, means vulnerability, gentleness, and respect for women. Further, to change his attitude toward women, Sean must first examine his attitude toward his own gender identity. In the process of his discovery, Sean gradually elicits an audience's sympathies.

Sean's views of and his relationships with women originate from two interconnected sources in his life. College educated and intelli-

gent, Sean spends time reading French literature. That his hero is
French novelist and dramatist Alexandre Dumas, who led a life of
roguish debauchery, underlies Sean's perceptions of his own manhood. In fact, Dumas' novels, *The Count of Monte-Cristo* (1844) and
The Three Musketeers (1844), to which Sean alludes during the play,
are romantic tales of adventure whose heroes overcome all obstacles
and are rewarded for their noble actions. Yet it is Dumas' personal
life that Sean desperately tries to emulate. To Michael, he offers
biographical notes on Dumas in efforts to explain his own professional ambitions:

> you know alexandre dumas waz a clerk
> who wrote at night & dreamed of joinin victor hugo's
>   salon
> his son/ alexandre dumas/ came by him accidentally
> a seamstress with clean firm hands loved him very
>   much.
> i'm gonna be the alexandre dumas of my time/ both the
>   father
> and the son. alexandre dumas waz a rogue
> . . . .
> his father's territories included the beds of paris
> & the stage/ women who turned heads with honeysuckle
>   voices
> & skirts lifted to the hips/ . . .
> . . . .
> alexandre dumas sent his son away from him/
> hurried to be famous/ his son waited til the moment waz
>   right
> & presented his father/ alexandre dumas/ with a man.
>   (62)

Sean, who has exhaustively studied the life of Alexandre Dumas,
defines success in terms of materialism, and manhood as having
multiple sex partners. Sean also celebrates Dumas' move from
anonymity as a lowly clerk who dared to dream to be a renowned
author. Dumas' dreams form the basis of Sean's dream of moving
from his position as a lowly "niggah" to that of the world's greatest

photographer. Until Sean can be commercially successful, he considers himself insignificant. His harem of female lovers means little to him as he dreams of matching Dumas' fame.

Still, Sean's feelings about Dumas the father are contradictory. On the one hand, Sean resents Dumas' callous treatment of his son and of his son's mother. Since Dumas considered his son an "accident," the son feels compelled to legitimize his existence by earning his father's acknowledgement and praise. Sean sees himself as the son anxious to prove his worth to his father. On the other hand, Sean admires Dumas' professional daring to excel. His inability to separate the professional from the personal in his own life contributes to Sean's confusion about what photography really means to him and what constitutes true manhood. Dumas' son's perceptions of manhood derive from observing his father's infidelity to his mother. Fearing his son's retaliation for this action, the father sends young Dumas away. The son's return becomes a personal goal for Sean, an assertion of his fame as an accomplished photographer who captures an essence of black life hitherto unnoticed. Sean clarifies:

> alexandre dumas tore his son from his mother's
> linen & sent his son away from him.
> the threat of his own blood too much.
> he sent his son to the forest to learn to disappear
> but sons come back/ sons come back from where they
>   are forgotten/
> these photographs are for them/ they are gonna see our
>   faces/
> the visage of the sons/ the sons who wdnt disappear
> niggahs who are still alive
> i'm gonna go ona rampage/ a raid on the sleeping
>   settlers
> this camera's gonna get em. (62)

This simultaneous admiration for and resentment of Alexandre Dumas offer a motive for his determination to succeed and a key to contradictions in his personality. His camera is, for him, the weapon by which he avenges his own perceived lowly position as a black male in a racist society. The image of sons sent away to disappear also symbolizes white patriarchy's historically documented efforts to render African Americans invisible, their experiences insignificant.

Sean's personal and professional predicament is the subject of the other characters' conversations. Earl reminds him: "it's just i dont understand/ i mean you were poor all yr life/ why you wanna be a poor starving artist" (59) and insists that Sean "can't forget how colored [he is] for a minute" (95). Claire says that "sean aint nothing but a niggah" and that "that's why he's never gonna be great or whatever you call it/ cuz he's a niggah & niggahs cant be nothing" (103). Even culturally arrogant Nevada describes Sean's hero Dumas as "common" and "the same as these wild niggah artists [Sean included] are today" (67). Only Michael recognizes Sean's potential for escaping the white stereotype of blacks as "niggahs"—lazy, unintelligent, morally loose, and destined to want and poverty. Sean has internalized these social restrictions. Despite professing to be "an artist/ committed to [his] art" (58), Sean has not quite defined for himself what it means to be an artist, what it means to be a black artist, and what he perceives as true art. One of his problems, which Michael helps him to articulate later in the play, is that he must assess positively his own self-worth, not allowing his identity to be socially defined for him. After witnessing Nevada's destruction of Sean's photographs as he stands passively, Michael challenges:

> i sat in this room & watched you take all this shit
> from some bitch cuz she's got money & you aint/
> cuz you think being a nigger is being nothing/ bein
> put upon & taken/ well i'm telling you i dont come
> from that/ & i cant watch you be that/ my people
> took care of themselves. (80)

In fact, Sean does break negative stereotypes concerning blacks' limited education, creativity, and ambition. As a photographer, Sean likens his power to create to the power of God. He recognizes his creative powers through photography in an otherwise socially and economically powerless role as a black man: ". . . my god i gotta world now/ i gotta world i'm making in my image/ i got something for a change/ lil sean david who never got over on nothing but bitches/ is building a world in his image/ YALL GOT THAT?"

(79).[12] Sean's acknowledgement of his perceived power over women does not diminish his need to prove himself to the white world since black women have even lower social status and respectability than he. The moment at once recalls spiritual texts:

> And God said, Let us make man in our image,
> after our likeness: and let them have dominion over
> . . . all the earth . . . .
> So God created man in his *own* image, in the
> image of God created he him; male and female
> created he them. (Genesis 2: 26-27)[13]

Sean recreates images of men and women limited by others' reflections and perceptions of black experience, manhood, and womanhood. What he chooses to represent as authentic experience, however, is laden with ambivalence.

Many of Sean's professional and personal problems stem from parallels between his relationship with his own father and the Dumas father-son relationship. At the end of Act I, Sean reveals his confused definition of manhood as derived largely from his father's promiscuous behavior. Abandoning his preconceived notion of manhood as granting immunity to emotional pain, he recalls:

> when you get to be a man/ you can go to the whore-
>   house
> with me/ that's what he usedta say
> tho he brought the whores home/ & fucked em
> & beat em & fought em & laughed all nite long
> . . . .
> when you can swim like me/ he said/ you'll be a man
> & stuck me in the water with my diapers on.
> at dinner time daddy waz asleep/ head on the table
> & bottle nearby
> . . . .
> soft-eyed child with good straight legs
> soft-eyed child with wet sheets every nite
> i lay there all day til they dried sometimes
> to be a man

. . . .
my daddy didnt like me/ daddy didnt like me
he usedta say/ mama neither but it dont matter
cuz i'm not theirs no how/ i'ma man
i am a man
& he wd cry & drink his vodka/ with the lady whose
        name
i cdnt know/ cuz i was running the hallways
looking for a daddy. (88-89)

Sean's boyhood memories are of an emotionally distant father who
had little respect for women. But the father's problems are as deeply
rooted as are Sean's. Sean recalls images of his drunken father crying
and distraught because he was emotionally neglected by Sean's
paternal grandfather. This neglect has crossed at least two generations of males, (mis)shaping their perceptions and subsequent manifestations of manhood. The independence thrust upon Dumas' son
and on Sean did not diminish the sons' needs for paternal approval
and affection, resulting in each son's compulsion to prove his legitimacy to another male. Meanwhile, each man's bitterness, resentment, and pain are manifested in his abuse of women. Still, these
physical and psychological expressions of power over women do not,
however, satisfy the men's emotional voids. In the stories of men and
their unresolved relationships with their fathers, Shange reassesses
and redefines manhood as gentleness, emotional vulnerability, and
sensitivity—the very qualities stereotypically attributed to women and
hence weakness.

Sean's driving hostility subsides when he admits his need for a
love that goes beyond physical lovemaking—what Shange's colored
girls seek also. But Sean's admission makes the play's ending perhaps too romantic. His profession of love to Michael is less convinc-
ing since we witness Sean's behavior at two extremes without evidence or warning that his attitude toward women and himself would
change so drastically. What is certain about Sean, however, is that he
is not an unredeeming, ruthless black man. Edith Oliver recognizes
Sean's dilemma, his character's complexity: Sean, whose camera
represents his manhood and his means of attaining fame—a Nobel
Prize for photography is what he has in mind—is haunted by a dread-

ful childhood, by Alexandre Dumas, [the father and son, who were themselves part black], and their literary and sexual achievements in nineteenth-century Paris, and by some dead soldiers he photographed on a hillside in Vietnam. For all his savagery to his women, he cannot be easily dismissed as just another male chauvinist; ". . . he appears to be as much a victim of his out-of-hand ambition and his bitter frustration as they [the other characters] are."[14]

Shange holds much respect for Sean the dreamer and works to refute the myth that "if you're black, there's an artificial ceiling on your ambition."[15] From the opening to the closing moments of the play, Sean refers to his future success as a great photographer. His confidence in his sexual skills are matched only by his belief that he will someday be "the greatest photographer in the world" (87). Yet despite his claims to limitless potential, Sean is immobilized by his own economic and social status as a black person, caught perpetually in the act of becoming rather than being a great photographer. There is no evidence, for example, that Sean has ever submitted a photograph for exhibition. He doubts his own artistic instincts and is unsure whether photographs should present truth in raw form or airbrushed images of that truth. Claire alone knows that "sean aint never tried to get no show or no/ recommendations or nothing" (102). While Sean says he is "an artist/ committed to [his] art" (58), he fears rejection so much that he bases his success as a photographer and his worth as a person on commercial appeal, just as his manhood depends on his lovers' responses to his bedroom skills. Only Michael dares to question Sean about his "art" and his manhood. In connecting the two issues, she forces him to reassess his alleged commitment to art. Having discovered Sean's hidden photos of the Vietnam War[16] and of fighting children from a neighboring black community—fighting becomes an appropriate metaphor here and connects with the Nietzschian idea of struggle presented in *spell #7*—Michael questions Sean's insistence upon photographing only that which sells commercially: pornography:[17]

> **sean**
> i told you i'm gonna be the greatest photographer in the
> world

michael
how abt being the photographer you haveta be . . . will
you love yrself to keep working/ if the muthafuckahs in
washington say yr work aint shit/ if the galleries in
northbeach say niggah/ yr work aint shit/ can you love
yr photographs/ sean/ if they dont get what you want?
(87)

Shange's own voice resounds through Michael in a challenge to all
artists, particularly minorities, to do as she continues to do: write
earnestly despite mixed public reception. As an artist of color true to
her art, Shange warns other artists of color against commercial
success and/or failure as a criterion for self-worth individually and
artistically:

> If one were in fact to believe that because you get
> awards or because people pay money to see some-
> thing you wrote that that means something about
> your life in a way that's not transitory, that to me
> would be a great mistake. Success in entertainment,
> particularly in the United States, is so highly transi-
> tory and in some ways [so] pernicious that it's bet-
> ter to simply skim over as much as possible because
> the only thing I can do for myself is to keep work-
> ing.[18]

The play does not resolve this issue of Sean's artistic commitment;
rather, it explores how artists, particularly black artists, must honestly assess themselves and their work in the face of unpredictable
and transitory fame.

Contrasting the machismo of Sean is the ambiguous sexual
identity of the other male character in the play, Sean's childhood
friend, Earl. While Sean has chosen the topsy-turvy artistic route to
success, Earl, a lawyer, is the more structured professional. The
extent of their friendship is evidenced in the opening moments of the
play when Earl reveals to Sean the problems he is having with his ex-
girlfriend Claire and his uncertainties about his identity as a male.
Allegedly unable to accept that the relationship with Claire has

ended, Earl voices his resentment: ". . . ever since she found out she
cd be a model she aint been the same/ i cant keep up with her any-
more/ not that i really want to/ how she's been acting/ it's not my
thing man" (60). Earl's intimidation by Claire's new professional
independence is camouflaged by his feigned lack of interest in her
now. He accepts one of Sean's pornographic nudes of Claire, view-
ing the photo's eroticism as an expression of Sean's art. Earl appears
indifferent to the possibility of a romantic or sexual relationship
between Sean and Claire, and actually seems to give Sean permission
for such a liaison, despite having had Claire abandon him instead of
the reverse, allegedly because he did not satisfy her sexually. Aside
from obtaining a law degree, Earl seems fully unable to direct what
happens in his life; he thereby creates an illusion of his empowerment.

Sean is also involved with Nevada, another woman for whom
Earl has special feelings. Although not romantically or sexually
attracted to her, Earl counsels Nevada, who is painfully attached to
Sean, on what qualities she should want in a mate: "[you need]
somebody quiet & concerned & rich & brown & never been mean &
wont be/ really nevada/ sean doesnt know bout much more than
women & cruelty/ i usedta wish i cd be half of what he feels in
women/ just a lil less correct" (91). All Sean has in common with
Earl's prescription of the ideal man for Nevada is that he is black.
The characterization of the gentle man that Earl alleges Nevada
needs is an inadvertent description of himself, while his wish to be
"half of what Sean feels in women" is possibly one of the first clues
to Earl's ambivalent sexual identity. Significantly, Shange has Earl
recommend a "brown" (as opposed to a dark toned black) man for a
culturally arrogant and educated Nevada, and there is no consideration of interracial relationships for any of Shange's characters. Even
though he pleads Nevada's case to Sean, against his better judgment
as a friend, Earl recognizes qualities in Nevada that Sean could never
appreciate. Earl expresses no interest in Nevada despite Sean's
half-hearted proddings:

> so/ since you made the best of our situation/ & find
> yrself a professional man now/ why dont you take
> nevada off my hands/ i dont have what she

> needs. . . . i really think you shd consider nevada/
> ya know her family cd help you a lot/ they've got
> all kinds of money/ from what she says sounds like
> they own the state of texas that woman's gonna
> bring some man a whole lotta power/ & if it's not
> me/ might as well be you/ . . . . her daddy wd love
> to see her married/ especially to a lawyer/ he might
> even give you one of his insurance companies for a
> wedding present/ he knows nevada's gotta be paid
> for/ she cant give much. (95-97)

Sean's flippancy towards Nevada directly contrasts with Earl's
respect for her. Yet, while Earl resents Sean's treatment of Nevada,
he envies the attention women give Sean despite his abusive behavior; he explains to Sean: "you've been stealing my women now/ i
guess all the way from poly high thru state college/ i waz always
hooking up wit the one you just left/ i cdnt figure if it waz the way i
looked/ that i studied too much or waz just scared" (96). Hence,
Earl's emotions toward Sean are a mixture of envy, admiration,
resentment, and sexual attraction. And while the two men seem to
have opposite personalities and interests—Sean is the attractive
playboy with women at his feet; Earl is the studious one who, while
respecting women, fears rejection from them—both men are ultimately intimidated by a woman's independence, be it emotional,
sexual, or professional.

Earl's fear of rejection by women strikes another ambiguous note
regarding his sexual identity. As aforementioned, Earl and Claire are
no longer romantically involved. Earl's lack of romantic interest in
Nevada, who in his eyes is the perfect female companion for any
sensible male, and Claire's open attack on his manhood leave Earl's
sexual orientation unclear. As bisexual Claire facetiously proposi-
tions Michael and Earl (Act II, scene xii), Earl's response and
Claire's retort further suggest Earl's homosexuality:

> claire
> oh my/ so yr both waiting for me/ how lovely . . .
> i've got something for you/ earl/ & you too/
> michael

> *earl (crosses to exit)*
> i dont want nothing you got
> *claire (following earl)*
> that's always been yr problem. (99)

On still another occasion, Claire, reiterating her subscription to gender roles and stereotypes, wonders why Earl does not respond to her sexually as other men do, ultimately questioning his sexual preference: "the little time i spent wit you/ if i tried to kiss you/ you got scared" (71). Such a comment is as revealing of Claire as of Earl. While she questions his sexuality, her own possible sexual attraction to women is hidden even from him. Hence, when Earl proposes that he and Sean become permanent housemates, the proposition substantiates Earl's potentially romantic interest in Sean. Having made an apparently insincere plea to Sean on Nevada's behalf because of his own self-interest, Earl offers Sean the financial security that Nevada provides; more importantly, he offers Sean shelter from "those crazy bitches":

> when are you gonna realize what's important? there
> are a million beautiful faces/ & that cd be all there
> is/ too. i've been practicing a couple of years now/
> & making some money/ i waz thinking you & i cd
> take a house up in the berkeley hills/ one of those
> glass & redwood split levels/ witta terrace & the
> fog rolling in at dusk/ it cd be like the old days
> sean/ when you & i were discovering & making a
> way for ourselves/ we cd still do that/ cuz i can
> help you out now/ some. i mean nothing to make
> you feel indebted/ but you cd leave those crazy
> bitches alone. . . . (96)

Earl's proposition presents him at his most vulnerable moment. His whole lifestyle could be restructured based on Sean's response, another manifestation of Sean's power over those who seek his affections.

Despite the sincerity of Earl's proposition, Sean's response to him is the same as his response to his female lovers when he feels

they want too much from him: he ignores them by changing the
subject, reading openness and honesty as vulnerability and powerlessness. In this instance, he flatters Earl by photographing him, not
coincidentally a technique he uses with the women as well. Observe
the exchange between Sean and Earl:

> *sean (grabs a camera)*
> hold it man/ i'm gonna do yr portrait. you got this face/
> man/ i haveta have
> *earl (sincerely flattered & hopeful)*
> really man? yr gonna do a portrait of me/ like you do
> claire? man/ give me the air of d'artagnan
> . . . .
> *sean (taking pictures)*
> here/ open yr shirt a lil . . . put that hat on right there/
> let yr sensuality lick the lens/ . . . that's it. i really think
> you shd consider nevada. . . . (97)

Shange's use of "sincerely flattered and hopeful" as description of
Earl reveals his excitement at having Sean's undivided attention.
Also, Sean's artistic use of Earl here parallels his artistic use of
Claire. Yet Earl is flattered whereas Claire is seemingly indifferent.
In these instances, photography and art serve as escapes from reality
rather than illusory chroniclers of those realities. Immediately sug-
gesting that Earl pursue Nevada clears Sean of any homosexual,
hence "unmanly," tendencies. In the final moments of the play,
Sean joins Claire in attacking Earl's manhood:

> *claire*
> look you faggot muthafuckah get yr hands off me . . .
> i dont like a man who doesnt like women
> . . . .
> *sean*
> . . . earl move your faggot ass on, man. (105-06)

Earl's behavior toward women borders on misogyny. Presumably
unable to maintain a steady relationship with a female and rejected
by both Claire and Sean, who question his sexual preference, Earl

threatens Claire, a threat that echoes Sean's earlier threat to have her gang raped. But even their threats connote different traits in the two males. Earl's threat is the more personally vengeful: "one of these days i'm gonna fuck you til you bleed" (106). While Sean wants to punish Claire as an assertion of his power over her, Earl's threat festers in his own attitudes about his masculinity. His potential hatred of women is thus manifested in a threat of physical violence; not coincidentally, there is no comparable threat against Sean for rejecting him. While Earl may prefer male sexual companionship over that of women, he is not promiscuous. In contrast to the stereotype of the "flaming faggot," Earl—a professional man who knows the value and necessity of conforming to social images—would only adopt a homosexual life discreetly and in a remote setting.

Just as the two men in the play offer contrasting images of manhood but parallels in their behaviors toward women, the three female characters offer variations on images of women and sexuality and on women and gender roles. Each is professionally independent, yet each woman's personal life is plagued by unfulfilled dreams and physical, psychological, or verbal abuse from the same man. Each woman fills a specific need for Sean as he asserts his perceived manliness.

Claire is a purely physical female, full of her own sensuality and bisexuality. A model whose body is her professional commodity, Claire prides herself on her promiscuity and seems just as proud of her own list of lovers as Sean is of his. Claire's unwillingness to have a monogamous relationship with Sean threatens and undermines his masculinity. Claire, whom Sean calls a "simple perverted bitch" (75), takes pleasure in detailing her sexual activities:

> *claire*
> . . . i think i might be coming down wit something
> *sean*
> well. i'm not
> *claire*
> coming down/ or with something?
> *sean*
> do you value yr life?

> *claire*
> maybe it's just the way i smell today/ i dont smell
> like you at all/ see/ these [breasts] aint yours/ &
> this [vagina] neither/ i know/ i know/ i smell like
> andrew/ no/ charlie/ oh that cdnt be/ i dont know
> anybody named charlie . . . i know/ i smell like
> willie/ wondrous willie. (64)

Claire's use of double-entendre when she questions Sean about his
"coming down" is appropriate for one who is not just interested in
but is obsessed with sex as is Sean. Yet Claire sees her body as
something to be possessed by men, and she taunts Sean with his
powerlessness to dictate her sexual liberties. She even revels in a
fantasy of being ravaged by several lovers at once, reminiscent of
Sean's threat to have her gang raped. The major difference here is
that Claire authors this sexual fantasy; Sean's is but a threat of sexual
violence to display his own power over her. Telling Sean that she has
rhinestones, palm leaves, and a magnolia flower in her vagina, she
teases:

> no. now let me see. who waz it/ i mighta forgot
> somebody john/ no/ andrew/ no . . . oh i know who
> gave claire all these treasures/ waz claire. i waz
> planning on being the sea & bein swept over by
> some pirates/ ya know/ carried on a rakish sea cap-
> tain's back/ into a lagoon/ ya gonna be a pirate
> sean/ i gotta treasure up in there/ a magic magnolia.
> (65)

Claire is as open with Sean about her lovers as he is with Michael
about his.
     Having little respect for Sean as an artist, Claire, as does Ne-
vada, attacks him and his hero:

> alexandre dumas waz still a niggah/ sean must know
> that alla those fancy waistcoats/ 2 bastards/ a boy &
> a girl by two different women/ he had women all
> over paris/ hanging out wit the fellas/ victor hugo/

> alfred de vigny/ alla them still thot he waz a nig-
> gah. some actresses usedta have all the house win-
> dows opened in the theater cuz when alexandre
> dumas showed up/ when he showed up she claimed
> she smelled an acrid stench/ the stench of a niggah.
> sean smells like a niggah/ maybe i'll tell him he
> smells like alexandre dumas. (70)

Claire is convinced that despite his fame, Alexandre Dumas never overcame the bigoted attitudes of French society—he was still considered a "niggah," although his mother was white and his father mulatto.[19] She applies her attitude about Dumas to Sean's professional aspirations and recognizes a truth about Sean that Earl and Nevada articulate at various moments in the play: that Sean is inherently trapped by his own social perceptions. And since the only real thing in Sean's life that he feels confident in is his sexual prowess, Claire's attitude suggests that Sean's artistic aspirations are little more than illusion and pretense.

Claire's brief soliloquy (Act I, scene vii) arouses our sympathies for her. As she "slugs some whiskey/ [and] rubs coke on her gums" (75), she acknowledges her confusion about what she wants in life and reflects on advice from her father about what it means to be a woman and womanly:

> be soft & brown/ be slick & claire
> remember who covers yr back/ yr backside
> is coverin yr back/ miz claire
> yr body is the blood & the flesh
> god gave his only daughter/ to save alla his sons
> daddy waz right/ daddy waz absolutely right/
> give a man exactly what he wants & he wants you/
> simple as that. but what about claire
> claire wants a present
> a lil jack daniels/ a lil blow . . .
> i know what feels good/ tender
> like the inside of my thigh
> but i dont know anybody who wd give claire a lil
> just a lil. (75)

Tenderness and romance are omitted from Claire's definition since she seems only to know the experience of physical love. Disillusionment prevails in her monologue for, having followed her father's advice concerning relationships with men, Claire is not content. She is left only with her ability to attract men and women physically. In this sense, her attitudes toward physical love parallel Sean's. In an attempt to fill this spiritual and emotional void, she turns to sexual excess, drinking, and drugs. Interestingly, Claire's father, not her mother, offers her advice on the meaning of womanhood, perhaps Shange's feminist assertion that women are left feeling empty and unfulfilled when they live according to patriarchal social and behavioral dictates.[20] Claire's monologue recalls the Lady in Blue's (*for colored girls*) sentiments upon experiencing spiritual rebirth into new selfhood:

> i know bout/ layin on bodies/ layin outta man
> bringin him alla my fleshy self & some of my pleasure
> bein taken full eager wet like i get sometimes
> [but] i waz missin somethin. (*for colored girls* 65)

There is no evidence in the play, however, that Claire finds what she is missing.

In contrast to Claire's physicality, Nevada represents intellectual and social status. While Claire is appropriately a model, Nevada is an attorney: well educated, intelligent, and arrogant about her social standing. She is the epitome of grace and breeding, socially adept and ultra-conscious of mannered behavior. Whereas Claire celebrates physical "soft[ness]" (75) as her prescribed definition of womanliness, Nevada is schooled in the art of stereotypical "femininity" or cultivated behavior—each female trying desperately to find spiritual contentment through their respective prescriptions. Nevada's extreme cattiness and arrogance, however, diminish an audience's initial sympathies toward her in her pathetic involvement with Sean. Note the exchange between Earl and Nevada when she first appears in the play:

> nevada
> earl/ do you see that/ i cant believe anyone is still

> wearing costume jewelry/ especially at my party
>> *earl*
>
> not everyone can afford real gold/ nevada
>> *nevada*
>
> then they shdnt wear anything. (67)

She clarifies her cultural ancestry:

>> *earl*
>
> yeah. see whatta niggah cd do when the rest of us
> were slaves
>> *nevada*
>
> no/ no. YOU all were slaves/ i keep telling you
> that/ earl. . . . (68)

and later exclaims to Sean: ". . . an artist/ an ass. that's what i've
been messing with/ i cd have anybody i wanted/ i am not an ordinary
nothing/ my family waz manumitted in 1843/ yall were still slaves/
carrying things for white folks/ just slaves/ that's what you come
from & i cd do better" (78). Nevada's intracultural disassociation is
certainly under attack by Shange who explains:

> I'm particularly sensitive to what I call "cultural
> arrogance". . . . when something in the culture I
> belong to is snubbed and/or abused, I respond as if
> it happened to me [personally]. It doesn't matter if I
> wasn't there or [if] it happened 200 years ago or if
> it happened in South Africa or in Iran or if it hap-
> pened in Mexico City. What matters to me is that
> something I am a part of has been injured. And if
> that happens, then yeah—it comes out of me in
> hopefully (at this point) a productive way which is
> through art in some fashion. I might dance it out or
> I might write it out or I might weave it out. It does-
> n't matter how it comes out as long as I get it out so
> that it brings something to the world as opposed to
> taking something from us.[21]

If Nevada "cd do better," as she alleges, in terms of finding a man who shares her social values and cultural background, why is she emotionally attached to Sean, who has little respect for her? This question lies at the heart of her unsatisfying relationships with men.

Nevada is as much a financial wellspring for Sean as Claire is his sexual pawn. Like Claire, Nevada is aware of Sean's involvement with other women, yet she continues to support him financially. Unlike Claire, however, Nevada wants to be the only woman in Sean's life. Upon finding Michael and Sean in bed when he is expected at her party, Nevada explodes:

> so. yr working/ huh. too busy to be bothered with
> me/ less the rent's due. or you need some film. or
> yr "model" needs whatever those kinda women
> need. you dont love me. you never loved me. me/
> nevada/ is nothing to you but a few bucks & a easy
> fuck/ niggah you never took my picture/ you never
> take my picture/ you dont think i'm beautiful or
> nothing, just these slut artist bitches/ . . . with good
> form. . . . (78)

Described by Sean as "a hysteric" (106), Nevada is not deceived about Sean's feelings toward her. Yet she is unaware of her dependence on Sean despite his emotional neglect of her. She claims: "i dont need you or nothing from you do you hear me tramp/ sean do you hear me/ i dont need you/ yr photographs/ yr dick/ nothing/ you've got nothing i want/. . ." (78), then later admits: "i just wanted you to take my picture . . . my picture/ make my face belong to you/ . . ." (78). But soon reverting to her socially correct behavior, where her emotions are always in check, she tells Sean that she will patiently await his call after Michael leaves. She even apologizes to him for destroying some of his pictures in her "unladylike" rage:

> sean/ i'm really sorry bout the mess i made/ but i'm
> on my way over to the museum/ and i wanted to
> know if you still want me to try to get that show for
> you
>   . . .

oh. here's the lens you were looking at last week/ it
might come in handy. (82)

Such contradictory behavior characterizes Nevada throughout the
play, at least in her dealings with Sean. Her frustrations with Sean
are manifested not only in her verbal attacks on Sean's other
women—she calls Michael a "slutty dancer" (91) and Claire a "low
down cunt" (78)—but also on Sean himself. She, like Claire, doubts
Sean's abilities and initiative in becoming a great photographer,
taunting him about his professional dream: "all by yrself/ yr gonna
build yr name with yr own ignorant lil self" (82). Later, as though
playing a game to get an upper hand on Claire, she defends Sean
against Claire's insults, insisting that "sean is a fine artist" (102).

    Nevada's contradictory behavior reveals her vulnerabilities, her
extreme loneliness perhaps caused by an image of "miss society"
(102) that she feels compelled to maintain. Nevada's profession as an
attorney—one which requires sound reasoning faculties—offers a
contrast to the irrationality and complexity of her emotional state.
While she admits on a rational level that "no. i dont need nothin else.
i gotta office/ i gotta porsche/ i gotta family & a name" (90-91), she
has not convinced herself that she does not need Sean; she acknowledges her loneliness and her craving for sincere love: "& i never had
nothin for myself/ just this stupidness/ running around being impor-
tant/ bein highfaluting/ all this time pushing for what isnt ever gonna
be mine/ i do i do/ need somebody" (90-91). Although Nevada has
what most would define as success—material possessions and social
status—she has no sense of her own identity apart from what her
family's money and name can obtain. Nevada and Claire, despite
their different personal and professional backgrounds, share this
emotional void. And while they represent opposing images of
females—forming a kind of mind/body dialectic—each becomes
vulnerable to Sean for different reasons. Perhaps Sean's role in
Nevada's life is to free her from socially appropriate behavior. She
comments on that freedom to Earl: ". . . you remember the nite i
passed my bar exam/ & we all three [Earl, Nevada, and Sean] got
drunk & went to the sapphire room/ & i danced on the bar & put on
one of the other girls' wigs/" (68). She further admits: "i need him
[Sean]/ he lets me breathe or something like i can feel/ i get close & i

haveta have that/ i haveta have that/ that's all i've got" (90). Nevada's soliloquy (Act II, scene xi) reveals her poor self-image with
an almost childlike innocence. Her daydream of being romantically
protected and coddled by a man resembling her father recalls Claire's
father's advice on how to "win" a man:

> mama mama/ is he gonna be like daddy?
> is he gonna buy me pretty things & take me
> round the world? mama/ will he be handsome
> & strong/ maybe from . . . / an old family
> of freedmen/ one of them reconstruction senators
> . . . maybe he'll buy me an orchid
> a silver orchid for my cotillion/ do you think
> i'm pretty enuf/ mama/ for a man like that?
> i'm gonna haveta get a figure
> aw ya know mama like you/ i wanna set my table
> pour the punch & make canapes/ & smile like you
> in an organza dress/ he cd swing me
> down by the lake/ & then he'll catch me almost
> in the air/ & rustle my dress round my shoulders
> not like he knew he cd take such a liberty
> just outta he cdnt resist me
> & then mama/ then i think he'll kiss me
> yeah/ there on the swing in the air
> by the lake/ he'll kiss me mama
> & whisper nevada . . . nevada. (97-98)

Nevada's is a stereotypical fairy tale romance of a beautiful, passive
female, totally dependent on a "Prince Charming" who "sweeps her
off her feet." This fantasy also highlights her extreme upper-class
consciousness. Impressed by her social etiquette, refined gentleman
callers would naturally shower her with lavish gifts and sincere
affection. Part of Nevada's emotional vulnerability to Sean and her
loneliness result from the fact that her image of "Prince Charming"
is an impossible one for any man to live up to. And since no man is
perfect, Nevada has no one. Until that Prince comes along, Nevada
contents herself with bribing Sean for his attentions, however destructive and abusive they may be for her.

In direct contrast to an arrogant Nevada and a lustful Claire is Michael, who represents for Shange—and in light of the play's ending, for Sean as well—a kind of "middle ground" image of women. Michael neither bribes Sean for his affections nor allows him to exploit her sexually. Seemingly perceptive, self-assured, and disciplined, Michael often becomes Shange's mouthpiece, provoking Sean to reassess his commitment to photography and to reevaluate his views on manhood and manliness. As a friend to Sean, Michael respects his work and his person and tries to convince Sean that he is not above needing, giving, and receiving a love that simultaneously includes and transcends physicality.

When the play opens, we witness Michael's coolheadedness when Sean insists that having one woman in his life is not enough. Immediately, we recognize that while Michael is not immune to jealousy over Sean's menagerie of lovers, she seldom bickers with him about the subject. Her indifference breaks the jealous-lover stereotype: "i cant do that ["get jealous & loud"]. i'm physically incapable of chasing & arguing abt a man/ i just cant. i dont have the energy" (69). This freedom that Michael allows Sean ultimately separates her from the other characters, all of whom want to possess Sean but are ultimately controlled by him. Michael reveals an independence of one who seems attuned to her own mental and emotional rhythms. Such is the case when she challenges Sean to define art, love, and the role of photography in his life. Enraged that Sean prostitutes himself to Nevada for rent money and camera equipment, Michael asserts:

> . . . i know what you are capable of
> . . . .
> . . . yr not even trying to be an artist/ yr trying to
> stay alive
> . . . .
> no. [Art is not survival.] it's love. it's fighting to
> give something/ it's giving yrself to someone/ who
> loves you. (84-85)

For Michael, Sean's best photographs are not the pornographic ones that he knows will be commercially successful but the ones that reveal truth about the human condition, the ones revealing suffering and realities unadorned. Unlike Nevada, Claire, and Earl, Michael does not criticize Sean's dreams or his talents as an artist. Instead, she encourages him to explore possibilities of his artistry. She implores Sean to seek satisfaction with himself as a photographer, not allowing an outside world to dictate his feelings about himself as a person or as an artist. Hence, in challenging his commitment to his art, Michael also challenges his manhood:

> i dont like thinking that you think yr dick means
> more to me than yr work/ you dont give yrself
> anymore than anyone is willing to give you
> . . . .
> [Rather than being "the greatest photographer in the
> world"] how abt being the photographer you
> haveta be
> . . . .
> when you work on yr pictures like you worked on
> me [sexually]/ i'll believe you/ right now i think yr
> fulla shit & i'm ashamed cuz i believed you at least
> loved photography. (86-87)

Not only does an articulate and seemingly rational Michael offer Shange's views on an artist's commitment to art as well as the nature of love and manhood, but Michael also celebrates an African American cultural past. Contrasting Nevada's cultural detachment, Michael prods Sean toward self-respect ancestrally; she reacts to Sean's passivity when Nevada destroys his photographs:

> . . . i am an artist too. i go to work/ in a nasty ol
> restaurant/ & you let some woman destroy yr
> photographs/ well/ my grandma carried a shotgun/
> do you understand me
> . . . .
> . . . it's our lives/ our grandparents & their uncles/
> it's how we came to be/ by taking our lives
> seriously/ we fight for every breath every goddam
> day/ do you know that

. . . .
it's ours. alla ours. dont nobody own history/ cant
nobody make ours but us. & look at what you've
done to yrself. (80)

Michael's comments on self-esteem for black people recall Maxine's
reflection in *spell #7*: "that surviving the impossible is sposed to accentuate the positive aspects of a people" (*spell #7* 51). Michael's
moment is one of the few in *a photograph* where Shange connects an
individual's positive personal identity with his or her ancestral,
cultural, and racial past. That Michael's grandmother "carried a
shotgun" becomes a metaphor for aggressively protecting and
defending one's racial heritage. In this instance, having to struggle
for a sense of belonging in a dominant white culture that alienates
and isolates blacks defines an individual's sense of who she is and
what belongs to her and her people.

Despite Michael's assuredness about her profession as a dancer
and about her views on art, love, and manhood, she appears to be
psychologically imbalanced, prone to losing control of her mental
faculties during certain chaotic moments in the play. Clearly, Shange
does not set Michael upon an heroic pedestal; evidence of such is
seen in Michael's blatantly manipulative advances toward
Claire—offering to give her a massage that would relax her body the
way sexual intercourse with Sean does—and even in her "sneaking
some of claire's cocaine" (74) when Sean is out of the room. Michael, too, battles inner turmoil, and while Claire turns to sex games
and Nevada to money and breeding, Michael keeps her frustrations
and confusions inside. Certainly, some ambiguity exists about Michael's mental stability when a stage direction describes her as
"rocking catatonically on the stool" (80) after Nevada's hysterical
outburst at Sean. While Michael is disciplined as a dancer, she becomes frantic when the order and structure in her environment are
threatened.

The final moments of the play further present the ambiguity of
Michael's emotional and psychological state. When all of the characters meet in a chaotic confrontation, Michael screams to Sean:
"they're crazy/ sean/ i dont wanna be crazy/ make it stop/ make it
stop" (100). Unlike the other characters, Sean seems to understand

her state and soothes her: "listen michael/ i'm gonna take care of it/
its gonna be awright/ you'll see" (100). Sean's final profession of
love for Michael is likewise ambiguous for he calms her in the
manner a parent might protect and soothe a distraught child. As Sean
speaks, one of the final stage directions continues this ambiguity:
"michael stops whispering. sean realizes that she is not 'with him' &
moves toward her" (108).

In light of Michael's apparent psychological problems, dance is
more than art for her; it represents order, structure, and discipline in
her life and is a means of creative emotional expression. The need
for order in her life that Sean fulfills is foreshadowed in her opening
dream sequence about her hero:

> all i know is his name . . .
> somebody very black & tall/ sophisticated for that time
> 'fore the war/ & he waznt born here either
> born in paris & carried to detroit when he waz five
> a french speakin niggah in detroit/ say 1926
> & he waz intense
> a rich colored boy in the Depression/ . . .
> who took a wife/ who didnt like just men . . .
> . . . .
> my daddy & his girl rode in the backseat of the newest
> & hottest car in nashville. . . . (63)

While initially it seems that Michael's hero is a fictitious black man
about whom she has read, it becomes clear that the man of her
dreams is her father. Recall Claire's advice concerning femininity
coming from her father, and Nevada wants to marry a man just like
her father. For Michael, Sean replaces her father. Michael's respect
for her father, despite his being socially mocked for having taken a
bisexual wife, ultimately transfers to Sean. Her dream, then, becomes a confession of her own bisexuality and of her love for Sean.
She essentially describes the state of her life with Sean:

> everybody knew abt her [Michael's father's wife]/ that
>   she liked to touch women's legs
> & mouths/ that there waz nothing cd be done

cuz she had connections/ & he waz so sharp & he took
   her
& the sorority took her/ & there waz nothing cd be done
cuz she was beautiful. & then there he waz & wd you
   mess
wit him who is anger/ a malignant fury in his glance
when somebody wanted to say/ what everybody knew
   abt her
& they did leave him alone. & how cd he not know
& if he did know/ it must be/ he really is a foreigner
not a whole man himself/ to have a woman so
a woman so fulla beauty/ she shared when a breeze fell
from her hands/ & he never left her. (63)

Michael's description of her father's wife, who is apparently not her
own mother, is actually a description of herself. Yet just as Sean is
unaware that she is describing her father's wife, he is equally unaware of her bisexuality. Recall earlier how he immediately attacks
Claire for her alleged 'perversion' when in fact Michael actually
suggests a relaxing massage for Claire. Although Sean grabs Michael's arm, questioning "why were you laying all over the girl just
to give the girl a massage" (74), he blames Claire for the episode.
The stage direction clarifies Michael's reaction—"michael smiles"
(74)—after Sean reproaches Claire and reveals Sean's gullibility and
Michael's skills at manipulating him. In the dream monologue,
Michael even suggests condescendingly something "unmanly" about
a male who does not know that he shares his female lover with other
females. She indirectly tells Sean of her love for him:

. . . i've kept a lover
who waznt all-american/ who didnt believe/ wdnt
   straighten up.
oh i've loved him in my own men/ sometimes hateful
sometimes subtle . . . / but who i loved
is yr not believing. i loved yr bitterness & hankered
after that space in you where you are outta control/
where you cannot touch or you wd kill me/ or somebody
   else

> who loved you. i never even saw a picture
> & i've loved him all my life
> he is all my insanity. (63-64)

Perhaps this double life with Sean is a cause of Michael's unwillingness or inability to play the jealous-lover stereotype. Perhaps it is this
double life she struggles with inwardly, deliberately hiding it from
Sean, that accounts for her questionable mental state. That "he is all
my insanity" is thereby paradoxical. While Sean may be a reason
Michael struggles to deny or subdue her bisexual longings, Sean is
also the force providing and sustaining some semblance of order in
her life. He is her protector, yet he does not control her.

One of the criticisms of *a photograph* is its potentially sentimen-
tal ending. For Shange, who insists that *a photograph* is generally
about "the ways people exploit each other emotionally" but more
importantly about "the possibility of learning love,"[22] the ending
seems appropriate if we accept the sincerity of Michael and Sean's
professions of love. Yet the motives for Sean's commitment to
Michael remain unclear. Is he merely soothing her emotionally for
the moment or does he genuinely understand the issues that Shange,
through Michael, has offered him? Based on Sean's consistently
abusive behavior toward Nevada, Claire, and even Michael throughout the play and considering Michael's emotional state in the final
moments, the former seems the more probable. And while his relationship with Michael at this moment takes on a stereotypical male
role as a woman's protector, this moment of gentleness with no
selfish motives attached conveys redemptive possibilities for Sean.

As an extension of the choreopoem technique, *a photograph*
incorporates Shange's characteristic use of music, dance, and poetry.
It is dramatically effective to have the dream sequences of Michael
and Sean as well as the characters' soliloquies in poetry. Such moments present a complexity of the characters when they are most
spontaneous, emotional, and psychologically revealing. Their confusions and uncertainties about their own personal past and present are
simultaneously immediate and distant as they struggle to satisfy
various needs and desires. *a photograph* is more visually oriented
than either *for colored girls* or *spell #7* since characters are continually physically interacting with each other—battling or embracing. In

addition, Michael, as a professional dancer, frequently rehearses routines—offering a subtle contrast to the chaos in Sean's life of characters coming and going. The closest thing to a song in a *photograph* is Michael's incantatory monologue about a woman's destructive powers (Act II, scene x). Contemporary music would serve not only as transitions between the scenes but also as the background in Sean's meticulously ordered and elegantly furnished apartment, offering further contrast to the characters' chaotic lives.

Unlike *for colored girls* and *spell #7, a photograph* is not about ideas but about the multiple complex dimensions of black people struggling toward sexual, gender, and racial identity. In commenting on these characters' identities, Shange again blasts racial and gender stereotypes that hinder the potential for an individual's complete personal development. And while the choreopoem is clearly a portrayal of black experience, complete with black language and a sense of cultural past that define the characters despite their various professions and levels of education, issues of infidelity, loneliness, rejection, sexuality, and focus on dreams, ambitions, and disillusionment—though influenced by race and gender—transcend both racial and gender boundaries. Shange's representation of confused and conflicting realities, here, is so complicated that she offers no easy resolutions, only a formal "romantic" one that may or may not undermine our trust in the momentary reform of Sean's character. Nevertheless, Shange's sympathies toward a confused black man are unquestionable. While Sean is a black man who abuses black women, he is also an individual in need of immediate self-assessment, as an artist, as a male, and as a human being. The women too must ultimately affirm themselves through their own eyes.

NOTES

1. Buckley, "The Three Stages of Ntozake Shange," C6.

2. Edith Oliver, "The Theatre: Off Broadway," *New Yorker*, 2 January 1978, 48.

3. John Simon, "Theater: A Touch Is Better Than None," *New York*, 16 January 1978, 58.

4. Martin Gottfried, "Theater: Playmaking Is Not Enough," *Saturday Review*, 18 February 1978, 42.

5. Dean Valentine, "On Stage: Theater of the Inane," *New Leader*, 2 January 1978, 29.

6. Quandra Prettyman, "Photograph (For L. McL.)," *The Poetry of Black America: Anthology of the Twentieth Century*, ed. Arnold Adoff (New York: HarperCollins, 1973), 259.

7. According to Shange, there had been six scripts of *a photograph* with three different casts before it reached its present form (Shange, *for colored girls*, audiocassette, side A).

8. See Timothy Murray, "Screening the Camera's Eye: Black and White Confrontations of Technological Representation," *Modern Drama* 28 (March 1985): 110-24.

9. Simon, "Theater: A Touch Is Better Than None," 58.

10. An exploration of Shange's presentation of men—Beau Willie Brown, Sean David, and Greens—can be found in my article, "Shange's Men: *for colored girls* Revisited and Movement Beyond," in *African American Review* 26 (Summer 1992): 319-28.

11. See both Richard and Lyle in James Baldwin's *Blues for Mister Charlie* (1964).

12. Recall from *spell #7* (discussed in Chapter III) Shange's focus on the issue of possession, spatial and territorial claim, and power as it relates to the African American experience. See also Ed Bullins' *How Do You Do* (1967), wherein Paul, the alleged Image-Maker, futilely tries to create representations of black people that are disconnected from stereotypes. Bullins concludes that revisions of one's thinking patterns and processes in and of the world are continual and necessary in creative expression and fuller living. Indeed, the stereotypes, Roger and Dora, threaten Paul's "ordered" ideological existence.

13. Holy Bible: King James Version (Camden, New Jersey: Thomas Nelson, 1972), 2.

14. Oliver, "The Theatre: Off-Broadway," 48.

15. Monroe, 57.

16. Perhaps some of Sean's social frustrations result as do Beau Willie Brown's from psychological and social traumas suffered as a Vietnam veteran. Shange does not highlight this as a major factor in Sean's development though his participation in the war indirectly affects his attitudes and ideas during and afterwards.

17. Sean does not consider the possible reality that pornography of blacks may not be as marketable as pornography of whites.

18. Shange, "A Colored Girl: Ntozake Shange," video-recording.

19. Shange reiterates the racist and illogical social (and sometimes legal) definition of black as derived from the contaminating "drop" of black blood (impurity) that when mixed with white blood (purity) results in impurity (defined as belonging solely in the black race). Hence, Dumas, in society's eyes, no matter that his ancestry is genetically closer to white, is nevertheless a "nigger."

20. See Shange's short play, "Daddy Says: A Play," in Woodie King, Jr.'s *New Plays for the Black Theatre* (Chicago: Third World, 1989), which examines the complex relationship between a father, confused by traditional and changing gender roles, and his two adolescent girls trying to understand the meanings of womanhood without a mother. Though the father, TDB, is not without Shange's sympathies—he admits quite honestly: "Well how am I s'posed to talk to two girls 'bout/ this woman business/" (248)—it is his woman friend, Cassie, who shows him that womanhood does not mean limitations: "Jus' what is yo' problem, Tie-down? You don' wanna woman good as you/ smart as you/ brave as you? Whatchu gonna do wit' them girls, huh? Give 'em some make-up & mo' free time so they can get pregnant & drop outta school . . . ?" (243) To this, TDB replies: "That's what gals is s'poses to do/ have babies & keep a good house/" (244).

21. Ibid.

22. "Future Subjunctive: Shange's New Song," *Horizon* 20 (September 1977): 70.

CHAPTER V

"dontcha wanna be . . .":
boogie woogie landscapes

Ntozake Shange's fourth published theater piece, *boogie woogie landscapes* (1979)—the third play in her *three pieces* volume—was performed first as a solo presentation at the New York Shakespeare Festival's Poetry at the Public series in December 1978. The published text with additional cast members was performed in June 1979 in New York at the Symphony Space Theater as a fund-raiser for The Frank Silvera Writer's Workshop. In 1980, it ran for four weeks in Washington, D.C., at the Terrace Theater of the John F. Kennedy Center for the Performing Arts, produced by Woodie King, Jr., and the National Black Touring Circuit. Sections of the play, constituting five "sketches," were presented as the unpublished choreopoem *Black & White Two-Dimensional Planes* in "An Evening of Performance Art by Ntozake Shange" at the Mark Taper Theater Lab, Los Angeles, during March-April 1982. As a companion piece to *for colored girls*, *boogie* is an in-depth character study that moves beyond the external person of the "reglar colored girl" (*for colored girls* 37) to expose a black girl's subconscious—her dreams, visions, memories, fears, and fantasies. Using expressionist techniques, impressionistic imagery, and her characteristic collage of dance, music, and poetry, Shange presents a choreopoem that is more complicated structurally, more theatrically complex, less idealistic philosophically, less naturalistic performatively, and more "entertaining theatrically"[1] than her previous dramas.

175

Key to understanding the play is an awareness of its structure as a dream—with dreams often becoming nightmarish—and the appropriateness and effectiveness of Shange's expressionist method of dissecting the persona she ambiguously identifies as an "all-American colored girl" (113). Is the image of the "all-American" colored girl or boy as conceivable as its blonde-haired, blue-eyed white counterpart? Unlike the all-American white person, the black person can be many possibilities, particularly in terms of skin tones and ethnicities. Using this premise, Shange signifies on the layers of contradictions that evolve when we are forced to image her central character. Use of a dream motif as a structural device frees Shange from an artificially ordered portrayal of a human mind at work, even when one's body and consciousness are at complete rest.

Shange's title announces the subject of the choreopoem and the manner in which it unfolds. "Boogie woogie," a style of jazz piano playing characterized by a steady rhythmic and melodic pattern, describes both the musical atmosphere of the piece and the piece itself as a kind of improvised jazz accompaniment.[2] Jazz and blues music also punctuate the action throughout and underscore the play's mood of dreaminess, temporality, fluidity, possibility, and memory while musician characters, during various moments of the play, "reflect her [Layla's] consciousness" (113). Additionally, "boogie woogie" is a type of dance done to "boogie woogie" music, "a fast-stepping blues in which the bass figure comes in double time" (Major 54). Shange's approach to exploring the character's unconscious is psychoanalytic. Whereas in *for colored girls*, Shange elevates and even glamorizes the social status of black women, in *boogie*, there is no final overwhelming celebration but rather a detailed exploration of a black woman's identity problems as derived from growing up in sexist and racist North America. Shange uses "landscapes," then, as significant gender and race regions of Layla's social and psychological existence. Brenna Ryan suggests that the landscaping metaphor, coupled with Shange's use of "geography" in the opening stage direction, is appropriate also because landscaping is a human means of ordering natural environment perceived as lacking order.[3] Since landscapes are created, they are thereby unnatural. They are also ever-changing and constantly in need of care and attention to maintain a landscaper's ideal of order. Layla's responses to and the social manifestations of racism and sexism that impact upon her identity are as ever-changing as are the emotional, physical, and cultural landscapes. Layla can only exist in the present—like poetry and music—because landscapes change without warning, and efforts to re-order permanently natural order are often futile and disillusioning. With a seemingly stream-of-consciousness presentation, Shange sets the play at night—conventionally associated with mystery, confusion, and even evil—and in Layla's bedroom as Layla dances, sleeps—a time when she is most physically vulnerable and consciously unaware—and dreams. Shange's introductory note clarifies the setting and intended effect of this choreopoem:

> this is a geography of whimsy, fantasy, memory & the night: a bedroom. the bedroom of layla ("born at night": arabic), an all-american colored girl. there is what furniture a bedroom *might* accommodate, though not too much of it. the most important thing is that a bedroom is *suggested*: the windows that overlook *somewhere*; an object that *might be* a bed; another that *might be* a night table. the mirrors that we see ourselves in/ comin in or goin out/ in our full regalia or in layers of our own sweat.
>
> the walls of the bedroom are designed to permit at least one or two of the night-life companions (dream-memories) to enter or exit at will. (113; emphasis mine)

Using such terms as "might," "might be," "suggested," and "somewhere" in the stage directions reinforces the inexactness of Layla's mental activities during the course of dreaming on this particular night. Ideas flow freely and uncontrollably in Layla's subconscious. There are also no clear distinctions or boundaries to separate her responses to being alive, however frightening and self-incriminating some of them are. Shange uses mirror imagery and speaks simultaneously of the "full regalia" of ourselves as well as "our own sweat" to suggest the complexity of any character study that treats an individual's self-reflective mental activities and physical and emotional ramifications of those activities. An image of sweating announces both the terror and the passion of Layla's existence and experiences. Such complexities arise from realities behind the public and private Layla, behind an image of herself that she daily prepares. Night-life characters who participate in Layla's fantasy sequences as narrators, role players, or chorus also concretize aspects of Layla's subconscious.[4]

Unsurprisingly, criticism of the structure or seeming lack thereof, as some reviewers insist, comprises most of the negative responses to this drama. For instance, Judith Martin argues that "Ntozake Shange's litany of complaints . . . is lacking [in] organization of its material . . . [and has] no dramatic point of view. . . . [The] playwright does not abide by her own definition [of the play as 'one night of dreams' or] observe any limitations of character or place."[5] Joseph McLellan adds that Shange's use of dream motif as a structural device is but "a formula [that gives] the author *carte blanche* to empty out her notebook of any odds and ends that might be passed off as dreams or memories (that is to say, anything in the world) without thought or structure, coherence or continuity."[6] Although Shange defines *boogie* as "one night of dreams and memories of a young woman who has grown up in America,"[7] that *boogie* is presented as a dream does not mean that the choreopoem is indeed unstructured. Rather, Shange offers an intentionally non-linear, loosely narrative dream structure that is coherent, though not perhaps by traditional dramatic standards. As does *for colored girls*, *boogie* traces a black female's growth from childhood perceptions about herself and her world to painful experiences associated with being black, a woman, and a black woman amid the flagrant social demons of racism and sexism. As Layla's dreams, visions, and fears are disclosed, personal issues in her life become political ones and she, too, learns that "bein alive & bein a woman & bein/ colored is a metaphysical dilemma" (*for colored girls* 48).[8] The choreopoem is essentially divided into three overlapping thematic movements: Layla's discovery of and acceptance of her blackness; Layla's awareness of the social and political injustices suffered by her femaleness, and Layla's recollections of times when neither gender nor race was an environmental determinant. Each movement reveals Layla's complex identity and proves that positive selfhood as a woman, particularly as a black woman, is always under attack by forces out to conquer and destroy. Accepting herself as she is despite forces that seek to deny her a legitimacy of being is her method of self-improvement.

Shange suggests through Layla's experiences that black females struggle with their racial identity before they struggle with gender issues. Shange's point here is not to argue that all black females experience race struggles before their gender awareness and the liabilities associated with it. This may be the reason we learn of Layla's struggles as she becomes a more politically and socially aware teen rather than earlier in her chronological years. Notably, Kay Lindsey, in her essay "The Black Woman as Woman" (in Toni Cade Bambara, ed., *The Black Woman: An Anthology* [New York: Mentor/Penguin, 1970]), argues that a black woman "discovers [her] sex sometime before [she] discovers [her] racial clarification." She adds: "Our first perception of ourselves is of our physical bodies, which we . . . compare with . . . those [of our families]." As does Richard Wright, in his autobiographical essay, "The Ethics of Living Jim Crow," black women and black men alike "discover what it means to be Black, and all that the term implies, usually outside the family" (Lindsey 87). Indeed, during the Civil Rights years, politically active black women chose or were expected to choose racial over gender oppression, especially as they followed revolutionaries like Malcolm X and Amiri Baraka whose political agenda, like that of Black Panthers' and other Black Nationalists', did not include black feminism as an issue. Shange's analysis of Layla deals first with the issue of race, with Layla's learning that she is black. Appropriately then, Layla's dream begins when she is an adolescent, confused and "trapped in [a] black & white" (114) one-dimensional existence. At age fourteen, Layla is aware of racial differences designated by skin color but not of her own place within that color scheme. Neither black nor white, she sees herself as "gray"—interestingly a combination of black and white—metaphorically a product of black physicality and white cultural dominance:

> *n.l.c.'s (in unison)*
> she is trapped in black & white/ she is trapped in black
> & white

> . . . .
> *n.l.c. #2*
> she never thought people places or ideas were anything
>   but black & white
>   *n.l.c. #1*
> . . . .
> . . . she's black too
> not tar like but a shade lighter than
> the sky . . .
> . . . .
> she is trapped in black & white/ without shadows
> she cannot lean against anything/
> the earth has no depth because she cannot hold it
> she cannot go away/ the horizon implies three dimen-
>   sions
>   *n.l.c. #3*
> . . . .
> she is a deeper gray than the shutters of her house. (114)

Clearly, Layla's blackness is distinguished from the "black as tar" images that allegedly presented black people physically in American minstrelsy and racist folk art. Darkness, despair, and images of death and non-existence beset Layla as a child trapped in a limited existence. The word "trapped" reveals a futility of Layla's predicament, unable to add depth or dimension to her life. During this period, Layla exists without the capacity to feel or taste. Even her home is not a place of familial love and comfort, but rather as "a house // more like a cave" (114)—emotionally cold, dark, dreary, threatening, and passionless. While she exists in a state of intellectual and experiential innocence, these limitations are a source of frustration for Layla, who desires greater self-awareness. Her efforts to define herself more fully in such a restrictive environment lead only to disappointment and eventual self-loathing:

> inside the cave i imagine i can
> cook something to eat/ but my hands dont work
> the skillet burns up/ my mother's smoke
> scars my arms/ my mouth blurts some phrase

> i wd have a fierce yellow
> but i dont know what that is.
> . . . .
> . . . i'm soft graphite
> i'm clumsy & reckless/ i'm a hazard to definitions.
>   (115)

One of the first lessons Layla must understand is that being a "hazard to definitions" is, according to Shange, reason for celebration because definitions themselves are limiting and restrictive. Human existence and her existence as a black female, on the other hand, is full of complexities and contradictions.[9] Despite Layla's desire for meaningful activities to substantiate her existence—cooking to eat, for example—the powers of her imagination are not strong enough to overcome her perceived physical powerlessness. While she wants to cook, to be productive, her "hands don't work" and the physical activity becomes self-destructive. Even her "mouth blurts some phrase" of which even she is unable to control or to make sense. Not coincidentally, Layla connects her mother with this suffering—particularly in the context of traditional female culinary responsibilities—using womb/oven imagery. At this subconscious level, Layla, even as a child, rejects the tragedy of becoming her mother, an oppressed and self-restricted black woman. In the single image of "my mother's smoke // scars my arms/"[10] (115), Shange offers a potentially feminist treatment of Layla's relationship with her mother. Shange explains:

> The breach between feminists and their mothers has been another issue that has torn the feminist community apart because if we [feminists] are in favor of the liberation of women from oppression, not just physical rape and battering but from the oppression of being the victim of the Other, and if it's okay to be half of oneself to serve someone else, then we have to look at our mothers again. Adrienne Rich addresses that issue in *Of Woman Born: Motherhood as Experience and Institution*. It's a very difficult thing for me because I know the last thing

many of us really want to do is grow up to be our
mothers. We reject the one who is most akin to us
and really mean it, not the way that men reject their
fathers and then become their fathers with pride.
When a woman becomes what she as a child saw
her mother being, she has then failed. She failed
just like her mother, so that there is a double sense
of frustration, incompletion, and shame associated
with that.[11]

Layla's frustrations are amplified by the fact that she longs for
something she cannot yet define; she wants to objectify an experience
through defining it, particularly in a language through which she can
speak to herself. Beyond definition(s)—which external forces use to
limit her creative possibilities as a black person, as a woman, and as
a human being—she is unable to accept her identity in her social and
familial surroundings. Hence, her response to this confusion is
inwardly directed, as manifested in her self-criticisms, her physical
self-torture, and in her description of herself as "clumsy & reckless"
Layla's psychological turmoil is manifested physically since her
physical body—in this instance, her skin color—creates this turmoil:

> she tries to stumble on something to stop
> this charcoal life/ she goes from room to room
> like a tractor in the grapes of wrath/ but
> everything she touches gets blacker & more
>   nondescript. (115)

The dramatic impact of Layla's predicament, the grotesque self-
destructiveness of "trying to stumble," is further intensified through
this image of black skin color as something that can be wiped away
or rubbed off.[12] Instead of making herself lighter, what she touches
becomes darker. If her skin color could be bathed or battered away,
she would do so.[13] Yet she despairingly accepts that she can only
darken her environment, making it less desirable even to herself.
Trapped in a limited existence of absolutes yet longing for a fuller
life that she can only vaguely imagine, Layla vents her frustration
and hostility in prolonged weeping and physical self-abuse:

> n.l.c. #5
> she threw herself on her bed & her sobs
> roused her so/ she began to beat the walls
> her fists matted the surface with grime/
> she turned to the doors/ rubbin her face
> across the thresholds/ she created ebony blurs
> that she cdnt even reach less she leave a furrow
> of slate fingerprints/ she made things black
>   n.l.c. #6
> indistinguishable. . . .
>
> . . . .
>
> she didnt want anything as black as the palms of her
>   hands
> to touch her
>   n.l.c. #1
> she waz black enuf awready/. (115)

Layla's inability to understand her existence in this environment produces self-alienation. Such details as her violently beating the walls with her fists and rubbing her face against thresholds graphically depict her psychological struggle and physical self-endangerment.

Layla hopelessly admits that she "feel[s] like an oven" (115), recalling the oven/cave description of her home environment. Oven imagery is particularly effective dramatically and metaphorically as it reiterates Layla's emptiness and her need to be filled with something to justify her existence and worth. On still another level, oven imagery recalls a myth that explained to black children that their skin is darker than white children's because they were "baked longer"; hence, the darker a black person's skin tone, the longer that person had been "in the oven." Yet the desired darkness of whites who tan is the very opposite for intraracist blacks. Within this imagery and mythic association is the reality of intraracism: "If you're light, you're alright. If you're brown, you can stick around. But if you're black, get back." Clearly, night-life companion #1's response to Layla's self-professed state reflects a black child's myth of skin color differences: "all black & crusty/" (116).[14] The image furthers negative connotations since a food that is overbaked to a hardness or crustiness is generally of lesser value, again a notion easily broadened to the issue of intraracism and its companion assimilation. Shange punctuates the night-lifes' description with appropriate images of darkness that visualize the experiential ignorance or negative self-association of Layla's condition: "charcoal life," "blacker & more nondescript," "smudges," "graphite," "grime," "ebony blurs," "made things black/ indistinguishable," "overwhelming darkness," "black as the palms of her hands," "black & crusty."[15]

To overcome this frustration and anguish, Layla turns to the outside world through the media, first to print, later to sound. As she moves from newspapers and gothic novels to tales of romance, her disillusion increases. Not only is the horror of her socially constructed world one of limitations, but these avenues further highlight her loneliness and passionless life. Describing Layla's spiritual or existential desires with food imagery, a narrator explains:

> . . . she ate newspapers/ the black & white pages/
> thinking news of the outside world wd soothe her
>   hunger.
> but she started to eat her books/ even the gothic novels/
> . . . .
> no one understood where the newspapers disappeared
>   to/
> but she knew it didnt matter/ cuz the outside world waz
> black & white & thin like where she lived. she cd
> read in the dark/ & eventually only ate the *new york
>   times*/
> the newsprint of the *times* waznt cheap like local papers
> or gritty like the *philadelphia inquirer*
> but as she tore the pages/ HELP WANTED first/ then
> REAL ESTATE/ stuffing them in her mouth/ she never
>   thought
> people places or ideas were anything but black & white
> no one printed books in colors. . . . (116)

Literally, Layla is distressed that the world through printed media is little different from the black-and-white dimension she already

witnesses. The black inked letters on the white page do nothing to
add emotional color to her world.[16] Hunger imagery accentuates both
the physical and the metaphysical intensity of Layla's spiritual and
emotional longings. The puns and free associational humor of rumi-
nating on literary ideas and devouring books take on potentially grotesque proportions. Shange presents an undernourished Layla who,
starving for spiritual sustenance in her world of limited experience
and perception, tries to find it through physical means, not unlike the
seven colored girls who first seek satisfying spiritual love through
physical lovemaking and social conformity. Shange's word plays
highlight two sections of the newspaper that characterize Layla's
youthful years: "HELP WANTED" is Layla's desperate cry for
assistance in understanding herself and redefining her world and her
place in it; and "REAL ESTATE" highlights Layla's need for
positive self-identity within the prison of her physical body as well as
her desire for both a multidimensional existence and a personal
territorial claim for herself spiritually and emotionally. In addition,
these two sections of the newspaper represent the two areas in which
blacks and women have traditionally suffered most discrimination
socially and economically in racist North America—employment and
unfair housing. In this movement, Shange stresses the futility of
anyone's efforts to find self-validation and self-actualization through
externals, particularly with prominent newspapers, gothic novels,
and romances render blacks generally and black women particularly
invisible.

Finding no solace in the printed word, Layla turns to the world
of sound; she discovers Jesus through the voice of a radio evangelist,
and the "religious experience" brings color to her life:

> *n.l.c. #1*
> . . . she waznt sure
> what colors were/ till she discovered jesus/ on the radio/
> . . . .
> *n.l.c. #2*
> as jesus came closer to her heart the way
> the deep voice waz sayin/ she knew the sun waz yellow
> & warm/ cuz the sun got in her throat & pushed a
>   brilliant

glow of shout from her/ not only heaven/ but the world
waz bathed in the gold of his love. she ran in the
sunlight of herself thru the house praisin god/
lettin her laughter wash thru the darkness of night.
    n.l.c. #6
& she stood in a arc of yellow so bright. (116)

The introduction of "yellow" marks a clear distinction from the dark
color imagery of Layla's pre-Jesus existence. With the voice of Jesus
in her life and the "great light shining in [her] soul" (116), Layla
understands and feels "yellow" as never before. Earlier, Layla
desired "yellow" but did not know what it was. Not only does she
recognize and experience "yellow" now, but she rejoices in it. The
darkness of her existence is replaced with images of light and
warmth: "the sun," "a brilliant // glow," "bathed in gold," "the
sunlight of herself," "a arc . . . so bright," and "a daffodil glaze."
The words "bathed" and "wash" in this account of Layla's discovery of the voice of Jesus recall a Christian baptism, being submerged
and cleansed and rising as a new person spiritually. While the women
in *for colored girls* rise from the ashes of despair, here, Layla experiences a similar conversion ritual and is spiritually reborn into new
momentary selfhood. Yet Layla's new identity is potentially narcissistic and not other-directed and still leaves her alone, lonely, and
void of spiritual fullness. What expands is her own sense of self-
worth, essentially what the women in *for colored girls* also achieve.
    Layla's discovery of the world's emotional colors through
religion—"the sun" and "the Son"—strikes an unexpected and
potentially ambiguous note in this piece. Until this play, Shange has
made no effort to include Christianity as any premise for self-actualization and self-realization. In *for colored girls*, for instance, Shange
repeatedly rejects the interpretation that the seven women experience
God in their rainbow vision.[17] Instead, the god they "love fiercely"
is an inner strength, a self-awareness that does not result from some
connection with an external spiritual force or being. Notably, their
experience in the end creates an atmosphere of communal fellowship
as they join hands chanting. The same atmosphere of religious
conversion characterizes the mental and intellectual conversion of the
actors in *spell #7*, who emerge with renewed racial self-awareness,

their experience being more like a spiritual revival than a conversion. In *boogie*, however, the role of religion is the one traditionally played in the lives of black people: that of providing solace and consolation from a hostile secular, materialistic, and white folks' world. The "shout" pushed from Layla's throat at her moment of conversion recalls the verbal and often physical show of emotion in traditional black churches when the Holy Spirit seduces and then consumes an individual into emotional unawareness of one's physical self and one's physical surroundings.[18] Through this religious episode Layla experiences color and herself as "colored," her first move toward greater self-acceptance. Having her transformation effected by a disembodied radio voice, rather than by an experience of communal worship, adds a satiric edge to Layla's conversion; a potentially parodic thrust at media evangelists exists in Shange's detail that "jesus came closer to her [Layla's] heart the way // the deep voice waz sayin." While Layla is not afraid of learning about the world, she is unable to become a part of it by actually joining a congregation or meeting an evangelist in person. Turning to a radio evangelist signals Layla's desperation and her move outside herself to find and accept herself. It is both interesting and problematic that Layla accepts an evangelist's voice as Jesus'. Such an acceptance on her part alerts us that this moment too is not all that Layla needs it to be. She allows another's voice to direct her actions rather than assume a more direct authority from her own spiritual ear. In this conversion moment, Layla's mother signifies further external opposition to Layla's self-awareness. That her mother's kitchen smoke scars her arms implies that the antagonism between mother and daughter thwarts Layla's self-discovery and underscores Layla's lack of support even within her home: "the mother waz cold/ & thought the rush of color // from her daughter's mouth/ too blazing & niggardly // for her household" (117). As in *spell #7*, Shange plays on the word "niggardly" to recall the derogatory term "nigger" and the potential cultural detachedness of Layla's own mother who may have problems accepting her own racial identity and its textured color. Despite the mother's opposition, however, Layla broadens her perceptions and her awareness, thus allowing her a more complete existence:

jesus had released her to the warmth of herself.
. . . .
. . . she had a glowin inside her that changed the world.
now she cd touch her face with the palms of her hands
she usedta sit on/ those black hands
now caressed her with forsythia delicacy
her soul waz filled with daffodils/ tulips spread in her
    cheeks. (117)

With religion, Layla experiences a newness of self and accepts her
physical blackness:

    layla
i waz growin beyond this singed & reluctant plane/
i discovered dimensions/ & hope
    n.l.c. #4
there are horizons. there are different dawns.
    n.l.c. #3
not here/ but out there somewhere/ or maybe
in my hands/ these black hands. (117)

Perhaps Shange is here simultaneously celebrating and attacking
religion as it has been traditionally associated with black people's
psychological and emotional survival in racist America. On the other
hand, traditional Westernized Christianity allows for the acceptance
of one's plight as a black person.[19] Shange effectively uses the same
images associated with Layla before and after discovering Jesus.
Before, there was no "horizon[, for it] implied three dimensions";
now there are "dimensions/ & hope. there are horizons." Before,
"dawn held no surprises"; now, "there are different dawns."
Before, her black hands "matted the [wall] surfaces with grime";
now, the horizons and dawns might be in "[her] black hands."
Before, she knew not the color and experience of "fierce yellow";
now, "the sun waz yellow," "she stood in a arc of yellow," she had
a "daffodil glaze," "the corn waz yellow," and she was caressed
with "forsythia delicacy" (117). No longer does she see herself as
"all black & crusty" but as "bright under the crust/ of herself"
(117). With this acceptance of her physical blackness, however,

come the physical dangers that threaten her because of her skin color, one of the ever-present 'troubles in paradise.'

Layla's new attitude toward her blackness paradoxically alienates Layla from other black people, a circumstance that separates her from the sisterly communion celebrated in *for colored girls*. Since Layla personally does not experience physical deprivation, especially that of black children, she is at once satisfied with her lonely living and is thereby oblivious to others' sufferings; she is detached from her own black family and from those black children who do not experience life as fully as her discovery of Jesus allows her:

> *n.l.c. #3*
> she had withdrawn from the hugs of her mother her
>   father
> her grandmother & those other lil blk things who lived
>   with her/
> the sisters & brothers who had found no colors/
> who still left huge slurs of gray all around/
> she held herself in her light/ feeling sorry for the rest.
> if she let them near her/ they might smudge this
>   precious secret/
> this soft fire she waz/ she wd never do that/ she waz
>   selfish
> she wd never tell them there waz something more
> than black & white skinny lives & black & white
>   shutters/
> & black cries & white yelps/ she wd never tell them.
>   (118)

The narrator's condescending tone—"those . . . lil blk things" and "black & white skinny lives"—reflects Layla's own momentary aloofness. Layla's discovery of existence beyond black and white becomes a source of selfish pride. No longer does she hide under the bed crying in despair; her rebirth leads her to hide beneath her bed, hoarding her newfound spiritual warmth and her illusion of personal completion. Though Layla wishes to keep her discovery secret, her humanity will not allow her the privilege of silence and passivity in the face of historical mistreatment of her race family at the hands of white racists. On one level she does not have the option of racial detachment since her skin color automatically connects her to the suffering and injustice that result from racial oppression; because of who, what, and where she is, she too can become a victim at any white person's whim. Hence, the pain that blacks generally and black children particularly suffered at the hands of whites who have historically burned blacks' property and persons, attacked blacks physically and mocked them crying, "niggahs/ niggahs/ go home/ go home/ niggahs!" (118)—all to maintain an alleged social order—stirs Layla's sympathies for other blacks and thus raises her own racial consciousness:

> i drew the lil black things with me under my bed
> & wiped the scarlet stains from their mouths
> with the light of myself. (119)

Layla's impulse to nurture and to protect overwhelms her initial self-ishness and creates a new core of racial identity, replacing religion. Herein is Shange's ultimate attack on Christianity as a force that removes individuals from the "masses," that artificially separates people into those who are "saved" and those who are not. Traditional Christianity, while it presumes to be other-directed—to have as one of its goals to bring the "unsaved" into the fold—is indeed self-serving, concerned not necessarily with others' alleged final destinies but with one's own spiritual destiny. Her actions reveal a movement from narcissistic self-love to agape; her new love reveals an encompassing sense of community, albeit a racially segregated one.

Such an episode associated with racial strife and psychological and spatial displacement of blacks recalls the St. Louis "territorial dispute" narrated by Alec and the minstrels in *spell #7*, as well as the autobiographical account of Shange's own call to racial consciousness. Some critics consider it paradoxical that Shange often writes of a class of which she herself was not a part. Since Shange was not poor as a child, nor was she subjected to the physical abuse inflicted upon the children in the throes of the sixties' civil rights movement, particularly in the South, some insist that her voice is less authentic in speaking about "ordinary" black people. For example, Robert Staples boldly but erroneously asserts that Shange's problem "is, that being middle-class, [she was] raised away from the realities of the black experience and tend[s] to see it all as pathological in the same way that whites view us [blacks]," adding that "Shange . . . put[s] down working culture without really understanding."[20] Never could Staples' assessment of Shange's race/ class consciousness be more off the mark. Rather, it was the ineffectuality of her upper middle-class childhood that allegedly moved her toward greater race consciousness and fuller awareness of her historical connectedness with those who did not necessarily share her intellectual and economic background. She explains her alienation within her middle-class familial setting:

> I found middle-class life terribly vacuous, incredibly boring. It doesn't interest me, and I can't write about something that I'm not interested in. . . . I'm not avoiding writing about my middle classness. There are just aspects of it that I haven't dealt with yet. When I understand them I'll probably write about them.[21]

Although Shange often recalls parental disapproval of her childhood friendships with "regular" colored people,[22] she resisted their objections. To Shange, even her parents had predictably misguided dreams as blacks in racist North America:

> My parents loved me and brought me up in a way black kids—any kids—can usually only dream about. . . . We were a true American success story —or at least they thought so. They thought they could assimilate into the American system and forget they were black. [This is not to suggest that they thought of themselves as white.] When they'd tell me I could do things other kids couldn't do they meant all other kids, not just black ones. They really think in those terms even today. They've seen the play [*for colored girls*] six or seven times and say they love it—not because they know what I'm saying but . . . because I'm their daughter.

> They're your typical NAACP blacks. They
> don't want to complain about things because they
> think those things are better left unsaid. They think
> they live the American Dream. I don't. I mean, I
> love them dearly but, to me, they've been duped by
> their own dreams.[23]

With cynicism and pain, Shange speaks of her "extraordinarily
privileged childhood":

> [We] had the best lives America had to offer. Both
> professionals [her parents], four kids, two cars. I
> was privileged, smart, comfortable, light-skinned.
> [My family] protected me from being colored. In a
> way, childhood was wonderful but I have been
> terribly unhappy.[24]

She continues to refer to her childhood as "a double life" and insists
that she was "living a lie":

> [I was] living in a world that defied reality as most
> black people, or most white people, understood
> it—in other words, feeling that there was something
> that I could do, and then realizing that nobody was
> expecting me to do anything because I was colored
> and I was also female, which was not very easy to
> deal with.[25]

She adds further clarification about not being "expected to do anything" as a child:

> It became clear to me that I had to do something
> when I was in the ninth or tenth grade (which would
> be 1961 or 1962—around then) because other young
> children my age were doing something, primarily in
> the South. They were boycotting stores, they were
> walking to schools, they were having people throw
> things at them—trying to get an education. Some of

> this I had experienced myself already in St. Louis. I
> think it was then that I decided I had to do some-
> thing. I did not really believe, with any kind of
> commitment, in non-violence; I never have. And I
> remember it used to upset me terribly to watch
> black people sit down and pray while "they"
> [white people] proceeded to hose us and beat us to
> death. I remember trying to run off to be on a Free-
> dom Ride because that seemed to be a more aggres-
> sive attitude than expressed in the marches since the
> Freedom Riders knew that these buses were going
> to be bombed. I don't know exactly why I thought
> that was more aggressive. . . . I don't think I was
> alone in wanting to be part of a group of young
> people who wanted certain so-called concessions
> from the white people in terms of where [we] could
> drink water and if [we] could stop in a hotel or not,
> or a restaurant; these were truly degrading, ridicu-
> lous things![26]

Layla questions racial injustices with this same intense perception.

Layla's physical development as a woman is Shange's emphasis in the second movement of this character study. As Helene Keyssar acknowledges, "To be black and a woman, to be each of these, is to have two distinct mountains to climb, and having conquered one, Layla must as a woman begin to climb again."[27] This ordering of gender and race oppressions does not seem primary in *for colored girls* since the adult women's experiences do not allow a "separation of soul & gender" (*for colored girls* 48). The women further deem a "metaphysical dilemma" the singularity of experience in "bein alive & bein a woman & bein colored." Shange's analysis of Layla follows the physical growth pattern of any child who first discovers his or her skin color then wonders about his or her physical body in terms of sexual identity. Yet recognizably as

n.l.c. #5
. . . .
she studied the legs & arms of herself/ the hair & lips

of herself/ before the burst of spirit let her hold herself.
. . . .
   n.l.c. #2
she got too big to hide under her bed/
she didnt really want to hide any more. (118-19)

Layla's discovery of her sexuality is succinct and dramatically effective because although the exact moments of any individual's physical changes are unobtrusive, the changes themselves are distinct and observable. Layla studies her own body: her legs, arms, hair, and lips. The growth of body hair on her arms, legs, and pubic areas signals Layla's gradual and abrupt crossing into womanhood. Still, Layla's discovery of her body is not as traumatic as the acceptance of her skin color; after all, she becomes aware of her body changes during the "burst of spirit."[28]

Layla's identity as an adult female is further defined by her attractiveness to men. Toward presenting the ambivalence often associated with a woman's sexual and gender awakening, Shange offers a warning to women about subsequent and consequential sexual victimization. Night-life companion #4 acts the part of a cunning lover who desires only sex with Layla, saying:

   you drink continually from a scarlet wine glass
   & let yr brazziere straps slip/ round/ yr shoulders
   . . . .
   with eyes as unfamiliar as your simplicity
   you rest your hands on light/ make yrself/ over & over
   you are your own mirror/ yr own deja-vu/ i, yr
        accomplice
   yr beauty is irreducible/ yr hair acorns.
   . . . .
   . . . yr wine glass barely braizes yr lips/
   . . . yr nails unpainted/ ridiculously inviting
   you sit here in carved glass/ in mirrors/ on light/
   in sepia caves/ only i imagine/ i sleep near you
   you are not afraid of the dark/ the wine simply eases
   the flowers from yr cheeks to my dreams/ the red goblet
   signals my white stallions to trot

now/ we are ready for the vision/ . . .

. . . .

a red glass so close to yr lips/ not unlike a kiss

not at all like my lips/ but constant & always possible.

you put yr hope where you can have it

you sleep with me on laced glass/ in caves swollen with
    beauty/

i put my dreams in yr goblet. (121-22)

The lover's appeal, full of sexual imagery and innuendo, arouses Layla's physical passions, as revealed in her gesture of undressing during the episode. While she responds flirtatiously to this man and is genuinely excited by his desire for her, her perception of his insincerity and her suspicions of his motives alert her to shun his advances. The seducer identifies himself as an "accomplice," implying that Layla is the instigator of her own victimization, he merely her willing partner. It mystifies her that the body she once despised is now an object both literally and figuratively of men's desire. Layla's refusal to sleep with this man does not imply a condemnation of female sexuality. Instead, Layla's hesitancy highlights a woman's need for caution in male-female sexual relationships. While in one sense, Layla's encounter with her would-be lover stereotypes men in matters of romance—that men want only sex from women and that men will use any manipulation toward that end, an issue raised in Act II of *spell #7*—the scene introduces and acknowledges the inevitable paradox in male-female sexual relationships, a paradox affecting primarily women: while acknowledging her sexuality as a positive force, that sexuality inevitably makes each woman vulnerable to the potential physical, social, and gender liabilities. The man, in contrast, experiences only the pleasures of the sex act, retaining physical, psychological, and social power. In fact, a male's sexuality is rarely a liability of any sort and is more often perceived as a form of social empowerment, even in this modern AIDS crisis. Just as Layla learns that being black means being oppressed, she discovers that being female also means being denied certain freedoms of existence.

This fundamental feminist assertion is set forth most vividly in Maxine's fantasy sequence in *spell #7*: as a child this female was free

in the world because contact with "made-up boyfriends" (48) was
not physically or socially threatening. As a child, she was "simply
another winged creature" (49) like the birds she observed. When she
physically became a woman, however, the outside world threatened
her safety, her very existence as an independent being:

> when i became a woman, my world got
> smaller. my grandma closed up the windows/ so the
> birds wdnt fly in the house any more. waz bad luck
> for a girl so yng & in my condition to have the
> shadows of flying creatures over my head. i didnt
> celebrate the trolley driver anymore/ cuz he might
> know i waz in this condition. i didnt celebrate the
> basketball team anymore/ cuz they were yng &
> handsome/ & yng & handsome cd mean trouble. but
> trouble waz when white kids called you names or
> beat you up cuz you had no older brother/ trouble
> waz when someone died/ or the tornado hit yr
> house/ now trouble meant something abt yng &
> handsome/ & white or colored. if he waz yng &
> handsome that meant trouble. seemed like every
> one who didnt have this condition/ . . . waz trouble.
> as i understood it/ my mama & my grandma were
> sending me out to be with trouble/ but not to get
> into trouble. the yng & handsome cd dance with me
> & call for sunday supper/ the yng & handsome cd
> write my name on their notebooks/ cd carry my
> ribbons on the field for gd luck/ the uncles cd hug
> me & chat for hours abt my growing up/ so i
> counted all 492 times this condition wd make me
> victim to this trouble. . . . (49-50)

Notice the confusion of this and potentially any female child who, in
addition to coping with normal physiological changes at puberty,
must also understand how these natural changes mandate complicated
and thereby cautious living for her. Before puberty, trouble for a
black girl involved racial tensions and natural disasters. The physical
"condition" of being female, however, changes her mother and

grandmother's definition of trouble—a definition with nuances so subtle, yet so confounding for a young black girl. Maxine's fears echo the Lady in Blue's (*for colored girls*), who lives always threatened by her immediate and remote male environment:

> i usedta live in the world
> then i moved to HARLEM
> & my universe is now six blocks
> . . . .
> i come in at dusk
> stay close to the curb . . .
> . . . .
> praying wont no young man
> think i'm pretty in a dark mornin . . .
> wdnt be good
> . . . .
> to meet a tall short black brown young man fulla his
>   power
> in the dark
> in my universe of six blocks
> . . . .
> i usedta live in the world
> really be in the world
> free & sweet talkin
> good mornin & thank-you & nice day
> uh huh
> i cant now
> i cant be nice to nobody
> nice is such a rip-off
> reglar beauty & a smile in the street
> is just a set-up
> i usedta be in the world
> a woman in the world
> i hadda right to the world
> then i moved to harlem
> for the set-up
> a universe
> six blocks of cruelty

piled up on itself
a tunnel
closin. (*for colored girls* 38-41)

For the Lady in Blue, the world is no longer physically accessible
without potential and substantial penalty. Her negative attitudes
about being female in a patriarchal society transform her from a free-
moving agent to one controlled by the onset of night. Consequently,
she, with reason, is less likely to celebrate being alive with the
passion of womanhood. Hers is a restricted existence and although
the poem cites Harlem as the circumscribed geography, such behavior might characterize any female anywhere whose life can be threatened at virtually any moment by the aggression of any "young man
fulla // his power" to make her powerless.[29] It is here that Shange
launches an attack on the social dictate that being born a female is
tantamount to and synonymous with being born a victim. Feminist
Susan Griffin's personal testimony summarizes potentially any
woman's fear and corroborates both Maxine's and the Lady in Blue's
assertions:

> I have never been free of the fear of rape.
> From a very early age I, like most women, have
> thought of rape as part of my natural environ-
> ment—something to be feared and prayed against
> like fire or lightning. I never asked why men raped;
> I simply thought it one of the many mysteries of
> human nature.
>
> I was, however, curious enough about the vio-
> lent side of humanity to read every crime magazine
> I was able to ferret away from my grandfather.
> Each issue featured at least one "sex crime," with
> pictures of a victim, usually in a pearl necklace,
> and of the ditch or the orchard where her body was
> found. I was never certain why the victims were
> always women, nor what the motives of the mur-
> derer were, but I did guess that the world was not a
> safe place for women. I observed that my grand-
> mother was meticulous about locks and quick to

draw the shades before anyone removed so much as
a shoe. I sensed that danger lurked outside.

At the age of eight, my suspicions were con-
firmed. My grandmother took me to the back of the
house where the men wouldn't hear, and told me
that strange men wanted to do harm to little girls. I
learned not to walk on dark streets, not to talk to
strangers or get into strange cars, to lock doors, and
to be modest. She never explained why a man
would want to harm a little girl, and I never
asked.[30]

As an adult woman, Layla becomes intensely aware of the
omnipresent potential for victimization of women individually and
collectively. Shange's attack of the perceived connection between
"female" and "victim" is never more poignant than in night-life
companion #3's feminist editorial:

it's not so good to be born a girl/ sometimes. that's
why societies usedta throw us away/ or sell us/ or
play with our vaginas/ cuz that's all girls were good
for. at least women cd carry things & cook/ but to
be born a girl is not good sometimes/ some places/
such abominable things cd happen to us. . . . infibulation is sewing our vaginas up with cat-gut or
weeds or nylon thread to insure our virginity. virginity insurance equals infibulation. that can also
make it impossible for us to live thru labor/ . . .
infibulation lets us get infections that we cant men-
tion/ cuz disease in the ovaries is a sign that we're
dirty anyway/ so wash yrself/ cuz once infibulated
we have to be cut open to have/ you know what/ the
joy of the phallus/ that we may know nothing about/
ever/ especially if something else not good that
happens to little girls happens: if we've been
excised. had our labia removed with glass or scis-
sors. if we've lost our clitoris because our pleasure
is profane & the presence of our naturally evolved

clitoris wd disrupt the very unnatural dynamic of
polygamy. so with no clitoris/ no labia & infibu-
lation/ we're sewn-up/ cut-up/ pared down & sore if
not dead/ & oozing pus/ if not terrified that so much
of our body waz wrong & did not belong on earth
. . . . it really is not so good to be born a girl when
we have to be infibulated, excised, clitorectomized
& STILL be afraid to walk the streets or stay home
at night. i'm so saddened that being born a girl
makes it dangerous to attend midnight mass
unescorted. some places if we're born girls &
someone else who's very sick & weak & cruel/
attacks us & breaks our hymen/ we have to be
killed/ sent away from our families/ forbidden to
touch our children. . . . to be born a girl who will
always have to worry not only abt the molesters/
the attackers & the rapists/ but also abt their
peculiarities: does he stab too/ or shoot? does he
carry an axe? does he spit on you? does he know if
he doesnt drop sperm we cant prove we've been
violated? these subtleties make being a girl too
complex/ for some of us & we go crazy/ or never
go anyplace. some of us have never had an open
window or a walk alone, but sometimes our homes
are not safe for us either. rapists & attackers &
molesters are not strangers to everyone/ they are
related to somebody/ & some of them like raping &
molesting their family members better than a girl-
child they don't know yet. this is called incest, &
girl children are discouraged from revealing attacks
from uncle or daddy/ cuz what wd mommy do? . . .
but infibulation, excision, clitorectomies, rape &
incest are irrevocable life-deniers/ life stranglers &
disrespectful of natural elements. . . . even though
gender is not destiny/ right now being born a girl is
to be born threatened; i want being born a girl to be
a cause for celebration/ . . . we pay for being born
girls/ but we owe no one anything/ not our labia,

not our clitoris, not our lives. we are born girls to
live to be women who live our own lives/ to live
our lives. to have/ our lives/ to live. we are born
girls/ to live to be women. . . . (135-136)[31]

Shange summarizes what is at the heart of the physical, psychological, and political problems that plague females: they are and have
historically been considered and therefore treated as men's property—
to be thrown away, sold, mutilated or played with—in short, objects
of male fancy. This status is evidenced in cultures that openly value
male babies over female babies. In some of these cultures, female
infants may be killed, or at best considered worthless—much like
spoiled fruit. Shange shows that this role of female as sex-object is
present in alleged "modern" industrialized societies as well. If little
girls are allowed "to live to be women," their value to society
increases through their ability to "carry things & cook," to carry
babies and to reproduce. Clearly, these responsibilities define a
woman's role in terms of how she can be used by men across cultures. To drive home the horrors of being born female in some
places, Shange itemizes the "abominable things [that] cd happen to"
females allowed to live after birth. She catalogues physical mutilation
of females through rape, excision, infibulation, and clitorectomy as
realities for females across centuries and cultures.[32] Against this
inhumane treatment of women and children, Shange uses such
graphic details as oozing pus and maimed female genitals to shock
and even repulse her audience into awareness of life as usual for
some females. A seesaw method of comparison unveils the silent fear
that forms a basis of female existence and shows how physical
mutilation in allegedly primitive societies is mirrored in modern
societies not only in physical abuse but in traumatic psychological
abuse as well. Whereas infibulation is "virginity insurance" for
females in 'undeveloped' cultures, that same purity is revered in
modern societies that condemn females' sexual liberties. Shange
recognizes that just as infibulation and clitorectomies make sexual
activity unpleasurable at best, modern social mores allow only men
the pleasure of sex without responsibility or guilt. Note the bitter
irony in her detail that "once infibulated we have to be cut open to
have/ . . . the joy of the phallus"; a female who has been pared, cut,

sliced, and reduced, finds little sexual joy left for her. Instead, that "joy" is reserved for the men ultimately responsible for the initial cutting and sewing and the eventual cutting and re-opening of the female's genitalia. While modern women are not necessarily killed for being sexually assaulted as in some ancient societies, they suffer social and hence psychological death in being outcast by families and communities.

This poem also questions legal systems that traditionally defend perpetrators of crimes against women, systems that justify or excuse men's behavior while further victimizing women. This patriarchal bias is evidenced by the passage of ever stricter anti-abortion legislation which reduces women's rights to control their own bodies— hence their own destinies—forcing them to accept the consequences of both sexual freedom and sexual assault; this same legal system is largely impotent in ensuring that males help support children they help create. Such responsibilities inevitably make it impossible for women to realize their full sexual identity. The same bitter sarcasm concerning the legal definitions of rape—"does he know if he doesnt drop sperm we cant prove we've been violated?"—recalls the tone and sentiments of the women in "latent rapists'" (*for colored girls* 17-21) who signify on the nature of rape and rapists. As if the physical mutilation suffered by females in some cultures were not enough to illustrate the hazards of being born female, women "STILL" have to worry about "walk[ing] the streets or stay[ing] home at night. . . . [or] attend[ing] midnight mass unescorted." The irony runs deeper given the fact that an escort (presumably male) is another potential attacker; the female may be turning to potential violators for protection from others. Shange offhandedly attacks patriarchal religions to which women are subjected as well. Such chauvinistic ideologies render them less significant and less capable spiritually and intellectually than men.

While Shange offers more clarification of men's responsibilities in helping create environments safe for women and children in *From Okra to Greens*, she does recognize that men are becoming more aware of and sensitive to women sexually, socially, intellectually, and politically. As a feminist who is also the mother of an adolescent daughter, Shange is steadfast in her commitment to address men who perpetuate patriarchal domination of women:

> . . . there is (in other parts of the population) an
> incredible rise in the number of physical attacks on
> women in so-called "domestic disputes" and at-
> tacks by strangers. Feminists first wanted to see this
> violence as a reaction to feminism. It's an uncon-
> scious response for men to say: "They [women] can
> earn the money; they can learn how to think and
> can go to school, but I can still kill them." . . .
> Rape and child molestation have to become as hei-
> nous to us as lynching was. We have to understand
> them as political crimes. That is where I think men
> have been cowardly because they have allowed the
> victims—the women who have been raped and the
> mothers of children who have been attacked—to be
> the voices of change in this matter when in fact
> we're not the perpetrators of these crimes. . . . Men
> have [to make] a decision that "I cannot simply say
> that I don't do that [abuse women and/or children];
> I have to participate in the reconstruction of a soci-
> ety where men know that other men will not look
> upon them kindly if I [a man] know that you
> [another man] continue to do this or that you did
> this."[33]

A woman's fears are further complicated and intensified by the
reality that a male's assertion of power does not always take place
outside her home. With increasing reports of incestuous molestation,
homes are often not safe either, leaving the female trapped, displaced, and afraid. Especially in cases of incest, the victim/survivor
again assumes responsibility for her attacker: "girl children are
discouraged from revealing attacks from uncle or daddy/ cuz what
wd mommy do?" Such realities, contribute to females' self-
alienation and confusion about their own right to exist in allegedly
free, democratic societies. The final lines of the poem affirm a
woman's right to exist without restriction despite these life-denying
and life-threatening conditions. The repetition of "live" underscores
women's collective and individual survival despite patriarchal efforts
to silence and to destroy. Given what has preceded the last lines of

the poem—the destruction of female infants in some societies, the physical mutilation of females in others, and instances of sexual violence and gender-specific social limitations in our own—the last line reaffirms women's right to exist: "we are born girls/ to live to be women. . . ." Such a simple statement encompasses a realm of complicated realities for potentially any female; Shange, then, gives legitimacy to being born a girl in societies where it is unjustly and devastatingly denied.

The ideal state for women to exist freely and without fear is proposed in the hypothetical Rape Prevention Month series (123-24), a list of ten alternatives that would create an ideal rape-free environment for females. Such a proposal forthrightly moves the issue of rape and female victimization from the level of the personal to the political. In this proposal, men and women would experience a reality reversal. Instead of women caging themselves in fear of their outside environment, "all . . . men [would be] locked in boxes with no windows & no doors/ we can come // & go as we please/ at any hour/ any day" (123). Such freedom of movement, taken for granted by males specifically and even by whites generally in racist North America, is one denied females and blacks. Shange recommends, among other things, that women and children be schooled fully in physical self-defense techniques and that governments rightfully honor rather than ignore survivors of sexual assault. The proposal offers that

> *n.l.c. #1*
> rape victims are given prime time 60-second spots to say
> what happened to them. the governor/ the mayor/ & the
>   entire
> city council will personally see the rape victim/
>   apologize
> for the municipal negligence/ . . .
> . . . .
> . . . in addition/ all women
> who died or who demonstrated remarkable courage &
>   integrity
> during rape attacks are given congressional medals of
>   honor.

> *n.l.c. #3*
> or the purple heart.
> *n.l.c. #1 & 3 (in unison)*
> we shall have streets/ schools & monuments named after
> all
> these women & children/ they died for their country.
> (124)

Centering on survivors' sufferings, there is neither excuse nor sympathy for females' attackers.

Recommending that victims be given "purple heart[s]" is an effective metaphor because, like those wounded in action in the United States Armed Forces, victims of sexual assault are in battle for their lives and their livelihood. Women's contributions to social development would be further noted if women went on strike in protest of these injustices. Shange's does not, however, leave women's empowerment in the hands of men. Instead, she offers that

> unless the streets are made safe for us/ we shall call a
> general strike/ in factories/ at home/ at school.
> we shall say we cannot come to work/ it is not safe.
> (124)

This detail recognizes the presence and impact of women in all institutions of North American society, in all parts of the world: the work place, the home, and the school. If women abandoned these roles altogether, she proposes, men would then realize women's value and respect their personhood.[34]

Shange's work makes clear that personal problems of racism and sexism are simultaneously broader political issues concerning people of color and women. While *for colored girls* attacks a legal system's further victimization of rape victims, *spell #7* cites the racial and hence political biases of the media which minimizes or ignores those relegated to social margins. In *spell #7*, Maxine's character recalls early childhood misconceptions based on media presentations:

> . . . during the polio epidemic/ i wanted to have a
> celebration/ which nobody cd understand since iron

> lungs & not going swimming waznt nothing to cele-
> brate. but i explained that i waz celebrating the
> bounty of the lord/ which more people didnt under-
> stand/ til i went on to say that/ it waz obvious that
> god had protected the colored folks from polio/
> nobody understood that. i did/ if god had made
> colored people susceptible to polio/ then we wd be
> on the pictures & the television with the white
> children. i knew only white folks cd get that partic-
> ular disease/ & i celebrated. (*spell #7* 50)

Obviously, the little girl of Maxine's character is misled by almost
exclusive images of whites in the media, learning later that blacks
too have this crippling disease. This character's misconception
reveals a political system controlled by a white patriarchy, reflecting
its values, ideals, and people. And the limited and popular roles of
people of color in the media reiterate myths and stereotypes, thereby
perpetuating cultural and social ignorance. In *boogie*, Shange, along
these same lines, attacks the print media, using *The New York Times*
as representative of social and political bias in North America.[35]
Personifying *The Times* as a prosaic and aloof white man—the American patriarchy—Shange challenges this bias in a political satire:

> the *ny times* has never asked me [a black woman] what i
>   think abt a goddamn thing.
> the *ny times* has never excused himself to take a leak
> no/ the *times* has never helped in times of need
> or offered his seat to a pregnant woman on the irt
> as a matter of fact
> at breakfast the *times* is quite rude
> interruptin conversations in any language
> unless i insist on sittin under the table
> so i cd talk to people's knees
> i've never been able to communicate with someone
> whose nose is in the *times*/ also i'd like
> to mention i've never seen the *times* dance
> can the *ny times* dance
> can the *times* get down

. . . .
. . . i wd like to get the *ny times* out of my social life
the next time someone asks me if i have seen the paper/
i'll say/ i've seen more news than is fit to print
& yes we have deliveries everyday/ discounts to
households that understand the rhythm of our lives
n speak colloquial universal language. . . . (124-25)

This attack on *The New York Times* extends to other media devoted
primarily to conservative white-middle class males' views. While
newspapers generally focus on "sick" perpetrators and not survivors, Shange resents this minimal coverage by mainstream presses of
issues that affect women and minorities around the globe. The
brashness of the language in the piece—"a goddamn thing" and
"take a leak"—contrasts the formality of the *Times* persona. Shange
concludes that the *Times* is really of little relevance to the lives of
people of color and women in North America. Notice the *Times'*
inconsiderate behavior in not offering his seat to the pregnant woman
on the New York subway. Rather than present empty headlines that
merely decorate North American media, Shange offers alternative
and more meaningful headlines for racially and culturally oppressed
peoples:

EXTRA EXTRA READ ALL ABOUT IT:
ZIMBABWE CELEBRATES FIFTY YEARS OF
    INDEPENDENCE
EXTRA EXTRA READ ALL ABOUT IT:
THOUSANDS OF WRITERS FLOCK TO
    INTERNATIONAL CONFERENCE
ON FREE SPEECH IN ARGENTINA
EXTRA EXTRA READ ALL ABOUT IT:
WHITE SOUTH AFRICANS DENIED ENTRY
    TO THE UNITED STATES
AS WAR CRIMINALS
EXTRA EXTRA READ ALL ABOUT IT:
NOT ONE AFRO-AMERICAN CHILD WHO
    CANT READ & WRITE/
CELEBRATION OF CAMPAIGN AGAINST

NATIONAL ILLITERACY
EPIDEMIC HELD IN BED-STUY
that's how i see it, today. now that's the news that's
fit to print. (125-26)

Such a proposition reveals Shange's own intense political consciousness, both nationally and internationally. Shange's headlines celebrate personal and public freedoms, literacy, opportunity, and the
possibilities for fuller living, now denied persons of color globally.
While recognizing the cultural rhythms of Havana and Soweto where
people of color have a sense of legitimacy, Shange resents African
Americans' constant struggle for that same legitimacy:

> The problem here for me and other black people is
> that no matter how many allegiances we form or
> how many politically brilliant spokespersons we
> spawn, we will nevertheless be a minority here,
> which I find very uninteresting. And it's not inter-
> esting to me to be a minority when the rest of the
> world is people of color, which is one reason why I
> think that I won't always be here in North America.
> I have a great deal more immediate emotional and
> intellectual satisfaction in countries where the
> means of production and national decisions are
> made by people of color. . . . There's no particular
> reason to imagine that one day all of a sudden it's
> going be all right to be a black person here.[36]

Shange's international political concerns are further presented in
From Okra to Greens. By offering the concept of "colloquial universal," Shange reiterates that the rest of the world is populated by
peoples of color rather than white Anglo-Saxons. The cultural
rhythms and experiences of over thirty million is colloquial only in a
predominantly white United States. The cultural influences and
experiences of blacks transcend, in Shange's view, North American
boundaries to encompass the lives of the rest of the world's peoples
of color. Additionally, Shange here redefines the boundaries of the
universe to exclude those are not people of color. Hence, for minori-

ties and other peoples of color, their alleged 'colloquial' is their universal. Shange's universe demands a conscious decentering of white folks.

Layla's dreams and visions, despite their presentation of potential gender and race victimizations, are not all nightmares. The third thematic movement of *boogie* recalls moments in Layla's past as a child and as an adult when neither race nor sex is a liability. Layla's childhood reveries are recognizably Shange's own personal ones:

> we waz a house fulla chirren who waz fulla the
> dickens cordin to grandma. there waz me & my 2
> sisters & my brother & my 2 cousins/ too smart for
> our own good & nothin but trouble for the ladies
> who looked after us while mama waz at work &
> papa went to the hospital. (130)

Details of Shange's family life in St. Louis contrast the play's more tense moments, the childhood epiphanies about racial injustices, the embittered awareness of the physical mutilations of females across cultures, and the attacks on white patriarchy. Using an adolescent black female persona, Shange renders entertaining accounts of her upper middle-class family's experiences with three women housekeepers. The emphasis of this reverie is on a young girl's growth toward maturity amid her youthful freedom and carefree innocence. Importantly, the childhood scenario focuses particularly on a young girl's relationships with women in the household—her mother, the three maids, her grandmother, and her aunts—who all function in one way or another as role models for the adolescent. The mother's implicit cultural arrogance conversely aids in the development of the child's strong racial consciousness. This female persona recalls being chastised by her mother for her choice of friends:

> . . . i never mentioned my feelins to mama/ cuz
> then she wd just remind me/ that i always pick the
> most niggerish people in the world to make my
> friends. & then she wd list mavis & freddie &
> charlenetta & linda susan (who waz really po white
> trash). . . . (134)

Such details might suggest clashes of racial consciousness between Shange and her mother, who admittedly "waznt no regular colored woman" (130).[37] The mother-daughter relationship also recalls Layla's with her own mother after Layla discovers Jesus.

Another unthreatening instance in Layla's life occurs at a disco party as dance and music transform her into another comic element. In this sequence, Layla revels in a freedom of the moment as she dances and sings with friends. Since Layla at this particular point in her dream sequence is "thinkin black & realizin colored" (126), she is at a black party with black people and music by black artists. Using allusions to popular music and artists—specifically to rock-and-roll, the blues, and rhythm and blues—Shange demonstrates her role as a black artist preserving and documenting positive black experiences. She cites the renowned Apollo Theater in New York, the James Brown Review, the Spinners, the Stylistics, Smokey Robinson, the Drifters, Archie and Frank Lowe, Chuck Berry, Ike Turner, Otis Redding, and even song-lyrics and specific dances—all as part of her own identity-defining and legitimizing experiences. For Shange, such allusions serve a two-fold purpose: (1) they allow for moments of mutual identification between Shange and audience members who connect emotionally and revel nostalgically in similar past associations, and (2) they preserve aspects of black cultural experiences that might otherwise be lost. She explains a commitment to documenting accurately the history of her culture:

> European writers continue to store vast amounts of information about themselves in their novels. As a writer of color, I have to do that too. Since my culture is a peripheral one here, the documentation of it is sparse and not terribly accurate. Even if I do it in a fictional manner, my characters—for the most part—live in the twentieth century and therefore their interactions with these cultural influences are real. If I can't document our lives as an historian because I choose not to, it doesn't mean that it's not documented. . . . [A]llusions to political events or cultural events of importance can give other people a sense of what it was like to be alive at this partic-

ular point in time, which is what I think most novelists do—regardless of where they're from or who
they think they're writing for or about.[38]

While Shange has been criticized for and presumably misunderstood
because of her extensive use of popular and political allusions, E.
Ethelbert Miller rises in her defense:

> [Shange's] work reflects (successfully) our [black]
> culture; it does not attempt to transcend or penetrate
> any further than the commentary offered on the
> evening news. It is a m[e]ssage, a new way of feel-
> ing and looking at things.
>
> Critics often have difficulty accepting literature
> that uses popular culture as a base. We still expect
> poetry to sound like something we can't understand,
> or something that should appeal to the intellect and
> not the emotions. . . . [Shange's] ability to draw
> upon popular culture for subject material and tech-
> niques has resulted in contemporary literature being
> as exciting as many of the other arts. If I prefer Bob
> Marley to Robert Lowell it is simply a question of
> which one is more a part of my life, not who is the
> better poet.[39]

Shange would argue that Bob Marley is every bit as important an
artist as Robert Lowell and more legitimate in her cultural realities
and experience than is Robert Lowell. "Mainstream" America
would be slow to accept Marley as a contemporary poet. Once again,
the density of popular allusions makes the alleged 'colloquial' legiti-
mately 'universal.'

This dance setting is also the occasion for Layla's existential
ponderings now that she has understood and accepted her blackness
and her womanhood, appropriately occurring in the final moments of
the choreopoem. Rather than have Layla confront a life-threatening
situation that leads to such thoughts, Shange allows Layla to question
the meaning of life in a context familiar to her—a disco. "Go[ing] to
Jonestown or the disco" (138) is here less of a choice than an image

in which Jonestown and the disco are paired as potentially self-destructive and Other-directed. Jonestown and the disco thus take on existential proportions for Layla. She could follow blindly a man who promises eternity in an afterlife, or she could experience life in the present at this moment at the disco.[40] To fully experience life in the present, according to Layla, is to glorify Jesus, the giver of life. And since she ultimately allows herself to live, it is Layla who redefines herself as Jesus, not in the sense that Adrienne Kennedy's Sarah (*Funnyhouse*) attacks a Westernized white male ideal, but Jesus as a holiness of her selfhood. Hence, at the disco Layla is able to "shout hallelujah/ praise the lord" (140) while "giv[ing] joy & form to the world" (139).[41] Shange, through this 'mystical' experience of the disco, presents Layla as a conjurer of sorts, a "neo-afrikan lady" (128) priest beckoning weary followers to consider her spiritual revival and celebration of feminine and cultural myth and ritual. As she replaces alleged prophets' words and voices with visceral responses to this music, mood, and movement, Layla perceives herself as the source of her own salvation. She urges black women to create for themselves a non-Western, non-patriarchal life-giving source:

> we need a god who bleeds now
> a god whose wounds are not
> some small male vengeance
> some pitiful concession to humility
> . . . .
> we need a god who bleeds
> spreads her lunar vulva & showers us in shades of
>   scarlet
>   . . . . .
> . . . . / i am
> not wounded i am bleeding to life
> we need a god who bleeds now
> whose wounds are not the end of anything.
> (*From Okra to Greens* 37)

Still, the disco and the Jonestown incident are situations where one's existence is defined in relation to an external governing force. Both environments present individuals who are enslaved either to another individual or to music: music does not deceive through intellect; instead, it seduces temporarily through emotion and physicality. Jim Jones and David Koresh offered their followers eternal life and salvation. With Jesus, Jim Jones, and David Koresh, desperate followers put their lives and their livelihood into the hands of per- ceived powerful males or male images. Layla in no way allows external forces to direct her life toward some afterlife existence. At this moment, she consciously chooses to "dance [her]self to death" (140), a death from which she is resurrected or 'reborn' in the present. At the disco, she can even merge with and become music— something that exists in the present like poetry. This final disco experience validates her existence in the present moment and helps to explain why Layla—at the play's opening—wants to "be music" (142); she wants to exist in the present and as a black woman whose existence is as natural as a rainbow, natural "like rain/ a cosmic event/ like sound . . ." (142). Becoming music, if only temporarily, allows her to transcend a physical world that limits her physical and creative possibilities. In much the same way that dance and music liberate the women in *for colored girls*, creative fantasy for the artists in *spell #7*, music allows Layla to unite with cosmic elements—the rain, sun, daybreak, and fog. The choreopoem thus concludes with an ideal proposition that to exist as a black woman, to be without limitations and restrictions is natural and divinely ordered. Music and the disco create this paradise, but the music ends as does the dance, and troubles of being black and a woman are once again Layla's threatening realities. Nevertheless, dance and music are readily available through her own creative energies, the souce of her own empowerment.

While *boogie woogie landscapes* presents a distinctly black feminist voice, Shange is not oblivious to a black male's emotional realities. And although black men are a significant source of black women's sufferings according to Shange, she presents a segment in *boogie* that considers a man's emotional vulnerabilities during the death of his child. As a contrast to the two near-seduction episodes where males want to seduce and objectify her—once when she is preparing for bed alone and again at the disco by "the man on the boat // from dusseldorf" (141)—Layla dramatizes a father's response to his child's death:

i lay in the cellar/ fractured/ crumbled/ over uneven
    casing
i crawled without my body/ thru sicilian ashes/
jewish cadavers moanin in the beams/ i crawled to my
    children. (137)[42]

Even his stereotyped and socially conditioned masculinity cannot shield him from personal anguish. This image of an emotionally distraught and physically broken father reduced by the very nature of human existence and his suffering in seclusion directly contrasts the previous image of fathers as molesters, rapists and baby-killers in *boogie* and in *for colored girls*. The allusion to Jewish cadavers suggests a parallel with the Holocaust, a socially inflicted and unnatural disaster. Death here contrasts with the metaphorical death through dance and music of temporarily transcending a world of disappointments, disillusion, and disaster.

There is little question that *boogie* is as much about Shange as is *for colored girls*. She admits: "[*boogie woogie landscapes*] is the secrets and traumas of an Afro-American childhood, a *double entendre* about myself, the many different places I have lived, and their varying psychological topography,"[43] and adds: "in *boogie* . . . i presented myself with the problem of having my person/body, voice & language/ address the space as if i were a band/ a dance company & a theater group all at once. cuz a poet shd do that/ create an emotional environment/ felt architecture."[44] *boogie woogie landscapes* is then another song of the inner rhythms of black female existence. Yet Shange, in *boogie*, goes beyond the layers of physical and emotional paraphernalia of *for colored girls* into the subconscious black womanhood. Details of Layla's life are set before a background of frequently dabbled color references that liken the choreopoem to an impressionist painting, here the portrait of a black girl. Shange justifies her use of a dream motif:

> *boogie woogie landscapes*/ [is] totally devoted to
> the emotional topology of a yng woman/ how she
> got to be the way she is/ how she sees where she
> is. . . . but she's no all-american girl/ or is
> she? . . . everything in *boogie* . . . is the voice of

> layla's unconscious/ her unspeakable realities/ for
> no self-respecting afro-american girl wd reveal so
> much of herself of her own will/ there is too much
> anger to handle assuredly/ too much pain to keep on
> truckin/ less ya bury it.[45]

In this sense, *boogie* resumes the study where *for colored girls* ends, revealing what is at the core of a black girl's innermost existence. And since the nature of dreams is such that they are unpredictable and seemingly disordered and non-sensical but can be interpreted, ordered, and related to the real world as well as to the unconscious, Shange plays the role of an analyst monitoring aspects of Layla's psyche, some of which even Layla is unaware. To bring order to those observations, Shange demands that her audience also become Layla's analyst. Although much of the night of dreams highlights the victimization of females politically, socially, and sexually, Layla's dreams are not all nightmares. Indeed, there are instances in Layla's life, both as a child and as an adult, when she celebrates life and her identity. Layla is a black woman who overcomes her dual victimization through dance and recollections of happier times. Despite Layla's complicated existence as a black female, despite Layla's inability to "stop smoking Kools/ forget // the militia in panama/ all brown & bald in gestapo boots/" (142), Shange affirms Layla's existence and affords her opportunities to celebrate that existence. Simply to be, to exist with possibilities, however temporal and illusory, is to defy a society that would render Layla and other women of color powerless or insignificant. To acknowledge and set forth candidly these experiences is also to reaffirm boldly that " we [women] are born to live to be women who live our own lives/ to live our lives. to have/ our lives/ to live. we are born girls/ to live to be women . . ." (136). That Layla's existence is further complicated and enhanced by her blackness once again makes the very fact of her existence an occasion for celebration.

NOTES

1. Judith Weinraub, "A Touring Black Troupe Begins Its Journey," *Washington Star*, 15 June 1980, H1.

2. Geneva Smitherman, in *Talkin' and Testifyin: The Language of Black America* (Boston: Houghton Mifflin, 1977), reminds us that boogie woogie was also a popular dance style during the thirties (256). Clarence Major, ed., *Juba to Jive: A Dictionary of African-American Slang* (New York: Penguin, 1994), hence Shange's prescription that Layla validate her existence in the present, in an immediate moment of music, dance, and poetry.

3. English graduate seminar on "Four Revolutionary Black Playwrights: LeRoi Jones, Adrienne Kennedy, Ed Bullins, and Ntozake Shange," The University of Alabama, Spring 1993.

4. Shange's presentation here is clearly informed by Adrienne Kennedy's complex presentations of black female existence. In both *Funnyhouse of a Negro* (1962) and *The Owl Answers* (1963), Kennedy explores the tortured psychological existence of educated black American females tortured by what they perceive as conflicting cultural, racial, and gender realities. In each play, Kennedy's protagonist endeavors unsuccessfully to unite her fragmented selves. As in *Funnyhouse*, Shange also incorporates mirror imagery here as part of the play's central imagery and symbolism. Both playwrights warn against the dangers of internalizing socially mirrored negative perceptions.

5. Judith Martin, "A Scattered *Landscape*," *Washington Post*, 27 June 1980, n.p.

6. Joseph McLellan, "Bungled *boogie*: Ntozake Shange's Lower-Case Editorials," *Washington Post*, 20 June 1980, C6.

7. Press Release Fact Sheet for *boogie woogie landscapes*, Terrace Theater at The John F. Kennedy Center for the Performing Arts, Press Department, Washington, D.C. (17 June-13 July 1980).

8. Adrienne Kennedy's *Funnyhouse of a Negro* (1962) dissects the psyche of a black female who is ultimately destroyed by confusion and self-hatred because of her biracial racial identity.

9. Poet Mari Evans, in "I Am a Black Woman," celebrates strength, defiance, and the fact that black womanhood is indeed

"beyond all definition" (275). See *No More Masks!: An Anthology of Poems by Women*, eds. Florence Howe and Ellen Bass (Garden City, New York: Anchor/Doubleday, 1973).

     10. Shange's detail about Layla's scarred arm contrasts with the Lady in Green's proud assertion: "i want my arm wit the hot iron scar" (*for colored girls* 53), a kind of war wound symbolizing survival.

     11. Personal interview, *Black American Literature Forum*.

     12. This same image of rubbing off the blackness of one's skin is present in *Betsey Brown* on the Brown children's first day in a racially integrated school:

> When Betsey got to her new school, it loomed
> like a granite tomb over her head. Nobody spoke to
> her, so she didn't speak to them. It was like they
> were all dead. . . . Wherever she stepped, the other
> children found somewhere else to go. It was the
> first time Betsey knew she was someplace, yet felt
> no evidence of it. Maybe they couldn't see her. No,
> Betsey knew better than that. They chose not to,
> like the color of her skin was a blight. Betsey wisht
> it would rub off. She'd rub coloredness all over the
> damn place. Then where would they go to get away
> from the niggahs? (98-99)

The attitudes portrayed are not parallel in the novel and in the play. In the novel, Betsey wants her coloredness to consume the white environment and views this as a positive change. In the play, however, Layla wants to rid herself of this coloredness altogether.

     13. African American literature and popular culture abound with instances of blacks' efforts to bleach away their dark skin tone. Everything from bleaching creams like Porsalona to bleach baths to Michael Jackson's alleged chemical skin peels document these physical and psychological dilemmas.

     14. African American "passing" fiction details the horrors parents who pass feel at their inability to predict their children's skin tones. This paranoia of producing dark children is vividly discussed in Nella Larsen's *Passing* when Clare, Irene, and Felise have gath-

ered at Clare's home for afternoon tea.

15. This imagery reiterates Ossie Davis' linguistic exercise with black/white and positive/negative. See "The English Language Is My Enemy."

16. In Adrienne Kennedy's *Funnyhouse of a Negro* (1962), mulatto Sarah, wanting to be as white as Jesus, the Duchess of Hapsburg, and Queen Victoria, "write[s] poetry, filling white page after white page with imitations of Edith Sitwell" (194). In *Contemporary Black Drama: From* A Raisin in the Sun *to* No Place to be Somebody, eds. Clinton F. Oliver and Stephanie Sills (New York: Charles Scribner's Sons, 1971).

17. See Shange's clarification of "i found god in myself" as feminist hedonist ritual rather than Christian theology in the earlier discussion of the final moments of *for colored girls*.

18. See Zora Neale Hurston's essay, "Shouting," in *The Sanctified Church* and Maya Angelou's details of black church shouting episodes in chapter six of *I Know Why the Caged Bird Sings*.

19. This same ambivalence toward Christianity is voiced by the Reverend Meridian in Baldwin's *Blues for Mister Charlie* (1964).

20. Staples, 32.

21. Michele Wallace, "Ntozake Shange: *For Colored Girls*, the Rainbow Is Not Enough," *Village Voice*, 16 August 1976, 109.

22. C. Gerald Fraser, "Theater Finds an Incisive New Playwright," *New York Times*, 16 June 1976, L27.

23. Ribowsky, 46.

24. Jacqueline Trescott, "Ntozake Shange: Searching for Respect and Identity," *Washington Post*, 29 June 1976, B5.

25. Allan Wallach, *Newsday*, 22 August 1976, as cited in *Current Biography 1978*, 381.

26. Personal interview, *Studies in American Drama*.

27. Helene Keyssar, "Communities of Women in Drama: Pam Gems, Michelene Wandor, Ntozake Shange," *Feminist Theatre* (New York: Grove, 1985), 146.

28. Such is Janie's case in Zora Neale Hurston's *Their Eyes Were Watching God* (Urbana: U of Illinois P, 1978), when Janie is stunned by her identity as a black person pictured amongst the other white children: "'Ah was wid dem white chillun so much till Ah didn't know Ah wuzn't white till Ah was round six years old. . . .

[B]efore Ah seen de picture Ah thought Ah wuz just like de rest" (21). In contrast, her womanhood, evidenced here in Janie's first period, seems to caress her: "The rose of the world was breathing out smell. It followed her through all her waking moments and caressed her in her sleep. It connected itself with other vaguely felt matters that had struck her outside observation and buried themselves in her flesh" (24).

29. In the P.B.S. television version of *for colored girls*, the Lady in Blue renders the monologue in a subway station. As the train races to a stop, the sound of the train creates an appropriate and tensely frantic closing-in effect.

30. Susan Griffin, "Rape: The All-American Crime," as printed in *Women: A Feminist Perspective*, ed. Jo Freeman (Palo Alto, California: Mayfield, 1975), 24-25.

31. Interestingly, this poem, along with its companion piece "otherwise i would think it odd to have rape prevention month (2)" was published in *Black Scholar* as a reaction to Robert Staples' "The Myth of Black Macho: A Response to Angry Black Feminists" [*Black Scholar* 10 (March-April 1979): 24-33]. In that article, Staples attacks the political theses of Shange's *for colored girls* and Michele Wallace's *Black Macho and the Myth of the Superwoman* (New York: Dial, 1979) and attempts to justify black men's abusive treatment of black women. In opposition to *for colored girls*, he argues:

> Ms. Shange does not care to tell us the story of why so many blacks feel their manhood, more accurately their feeling of self-respect, is threatened by black women. We are never told that many of these men are acting out because, of all groups in this society, they have no basis for any sense of self-actualization, or somebodiness.
>
> There is a curious rage festering inside black men because, like it or not, they have not been allowed to fulfill the roles (i.e., breadwinner, protector) society ascribes to them. . . . Some black men have nothing but their penis, an object which they use on as many women as possible[, and] in

> their middle years they are deprived of even that
> mastery of the symbols of manhood. . . . (26)

Shange's poetic responses to men's sexual abuses against women underscore Staples' failed efforts to justify men's sexual aggressions. Staples posits that black men need black women as scapegoats since black men are socially and economically inferior to white men. He even admits a self-deception when he suggests that "on the institutional level, most black men do not have the power to force women into subordinate roles."

32. Evidence abounds documenting the devaluing and mutilation of women's bodies in other cultures. In "The Women of Eritrea Literally Are Fighting to Gain Their Equality" (*Birmingham News*, 28 February 1988, 8E), Blaine Harden details circumstances in Eritrea where young girls are circumcised at the age of two, are forced into polygamous marriages at the age of eleven, and can be divorced at will by their husbands. In "'Bride-burning' Said Increasing in India, Though Police Deny It" (*Birmingham News* 24 January 1988, H2), Seema Sirohi explains that "dowry deaths" (wherein women with meager dowries are burned to death) of women are dismissed by legal authorities as "cooking accidents." Alice Walker's novel, *Possessing the Secret of Joy* (Harcourt Brace Jovanovich, 1992), deals graphically with the subject of female genital mutilation within the context of historical evidence showing this to be a reality for millions of women and girls in Asia, the Middle East, and Africa.

33. Personal interview, *Black American Literature Forum*.

34. Such a proposed strike is drawn along racial lines in Douglas Turner Ward's satiric play, *Day of Absence* (1966), where the self-centered white people—actually and importantly blacks in white face—are paralyzed and hysterical because the blacks have mysteriously disappeared. Ward suggests that black empowerment has come about through the uncertainty of other disappointments.

35. See Shange's poem "with no immediate cause" in *Nappy Edges* (114-17) where she describes the prevalence of physical abuse by men toward women and children and recognizes the one-sided media attention to such instances. Too often rape, child abuse, and molestation share equal media billing with purse-snatching and theft.

That the lives of children and women who survive these assaults against their persons are often traumatized is glossed over in 'standard' impersonal crime reports.

36. Personal interview, *Studies in American Drama.*

37. This episode of childhood revelation is undoubtedly the kernel of *Betsey Brown* (1985). In the semi-autobiographical novel, Shange details the differences between the responses of Betsey's parents to issues of race during the throes of 1950's integration in St. Louis, Missouri. The Browns too are an upper middle-class black family with a psychiatric social worker mother and a physician father. While Betsey's northern-bred and conventional mother "not only frowns on the habits and behavior of uncouth blacks but also those she calls poor white trash," [Edwina Rankin, "Much of Poet Ntozake Shange is in *Betsey Brown*," *Pittsburgh (Pennsylvania) Press*, 7 July 1985] and "still insisted on having her good china and cloth napkins for her (morning) coffee upstairs" [Adrienne Y. Welch, "Shange's *Betsey Brown* Mixes Poetry, Humor," *Miami (Florida) Herald*, 11 July 1985], Betsey's father is "bent on making sure that his children know, love and respect their black roots. He . . . drills his offspring with questions such as 'Who invented the banjo?' and 'Where is Trinidad?'" (Ibid.). Judith Stewart suggests one of Betsey Brown's immediate conflicts lies in being "caught between Mama's nearly white, genteel past and Daddy's kinky, dark and militant hold on the present" [Judith Stewart, "Growing Up Black in the Tumult," *Grand Rapids (Michigan) Press*, 2 June 1985]. Elizabeth D. Dickie adds that while Betsey's father is "calling the children together for their morning quiz on black history," Betsey's mother is "much more interested in appearances and her children's safety, than in the saving of the race" [Elizabeth D. Dickie, "*Betsey Brown* Rich and Realistic," *Richmond (Virginia) Times-Dispatch*, 9 June 1985]. Shange's keen sense of racial consciousness and exposure to and vast cultural knowledge of peoples of color was influenced by a father who routinely "mount[ed] his conga drums on his shoulders and march[ed] through the house beating a latino rhythm and reciting a poem that contains the . . . lines: 'The Negro race is a mighty one / The work of the Negro is never done / Muscle, brains and courage galore.'" Michael Weaver adds about *Betsey Brown* (and the comment applies to Shange herself): "the

whole black self-concept that [the father] attempts to weave for the children and reinforce for himself is like a set of clothing made from the stuff of history. Betsey goes out in the world wearing her colors proudly . . ." [Michael Weaver, "Authors Outline the Coming of Age of Two Black Girls," *(Baltimore, Maryland) Sun*, 21 April 1985].

38. Personal interview, unpublished, August 1986.

39. Miller, 29.

40. In *Betsey Brown* Shange also introduces the blending of dance and religion metaphysically as Betsey studies her Bible and listens to "nasty colored music" (114): "Betsey was in her own time, practicing her dancing and proverbs: the Bible and a little dance were a girl's way to salvation . . ." (115).

41. Clearly Shange blends effectively images of dance and African culture with the rhythm and movement that characterize not only dance events such as discos but also religious service. And indeed the body becomes in both instances a means of venting external secular frustrations as well as a means of signifying an inner spirituality. Ishmael Reed, obviously a major influence on Shange, connects this ritual and mythology to what he calls Neo-HooDoo, and defines it thusly in *Conjure: Selected Poems, 1963-1970* (Amherst: U of Massachusetts P, 1972): "Neo-HooDoo is a 'lost American Church' updated. Neo-HooDoo is the music of James Brown without the lyrics and ads for Black Capitalism. . . . Neo-HooDoos would rather 'shake that thing' than be stiff and erect. . . . The power of HooDoo challenged the stability of civil authority in New Orleans and was driven underground where to this day it flourishes in the Black ghettos throughout the country. HooDoo is the strange and beautiful 'fits' the Black slave Tituba gave the children of Salem" (20).

42. This poem sequence appears as "frank albert & viola benzena owens" in *Nappy Edges*, 61-64.

43. Weinraub, H1.

44. Shange, foreword to *three pieces*, xi.

45. Ibid., xiv.

CHAPTER VI

"to make/ our daughters' dreams/ as real as mensis":
*From Okra to Greens/ A Different Kinda Love Story:
A Play/ With Music & Dance*

That virtually everything Ntozake Shange writes is rooted in a poem or poem kernel is evidenced most clearly in her fifth published theater piece, *From Okra to Greens/ A Different Kinda Love Story: A Play/ With Music & Dance* (1985), an example of Shange's reworking materials to accommodate another medium of creative and political expression. As does *for colored girls*, *Okra* uses dance and music as cardinal structural components and characters that personify abstract ideas. Of her theater pieces, *Okra* resembles *for colored girls* most as a collection of independent poems that Shange has rendered at poetry readings and that have appeared in other published and performance pieces. Unlike Shange's other published pieces, however, practically every poem in *Okra* has appeared almost verbatim, even typographically, in other Shange publications, particularly her volumes of poetry, *A Daughter's Geography* (St. Martin's Press, 1983) and *from okra to greens: poems* (Coffee House Press, 1984). Even the poem sequence "some men" was published in a limited edition as *Some Men: Poetry as Art Object* in collaboration with Wopo Holup, New York City (1981). Before the publications, however, sections of what now constitutes *Okra* had been produced across the country. For example, *From Okra to Greens* in play form was first produced at The Kitchen in New York City (April 1981) under the title *Mouths. It Has Not Always Been This Way: A Choreo-*

poem, another section of the play, was produced at The Symphony Space Theater in New York (June 1981) in collaboration with the Sounds-in-Motion Dance Company. In March-April 1982, *It Hasn't Always Been This Way* and *Mouths: A Daughter's Geography* were presented as part of *Triptych & Bocas: A Performance Piece*, "An Evening of Performance Art by Ntozake Shange," at the Mark Taper Theater Lab in Los Angeles. As an abbreviated history of this piece reveals, the poems sustain themselves both as literary text and as dramatic performance. *Okra*, then, is Shange's final published effort to bring these poems together in an extension of the choreo-poem form.[1] Whereas in *for colored girls* she arbitrarily distributes the monologues among seven characters who represent a black female voice, in *Okra* she divides the various poems into two voices—a black female and a black male. Using no prose sections and paying conscious attention to dance and music, Shange presents a cultural and political variation of the traditional boy-meets-girl romance. Toward this end, she transforms dramatic monologues into poetic dialogue, offering emotional dimension to seemingly uncon-ventional characters.

A potential problem with this play lies with its coherence as Shange endeavors to rework an entire volume of poems into a single play. While the poems work independently in the three-sectioned *A Daughter's Geography*, the ordering of some of the poems and the inclusion of others often seem to break thematic and dramatic conti-nuity. Shange's intensely political poems, for example, may seem arbitrarily placed in the love story, although they do present further commentary on the realities of oppression and the need for women's sexual liberation. In independent poems about Haiti and Atlanta, Shange becomes the spokesperson for the vulnerable and the poor, for women and children across transcontinental borders. Her explora-tion of international politics suggests that a "true" marriage cannot exist between an artistically sensitive couple without some degree of political consciousness on their part as well. And while the characters represent sometimes opposing, sometimes joint sensibilities about the nature of female existence, they are above all believable articulators of Shange's poem-dialogues. To understand both content and struc-ture, one must see the play, in Shange's words, as a "feminist poem in motion"[2] within a love story framework.

The title of this piece characteristically announces its outer and inner structure. The subtitle, "A Play/ With Music & Dance," signals it as another choreopoem, but also personifies music and dance as though they are featured characters in the piece, sharing the stage with the named-after-foods characters. Music both punctuates the action of the play and introduces specific themes and moods of the action.[3] Dancers dramatize the action as well as announce scenes. At no moment during the play are music and dance vague and abstract; instead, both elements consciously complement characters' words and actions. In this sense, music and dance function in much the same manner as the Greek chorus.

Aside from the innovative form of her theater pieces, Shange's unconventionality as a playwright appears also in the names she assigns this play's two leading characters, names that refer to a vegetable combination popular among southern blacks. That Okra, whose name is of African origin, is a black female and Greens a black male is the first clue that this piece is indeed "A Different Kinda Love Story," one based on realities of a distinctly black experience and culture. And while romance itself is not necessarily relegated to race or ethnicity, these characters' experiences are definitively connected with their existence as African Americans in North America. Shange's use of "Kinda" presages the characters' colloquial language. It is "different" in that *Okra* offers a distinctly female perspective and is not a simple or traditional love story of boy-meets-girl, arguably a white cultural mythic creation. As suggested in the prepositional phrase "From Okra to Greens," it is an introduction to female sensibilities that Okra "gives" Greens in the form of a gift, a gift that allows Greens a fuller and more complete existence. More specifically, a black female gives this black male her socio-political views on a black woman's existence within a local, national, and international scheme. In the end, it is a baby—metaphorically this feminist poem—that Okra offers Greens, that Shange offers her theater audience. This love story is different finally because of Shange's candid and poetic portrayal of a heterosexual couple's romantic and sexual experiences as well as of their social and political realities as minorities living in racist North America.

A Daughter's Geography, the collection of poems from which Shange drew for *Okra*, sets forth in its third section the story line of the Okra-Greens romance in this play version. The sequence of events is summarized in the collection's table of contents:

> From Okra to Greens/ A Different Kinda Love Story
>> Crooked Woman/ Okra Meets Greens in Strange Circumstances
>> From Okra to Greens/ A Different Love Poem/ We Need a Change
>> Synecdoche/ Asbury Park in October
>> In the Blueness/ Says Greens
>> Okra to Greens Again (Special Delivery)
>> Fiction/ Non-Fiction (Okra's Intellect Addresses Greens' Mind)
>> Okra to Greens: A Historical Perspective of Sound/ Downtown
>> Okra to Greens/ An Aside on Amsterdam Avenue
>> Revelations (The Night Greens Went Off with that Hussy, Rutabaga)
>> From Okra to Greens: A Personal Invitation (Reconciliation in Casablanca)
>> Rise Up Fallen Fighters (Okra Takes Up with a Rastafari Man/ She Cant Hold Back/ She Say Smilin')
>> The Beach with Okra & Greens/ On Their Honeymoon/ Banda Abao, Curacao.[4]

The poems from the two other sections of *A Daughter's Geography*—"It Hasnt Always Been This Way" and "Bocas: A Daughter's Geography"—also appear. Even in the presentation of this table of contents, it seems that *Okra* was destined for the stage, and more often than not, the poems simulate dialogue between the two characters. The changes that occur in the move from poetry collection to play are ones of dramatic perspective and of occasional word choice, while the actual lines of the poems themselves remain virtually unaltered. Reordering the poems for a more linear development of this love story, Shange gives *Okra* the following dramatic structure, a structure that is not coincidentally woman centered:

   I. Black woman exists alone.
   II. Black woman meets black man.
   III. Black woman and black man court and then marry.
   IV. Black man is unfaithful to black woman.
   V. Black woman and black man are reconciled.
   VI. Black woman becomes pregnant.
   VII. Black woman and black man, as husband and wife,
       honeymoon on beach.

As a comment on the condition of the black woman in ancient and modern patriarchal societies, *Okra* appropriately and ironically begins with a male's (Greens') uncompassionate assessment of her existence. Rather than have Okra profess self-pityingly the woes of her plight, Shange uses Greens to describe Okra's condition as Okra's body importantly dances (or painfully contorts) to visualize either or both a black woman's social, psychological, and emotional suffering and her dance as spiritual coping. Greens cynically delivers his narrative, implicating himself—his own social and gender "crookedness"—and his role as a black male in contributing to this black woman's troubles and resultant poor self-image. His portrait of an African American woman is entitled "the crooked woman" and appears as such in *A Daughter's Geography* (57). According to Greens, a black woman's main problem is her poor self-image because of society's hostile treatment of her. She is doubly oppressed because of her race and gender, and her oppression leads to self-alienation, isolation, and thoughts of suicide much like the women in *for colored girls*. Unaware of her own value, she thinks herself an object for men's lusts and of social ridicule. Okra's physical movements and contortions vivify the image Greens sets before us:

> the woman dont stand up
> straight
> aint never stood up
> straight/ always bent
> some which a way
> crooked turned abt
> slanted sorta toward
> a shadow of herself.[5]

Greens' tone implies that this black woman could stand straight if she wanted. He does not say that the woman "can't" stand up. If she accepts her own powerlessness, then perhaps Greens' cynical tone is his attempt to spur the "crooked" woman into positive self-awareness. Like the abused and powerless women in *for colored girls* who consider suicide, Okra, according to Greens,

> seems like she
> tryin to get all in the
> ground/ wit the death
> of her
> somethin always on her
> shoulders/ pushin
> her outta herself
> cuttin at her limbs. (8)

This death-suicide imagery parallels that in *for colored girls* when the Lady in Red professes: "i wanted to jump up outta my bones // & be done wit myself" (*for colored girls* 66). The crooked woman wants to crawl back into the earth, a possible death wish or a natural and safe refuge like a mother's womb. The blurring of dance and physical contortions from pain works effectively on at least two levels. Perhaps this woman creates her own survival through dance. Perhaps her sufferings are so great they have literally taken their toll on her physical body. In either case, Okra's inner rhythms are physically manifested. Her self-alienation leads to isolation and withdrawal:

> folks wd just go play
> wit her/ get they kicks
> watchin the crooked lady
> do her thing/ & her bones
> gotta crackin
> shatterin/ mutilatin
> themselves til she
> waz lookin so weird
> to herself she
> locked herself up in
> a closet. . . . (8-9)

Society's callousness and ostracism ultimately lead to this black woman's private misery and psychological suffering—made even more vivid here through images of bones cracking, shattering, and being mutilated while those around her remain oblivious to or deliberately unmoved by such suffering.

In her isolation, however, Okra encounters a black man, Greens, and their romance officially begins. Interestingly, their earliest encounter, a sexual one, temporarily allows this crooked woman to escape her social and personal pains. That sexuality is part of this relationship early on is Shange's move to legitimize once more raw passion, or perhaps a natural order in matters of romance, in the face of social standards that revere virginity only for females. Greens comments on their union:

> . . . she
> met a man/ . . .
> . . . .
> we curled round/
> nobody cd tell anymore/ what to
> get outta the way of/ & we
> never once spoke
> of our condition. (9)

Some feminists might take issue with Shange in this suggestion that a man is a woman's savior. That this is not Shange's feminist perspective is clear from *for colored girls*. Here, Shange legitimizes and celebrates grandly and unapologetically a heterosexual negro love story, one all too often not seen or realized in a white-dominant social order. At first, Greens is aware of though removed from this crooked woman's existence. Before this encounter, "he didnt know what a stood // up straight man felt like" (9). Such a detail suggests that spiritual union accompanying physical love is a new experience for him, an experience that allows him to stand upright also. That Greens finishes the narrative with first-person plural pronouns "we" and "our" evidences his spiritual connection to Okra beyond but growing out of their physical intimacy. Their meeting constitutes the first section of the choreopoem; their life together as a couple constitutes the second section and the greater portion of the play.

A modern couple with liberal morals, Okra and Greens establish their relationship upon sexual compatibility. Only after their first intimate encounter, which importantly involves no power plays or gender role prescriptions, are they able to disclose their fears and fantasies to each other. Not coincidentally, their identity as sexual beings is present even in their conversations about politics, about life in general. Indeed, the candor with which Shange allows her characters to speak of their sexuality is punctuated with erotic imagery:

> OKRA.
> you take my tongue outta my mouth/
> make me say foolish things
> GREENS.
> you take my tongue outta my mouth/ lay it on yr
>   skin
> like the dew between yr legs
> . . . .
>   OKRA.
> oh you are sucha fool/ i cant help but love you
>   GREENS.
> maybe it was something in the air
>   OKRA.
> our memories
>   GREENS.
> our first walk
>   OKRA.
> our first . . .
>   GREENS.
> yes/ alla that
>   OKRA.
> where you poured wine down my throat in rooms
> poets i dreamed abt seduced sound & made history/
> you make me feel like a cheetah
> . . . .
> you make me remember my animal sounds/
> . . . .
> my body loosens for/ you
> . . . .

you wet yr fingers/ lay it to my lips
that i might write some more abt you/
how you come   into me

. . . .
    GREENS.
how i come into you like a rollercoaster in a
dip that swings
leave you shattered/ glistening/ rich/ screeching
& fully clothed. (10-12)

In discussing their spiritual connection to each other, both Okra and Greens acknowledge the irresistible power of love, using such phrases as "you take" and "make me." Although not spoken despairingly, Okra admits that she "cant help but love" Greens. Their exchange is both tranquil and passionate as they speak of deep kisses, animal sounds, and wet fingers. The scenario describes an act of sexual intercourse itself without offensive language—the stages of foreplay, the act itself, and their mutual climaxes.[6] From their discussion, it would seem that Okra is the more sexually expressive partner, the partner who seems more at ease with her sexual identity. Yet while both speak openly to each other about their sexual desires, Okra (not coincidentally a poet), in this instance, speaks of intercourse within the context of sensual images: "pouring wine down my throat," "seduced sound," "feel[ing] like a cheetah," and "animal sounds." Greens' emphasis, on the other hand, focuses on the physical act itself as it involves kissing, Okra's vaginal wetness, his ultimate ejaculation. Perhaps Shange offers here commentary of gender-specific attitudes toward sex and sensuality. Such a distinction might easily remain stereotypical—that women are more romance-focussed, men more intercourse-focussed—were she not to show Greens' ultimate sensitivity to a woman's full passion and selfhood. Considering the fact that Greens opens the choreopoem with a definition of a black woman's problems, it is clear that he is sensitive, gentle, and open to learning of this black woman's emotional and physical needs.

In acknowledging and celebrating their own sexuality, Okra and Greens also recognize and attack the double standard that sexually liberated women are subject to greater risks socially, physically, and emotionally than their male partners. As a sensitive black male, Greens recognizes the potential power play between male and female even during moments of private intimacy. In the poem sequence "some men," which also appears in *A Daughter's Geography* (37-44), Shange offers a feminist tract on the abusive behavior of too many males. Careful not to stereotype all men as insensitive and abusive to women, Shange itemizes the behavior of "some" men who possess inappropriate definitions of manhood. In both *A Daughter's Geography* and the published booklet of *Some Men*, a female persona abbreviates a history of some males' behavior toward women. As a participant in the exchange in this play version, Greens offers an alternative male perspective to the one being attacked in the sequence. Greens, then, represents those men who do not behave and think as do these men. Perhaps the published edition with its parodic dedication and format best captures the impact of the piece. Since the poem is about tragic ironies in the lives of "pretty men," Shange appropriately formats the poem as though it were Scarlet O'Hara's dance card.[7] With cartoon illustrations by Wopo Holup that underscore the deliberate contradictions within the piece and in male behavior, the poem is divided into five dance movements—the First Dance, the Waltz, the D.C. Bop, Ladies Choice, and the Slow Drag—and is dedicated generally to "Tom, Dick and Harry" and more specifically to:

> George, Bob, William, Michael, C.L.,
> Bill, Gene, Kevin, Tim, Lynn, Peter,
> Jim, Robert, Walter, John, Paul, Keith,
> Sam, Jeff, Lionel, Milt, Adam, Larry,
> Andy, Wayne, Newton, Saul, Ronnie,
> Mitch, Bruce, Robin, Joe, Larry, Amos,
> Trevor, David, Jose, Steve, Ira, Edward,
> Gale, Matt, Smitty, Jack & Eric.[8]

Such a dedication is a clear example of Shange's artistic efforts to move the specific to the general, the colloquial to the universal, signifying on the potential abusive behavior of any male. Shange includes names associated with different cultures and ethnicities to show that men's abusive behaviors toward women transcend cultural and racial boundaries. While the various movements of the poem categorize different types of male behavior, the composite portrait details senselessness and selfishness of men's abuse of women. For Shange, abusive behavior is an attempt to exert control—this desire to control being deeply rooted in these males' inadequate feelings about their physical and sexual selves. Okra's opening lines summarize what is at the heart of the poem and at the heart of "some" males' perceptions of manhood:

> some/ men
> dont know anything abt that.
> the manliness inherent at birth[9]
> is lost as they grow or shrink
> to size. (18)

Very matter-of-factly, Okra comments on the irony that men do not know what it means to be a "real" man. Shange's use of erect/flacid penis imagery appropriately and sarcastically attacks those men whose manhood is not defined by gentleness and sensitivity but by sexual performance and penis size. The image of growing and shrinking in size also foreshadows the "pretty men" scenario later in the "some men" sequence and highlights a movement between powerless and powerful that structures the poem. Shange is quick to assert at the outset that the phallus does not necessarily define manhood, a point Michael tries to make clear to Sean in *a photograph*. The poem also highlights the shallowness of men whose egos depend on a their perceived sexual performance and undercuts those men who pride themselves on their sexual prowess:[10]

> some/ men
> dont know . . .
> a well-dressed man is a good female impersonator
> that machines replace them & do a better job. (18)

In Shange's reversal of stereotypes, men concerned with appearances and superficialities—those things deemed only important to and contributing to the alleged shallowness of women—are men whose relationships with women exist only as enhancements to themselves.

Economically, the threat of machines exacerbates a male's anxiety of losing his job—both in and out of the bedroom—to technology. Physiologically, the fact that a woman may get as much or more sexual pleasure from a dildo comments on the fragility and self-delusion of men who define themselves in terms of their penile performance —particularly a man like Sean David, who, whenever he perceives he has lost control over his environment or himself, turns to sex, or physical or verbal abuse of his challenger. Undeniably, Shange affirms in this poem sequence that men's sexual prowess does not determine their self-worth or manliness.

Shange also highlights "some" men's inability to communicate with women in and outside the bedroom. These men are victims of a patriarchal society that identifies sensitivity, gentleness, and emotional vulnerability with females and weakness. Because men and women are early in life indoctrinated into gender roles with prescribed standards of masculinity, they are often unable to articulate true feelings, or they equate verbal abuse with meaningful communication, particularly in situations of intimacy. Okra explains:

> some/ men
> have no language that doesnt hurt
> a language that doesnt reduce what's whole
> to some part of nothing. (18)

For Shange, men's language is another instrument by which to demonstrate their power. Hence, the language that many use does not recognize gender equality but rather reduces women personally and socially. Exploring these "linguistic imbalances," Robin Lakoff maintains that language represents the "sharper focus real-world imbalances and inequalities"[11] prevalent in modern society. Yet "some men" is importantly not about how males have been victimized by their own power system; instead, the poem details instances of rampant victimization of women by men.

Aware of some women's experiences with some men, Greens joins Okra in offering as the first portrait in this gallery, an unusually handsome man who surrounds himself with expensive, beautiful furnishings that complement his own self-perceived and celebrated physical attractiveness. This "pretty man" considers and thereby treats his female victims as other less valuable apartment decorations to be rearranged or even discarded at his whim:

> he was a pretty man who liked pretty things.
> surrounded with beat-up luxuries/ old mantillas
> from women's heads lay across his mahogany tables/
> bronze nymphs, bulbs in their mouths, lit up
> his quarters/ onyx vases steadied scarlet tulips before
> french windows he opened when he had expresso
> in early morning. (18-19)

The apartment's luxurious furnishings are appropriate for this narcissistic man who has only the finest that money can afford. "[O]ld mantillas . . . across his mahogany tables" may symbolize past romantic conquests, displayed like so many sportsmen's taxidermic trophies mounted on walls. Women are further objectified in the image of "bronze nymphs," women who, in this man's perception, exist solely for his enjoyment. The dark hues of the furniture and decorations, mahogany and bronze particularly, reiterate the owner's emotional and psychological detachment from his lovers, the sterility of his immediate and valued environment:

> he waxed his floors til they shone & covered them with
> near eastern rugs/ the kind little girls spend whole
> lives tying. (19)

The care he takes with his floors and his carefully selected and valuable art collectibles contrasts with his treatment of his female partners. His casual use of rugs "little girls spend whole // lives tying" further symbolizes his treatment of women: while he appreciates the beauty of a rug, he is oblivious to the life energy that went into its making. In addition, the rug—which in other circumstances might be displayed on walls and not meant to be trampled upon—protects a shiny floor that mirrors his perceived perfect reflection, another connection with the Echo and Narcissus myth. The floor is the greatest source of satisfaction for him, not the eastern rugs. Shange's emphasis on size in the narrative relates not only to physical stature but again to the phallus as an empty symbol of manhood:

> he walked about grandly.
> though he was a little man/ he liked to think
>   himself
>   large.
> he had so many pretty things.
> . . . .
> old pretty things/ used abused beauties
> like the women who decorated his bed from time to
>   time. (19)

Despite this man's efforts to think and endeavor to make himself appear physically larger than he really is, Greens reminds us that he is "a little man" who nevertheless can only "think // himself // large." Such a man, who ultimately loves only himself, after achieving his own sexual gratification, treats his companion as a used condom. Since this woman has served his purposes, he almost ritualistically follows through with a game that almost assures him that he is the controlling force in this encounter on all levels:

> he was a little man
> & straightening his legs in the bed added nothing to
> his stature. he sat up & crushed the frailty of
> the morning
>   "suck my dick & make some coffee"
> he squealed. (20)

To greet a lover in this way illustrates this man's premeditated cruelty. That this woman may have enjoyed this sexual encounter is perhaps the beauty that disrupts this man's self-ordered world. The tranquility of the morning contrasts with the deliberate harshness of his words and tone—"suck my dick and make some coffee"—establishing a master-servant relationship and further objectifying his view of women. Shange quickly reduces this man's exaggerated self-grandeur through Greens' use of "squealed" after the crude remark. She attributes a kind of piggishness to such unacceptable male behavior, particularly in the context of sexual intimacy. This man's self-esteem is undermined by a feeling that this woman in some meaningful way may be his equal or his superior; this man's self-esteem is then bolstered only through blatant power plays with an unsuspecting female partner.

Males' use of language indicates still another issue Shange examines regarding alleged differences in male and female emotional experiences.

> It seems perfectly reasonable that if one were raised in a patriarchal environment and accepted that as one's definition of one's manhood, then a struggle would evolve against patriarchy because it is anti-human. But if you don't have any other value system, then, of course, you are at a loss for a vocabulary. Men don't have an emotional vocabulary that is as highly developed as women's because women have been taking care of other people all their lives. Therefore they are able to know *immediately* how they're feeling and what they're feeling; whereas men, certain men, not all men but *some men*, are unable to express such feelings—unless it's related to humiliation or anger or pride or revenge or their domination over some other being. Things of that nature men, generally, can do pretty well with.[12] (emphasis mine)

This "pretty man's" behavior conveys a shallowness of males who degrade women to assert their power over their environment, metaphorically representing another form of rape. Greens repeatedly describes this man as "small" and "little" in more than just physical stature and perhaps even penis size. True manhood, Shange would argue, manifests itself quite differently. Greens assesses the irony of this scenario:

> the beauty of it all
> was it cost him so little. imagine him
> so small a man getting away with all that.
> . . . .
> but
> he was a small man

> & cd handle only damaged goods. he sat in his big
>   bed
> with his little legs bent/ quite content.
> now/ there was something someone else cd collect/
> an abused/ used luxury/ a woman
> with a memory of daybreak in a near perfect place.
>   (19-20)

From the perpetrator of this emotional assault, Shange calls attention
to those women who, treated as possessions, rightfully come to
distrust and even deny their sexuality and sensuality in the presence
of men. Such abuse leads female victims to feelings more often associated with sexual violence. In a final effort to deny this self-
absorbed man any chances at redemption, Greens concludes:

> & he was a little man/ a pretty man
> surrounded with beat-up luxuries/ creating blemishes
> scratches   fraying edges/ illusions
> of filling the bed he slept in. (21)

Throughout Greens' monologue, Shange strategically and metaphorically identifies this pretty man's female lovers as "pretty things,"
"beat-up luxuries," "bronze nymphs," "used abused beauties,"
"manuscripts he collected," "vintage photographs," and "violated
thrown out pieces of lives." These abused women nevertheless
retain a beauty and a high value despite their mistreatment, as do the
women in *for colored girls*. This beauty of the survivor reiterates
Maxine's comments on African American's positive blackness
existing despite blatant racism in *spell #7*. In both *for colored girls*
and *Okra*, Shange reverses the "used" and hence "worthless"
image to one of increased worth and value. Just as the women in *for
colored girls* emerge all the more triumphant and hence beautiful
despite as a result of their sufferings, Shange in this poem sequence
further celebrates a beauty of women who survive such physical and
psychological attacks on their person:

> what's to value in something unblemished?
> porcelain must be cracked/ to covet. rugs frayed/

> to desire. there must be scratches on the surfaces/
> to enjoy what's beautiful. (20)

A poignant statement on the condition of women in the presence of some men, Greens' account reverberates with such words as "beauty" and "pretty" in a scene that is quite the opposite. This kind of common and even ritualistic objectification of women by some men, according to Shange, is "nothing new. not a new *thing*" (20; emphasis mine); her poem therefore offers an alternative standard of manhood, prompting men and not a few women to become aware and intolerant of other men's "unmanly" behavior.

While some men are content using women as sexual toys, others are intolerant of women altogether. Okra describes misogynists who, like "pretty men," abuse women selfishly and unashamedly:

> there was nothing he could see in a woman that was
> of any use at all. she was forever silly.
> . . . .
> everytime she'd try to do what pleased him/
> he'd find a more indelicate failure.
> . . . .
> he liked pornographic still-lifes.
> when he cant afford the quarter machine/ he invites
>   women
> to keep him company/ then he makes them ugly. (22)

Here is a man who exploits women sexually and psychologically through harsh and arbitrary criticism. Women, in his extremist's view, are worthless, unintelligent, and physically unattractive. For this man who experiences life in terms of negative absolutes— "nothing," "forever," "everytime," "failure," and "ugly"—contact with any female is a power struggle from which he sees himself the emerging sadistic victor. Being around such worthlessness and inferiority highlights his own perceived strength and power. Note his sexual objectification of women also serves his own ends.

Still categorizing some men's abuse of women as shallow exhibitions of their manhood, Shange recognizes some men's mythic notion of impregnating women as a sign and determinant of their manhood.

For such males, impregnation comes not from a desire for responsible fatherhood but from a desire to control a woman's life, and by extension, a future child's. Unable to assert control over his environment otherwise,

> he said/   she had too much for her own good.
> too much what/   she asked
> everything/   he said
> but what/   she asked
> money/   he shouted/   too much money
> yeah/ too much energy/ just too much/ you/
> dont need all that.   you should give it to me
> i'm a man/   he said
>   she said nothing
> he turned around
> his eyes sparkled when he told her what she really
> needed to do was have a baby/   she needed
> something to tie her down. (21-22)

Obviously suffering from low self-esteem and personal inadequacies on a number of levels, this man resents and is ultimately intimidated by an independent woman.[13] Impregnating her substantiates his worth as a male whose sense of power comes not only from creating a child but also in altering the lifestyle of this woman. Notice that Shange's emphasis here is not on the responsibility—or lack thereof— of a woman who finds herself pregnant by such a man. Rather, the poem emphasizes the characteristic behavior of some men and their methods of manipulating and controlling women's realities. Even after the woman's pregnancy, this man continues to be dissatisfied with his female partner, this time because she attends to the needs of her newborn before his own sexual needs. Ironically, pregnancy might even increase this man's sense of inadequacy and powerlessness since the woman carries the fetus inside of her body and thereby has sole responsibility for its growth and development. Okra describes a mother's devotion to her child as another source of resentment for insecure men. She describes this father's selfish feelings of sexual neglect in a way that reduces him to immaturity in the same way that her "pretty man" earlier is reduced through his squeals:

the baby . . .
.... she needs to
  nurse
& her mama's right there. without sleep or no/ the
  milk flows.
      he doesnt like that. he said.
there's no one taking care of me. ....
it dont hurt her/ it wont hurt/ he said/ it wdnt
  hurt.
dont you remember before that damned baby? it was
  me.
it was me & you. there's always milk for the baby
none for me/ never too tired for the baby/ never too
tired for the baby/ he didnt understand
. . . .
he hadnt done nothing but hold her arms back/ & bite
on her titties/ how did he know his teeth wd hurt
how cd he know/ shit/ she always has time for the
  baby
what was he sposed to do/ the milk flows whether
  she tired
or not/ when was he gonna get some. (22-23)

Shange attacks the outrageous insensitivity, irresponsibility, and
emotional selfishness of men who father children only to affirm their
own alleged manhood—again, largely defined through their control
over women. Such men are fathers only in the biological sense. This
behavior contrasts sharply with the almost overwhelming duties of
motherhood portrayed in this episode. Not only is this man's insensitivity manifested in his criticism of the mother's priorities and of her
physical state after the trauma of childbirth, but it is concretized in
his restricting her arm movements and biting her breasts. On the one
hand, Shange points out a truth about fatherhood generally: on a
purely physical level, fatherhood cannot be experienced as is motherhood through gestation, childbirth, and breast-feeding. Yet this
man's insensitivity is not founded in the reproductive differences that
separate males from females. Instead, his objections to the new life
he himself suggested and helped to create only highlight his own

"manhood." The narcissistic image created recalls once again the portrait of the "pretty man." Biting his lover's breasts combines images of lovemaking and of a child suckling at his mother's breast, further reducing this "spoiled" man's alleged manliness and elevating Shange's nurturing mother image. Shange's scenario of "new parents"—with the neglected father and the exhausted and frustrated new mother—is a version of what even "good" men may experience as new fathers.

Aside from verbal and psychological abuse of women by "some" men, Shange also considers forthrightly the everpresent reality of men's sexual assaults on women, a reality against which Greens speaks out in his narrative of a female's encounter with a male flasher. Although the flasher does not physically attack this female, his stalking, his invasion of her physical, emotional, and psychological space, and her fear of being caught unawares and trapped, create similar emotional and psychological consequences as would a physical assault. Greens describes the calculated terrorism of this exhibitionist:

> he waited
> til she got out of her car
> & pulled his dick out   exactly 6 ft
> from her doorway.
> the car was locked
> the front door was locked
> there was a man with his dick out
> freezin winds
> her hands trembling/ her mouth falling over her
> scalp
> his laughter came all over her coat. (23-24)

In such a brief but tense scenario, Shange dramatizes traumatic complexities of such a threatening moment. The typography and the choppy lines create this woman's sense of terror and powerlessness. Although she is physically able to move between the locked car door and the locked house door, she is nevertheless trapped by the circumstances of his unpredictable actions, the man's perverted glee contrasting with the woman's sense of panic and fear. In any given circumstances, this flasher might well be the perpetrator of rape—his laughter then analogous to ejaculation—and the victim's fear is justifiably similar to a survivor's spiritual and physical invasion. Shange drives home the fact that while men may consider such behavior inconsequential and even amusing, it is quite the opposite for women easily and frequently trapped by such circumstances.

Such outlandish displays of a man's power(lessness) through physical violation can lead women to live in paranoia, to distrust any male, friends and strangers alike. A man's "latent rapists' bravado" (*for colored girls* 19) might also manifest itself in an obscene phone call, again an action perceived as harmless and amusing by typically male perpetrators. Just as a flasher can at a whim throw his victim into sudden panic, an obscene phone caller achieves this same end without his physical presence:

> it was best to call in the middle of the night.
> women living alone are startled by noises at late
>   hours.
> it was best to ring twice & hang up.
> then ring back/ say nothing.
> women living alone are familiar with perversions.
> he decided to ring twice & hang up three times.
> he felt once she answered/ heard a man breathing/
> she'd hang up quickly.
> then
> he cd call back & she'd be so glad
> finally a man she knew
> a man she cd trust in the middle of the night. (21)

This caller's calculated methods of arousing fear in this woman arbitrarily and with no provocation except his own satisfaction recall the flasher's calculated actions in the previous episode. Hence, for women, no man can ever be fully known or trusted; Shange's warning then is that potentially deceptive male behavior is something of which all women must become aware. Still, to offer such a statement of fact is clearly not to indict all men. While individual circumstances directing and affecting male behavior change in each of the above scenarios, the male perpetrators' ultimate manipulation of power and the female victims' feelings of fear are the same. As each scenario represents one of five dance movements on a dance card, Shange creates a profile of a pretty man, a misogynist, a selfish father, a flasher, and an obscene phone caller as one and the same. The dance card metaphor highlights the ritualistic behavior of men who lead unsuspecting women into regions of emotional abuse and physical insecurity.

Shange also recognizes that even sexual intimacy that is mutually satisfying for both male and female partner can often and very easily become a power play for some men. In this final scenario, the initial naturalness of this couple's lovemaking is reflected in Shange's paradisiacal imagery:

> OKRA.
> he felt her thighs/ strong & wet.
> her body arching like ferns reaching/ she was
>   smiling
> & feverish with desire
>   GREENS.
>   strange sounds fell from her mouth
> gurgling innocent hot sounds/ crept along his back
> her fingers
>   OKRA.
> sought out the hairs long his neck/
>   GREENS.
> the evening fog laced kisses round their bodies/
>   OKRA.
> she thought she heard piano solos/ she thought she
>   heard
> trumpets gone marvelously wild in nature's
>   murmurings
>   GREENS.
>   she felt him coming
>   OKRA.
> & let go all *her powers*
>   GREENS.
> when without warning
> he shot all his semen up her ass

OKRA.
she kept screaming
WHAT ARE YOU DOING WHAT ARE YOU DOING
to me
GREENS.
he relaxed/ sighing
"i had to put it somewhere. it was
too good to be some pussy." (24-25; emphasis mine)

The sensuality and beauty of lovemaking for both partners contrasts
with the unnatural abruptness of this male's decision to release his
semen anally rather than vaginally. Threatened by this woman's
sensual "powers" or the reality of her pleasure—much like the pretty
man "overpowered" by his female lover's beauty in the opening
segment—this male again calculates how best as a man he can make
this woman powerless, thus allegedly making himself more powerful.
Not only is anal penetration solely this man's decision, but it also
demonstrates his power to destroy this woman's complete sexual
experience by inflicting physical pain. Such a violation in this case is
not far removed from rape.[14] Prior to this moment, the sexual act for
this female moves far beyond the sweat and grinding of raw passion.
She had heard and responded vocally to the music of lovemaking—the
"piano solos," "trumpets gone . . . wild in nature's murmurings."
This male's emphasis, however, seems almost exclusively on the
physicality of the sexual act: "he felt her thighs/ strong & wet. // her
body arching." The female's orgasm, her moment of "let[ting] go
all her powers," contrasts with the male's decision to control a
female's pleasure. His crude and passionless response—the troubles
in paradise—like the "pretty man's" demands for fellatio and coffee
earlier, undercuts any sense of romance and mutual satisfaction that
may have been connected with the sex act. Throughout this presentation on the behavior of some men, Shange at no point condemns a
sexually liberated female. Nor does she point a critical finger at
unsuspecting women who find themselves trapped in such circumstances. Instead, this entire "some men" sequence considers some
males' misconceptions about masculinity, sexuality, and their treatment of women. Although some critics insist otherwise, Shange does
not condemn all men, even in this poem. Rather, she calls for a

revised definition of manhood as it relates to respecting and being
sensitive to women. In her myriad conversations about black feminists portrayals of black men, she acknowledges that they too are
victimized by a patriarchal society that prescribes, tolerates, and
even celebrates abusive behavior toward women. Yet men's victimization does not justify their abusive treatment of women:

> Men are confused and frightened. As women
> change and we change what our desires and our
> options are, as we become more self-sufficient, a
> lot of men lose the idea of taking care of one's
> family. They [men] can find something else that
> they can take pride in. The other [notion of
> manhood] deals with men's being sensitive sexually
> and intellectually. That can be confusing for a man
> if a woman wants to be self-reliant, not to be taken
> care of. How do [men] manifest care in a situation
> like that? I don't know. . . . I do think that there
> are more experiences available for men because of
> the way their orgasms come. But there's more to
> sexuality than having orgasms. And I think that's
> becoming part of more men's lives and their
> realities whether they like it or not. It has just
> started to happen because women demand it.[15]

Shange's sensitivity to black men is evidenced in her portrayal of
Greens. Okra knows that Greens is not a male who abuses women as
displays of his manhood. As much as he is able, as a male, he seeks
genuinely to understand and be sensitive to Okra's feminist perspective.[16] As their relationship develops, they realize and express their
full emotional attachment to each other, an attachment that transcends infatuation and sexual involvement. The time they spend apart
makes each partner realize and articulate the fullness of their mutual
commitment. Especially when he is alone at night does Greens
acknowledge his true feelings for Okra:

> in the middle of the nite
> is a blue thing

> a blue thing in the nite
> which covers me
> makes music
> like leaves that havent shown/
> themselves &
> when i dont know where i am
> when i dont know when i'll see you
> what time it is
> i lay
> in the middle of the nite
> covered up with   this   blue-ness
> this memory of you. (25-26)

For Greens too, their relationship has moved far beyond the sexual passion which ignited it. He even admits a disorientation when away from Okra and recognizes these emotions as new experiences for him. Okra, too, declares an emptiness when apart from Greens. Although a poet, practiced in the manipulation of words and the impact of language in expressing her realities, Okra nevertheless recognizes the inadequacies of verbal language when trying to fully express her affections for Greens:

> what language is it in
> why my bed is /   too big   cuz yr not in it
> how cd i say
> my synapses remember where yr lips
> linger/ unaccompanied bach/ . . .
> . . . .
> . . . what language is it
> big enough/ to say yr name
> how many colors is the sound of you put to
>   skies/ dusk/ in amber & midnite reds/
> . . . .
> . . . what language fits our needs
> . . . .
> say how to reach you so i am clear/
> . . . .
> say how to reach you with love. . . . (27)

In this instance, Shange reverses gender stereotypes in Okra and Greens' professions of their love. Rather than have Greens talk of the sexuality that is manifested in his love for Okra, Okra is here the more deliberately sexual being. Giving her physical body to a man becomes an ultimate profession of her love, as she requests of Greens: "give me yr tongue/ darling" (28). Regarding their particular use of verbal language to articulate their experiences and realities, Shange presents Okra as the more abstract thinker. For example, while Greens expresses his emptiness primarily through single imagery associated with color, Okra questions the adequacy of language altogether in expressing emotions. Her use of multiple images—sound, color, and the physical body—reveals more complex thought patterns than Greens'. Though Shange is certainly not suggesting that Okra is more intelligent than or intellectually superior to Greens, perhaps this detail reflects Shange's belief that female poets' visions of the world are of political and personal necessity more complex than male poets'. And finally, while Greens, here, expresses a need to have Okra structure his environment, Okra's concern is how to express the fullness of her passion to Greens at this moment since their existence to her is defined in the present.

Okra and Greens' marriage is a legal symbol of their emotional commitment to one another. Yet the marriage relationship is a complicated one as each tries to retain an independence of self while becoming one social and psychological unit. For Greens, caught up in the mystical powers of love, their relationship as husband and wife is primary. He admits having fantasized about being married before their actual marriage later in the play:

> i dreamed myself in a house of yr paintings
> fore you even said diagonally yes
> yrs/ mine you/ me/   this cant be simple
> this is non-fiction
> most of the world is make-believe & predictable
> . . . .
> . . . i want to know
> what we make
> in the world/ survivin us/ makes us. (31-32)

Greens insists that facing and resolving any problems external to their relationship will only reinforce their mutual commitment. With unyielding optimism, the couple begins their new life together, insisting that "the last heavy breaths of day belong to [them]" (33).

And indeed their relationship is not without both internal and external conflicts. Once the idyllic bliss of their wedding day fades into their mundane existence as a black couple, Okra and Greens consider their relationship within greater socio-political contexts. Consciously the more perceptive and sensitive partner as well as the more oppressed of the two, Okra, having explored the issue of sexism, now examines racism in North America. She resents the political and cultural bias of the media and combats the injustice through reveling in her own personal and their collective rich cultural heritage. In discussing the problem, she notes:

> i haveta turn my television down sometimes cuz
> i cant stand to have white people /shout at me/
> sometimes i turn it off
> cuz i cant look at em in my bedroom either/
> bein so white/
> . . . .
> i gotta turn the TV off cuz white people
> keep playing games/ & followin presidents on vacation
>   at the war
> there's too much of a odor problem on the TV too. (12-
>   13)

To combat her sense of violation and to register her resentment that more people of color, particularly black people—their culture and experiences—do not appear in the media outside of myths and stereotypes associated with athletics, crime, and entertainment, Okra re-directs those energies into pleasant dreams and reminiscences that are culturally and uniquely her own, a notion that recalls *spell #7*'s redefinition of "black magic." Okra notes that just as "white" life projected by the media is of no personal experiential significance to her, certain moments and lifestyles in her own personal history as a black person are distinctly hers and have no experiential significance to whites. Okra's cultural identity is thereby substantiated in her memories of the particular foods and eating habits of her family, of her black people. Personifying the leafy vegetable turnip greens, she explains:

> that's why i like/greens/
> they [white folks] cdnt even smell you/ wdnt know what
>   you taste like
> without sneakin / got no
> idea you shd be tingled wit hot sauce & showered wit
>   vinegar
> yr pot liquor spread on hot rolls. (13)

Her description savors of both the specific taste of the dish and the specific moment of the experience. Memory, the past, and ritual sustain Okra when she is feels culturally insignificant, marginalized, ignored, or otherwise violated. Consequently, dissatisfaction with dominant white culture in her environment always "brings [Okra] back to greens" (13), her spiritual and physical sustenance. Okra admits that a significant part of her identity as a black female lies in the seemingly insignificant ritual, passed down through generations of black women, of preparing greens as a meal. Notably, this activity as nurturer and preparer of meals does not stereotype women into gender roles so much as it reiterates a cultural reality that empowers and sustains. She recalls with celebration:

> i remember my grandma at the market pickin turnips
> collards kale & mustards/ to mix-em up/ drop a 1/2
>   of strick a lean
> in there wit some ham hock & oh my whatta life/
> i lived in her kitchen/ wit greens i cd recollect
> yes the very root of myself
>   the dirt & lil bugs i looked for in the fresh
>   collards/
>   turnin each leaf way so slow/ under the
>   spicket/ watchin
>   lil mounds of dirt fall down the drain
> i done a good job
> grandma tol me/ got them greens just ready for the

        pot
        & you know/ wdnt no white man on the TV/
        talkin loud n formal make no sense o the miracle
        a good pot a greens on a friday nite cd make to me. (13)

Such a detailed recollection, a kind of recreation, not only empowers
Okra through the very act of remembering and transfers Okra to a
unique realm of cultural experience, but it also fulfills another
responsibility of her work for Shange: it consciously teaches and
entertains. Her comments on her theory and practice of writing
further explain why she details Okra's recollection:

> I really believe that novels should teach you some-
> thing. In *Sassafrass, Cypress & Indigo*, that's one
> of the reasons I taught the women weaving and
> violin playing and cooking because novels should
> impart knowledge—not necessarily knowledge that
> is intellectual knowledge but practical knowledge
> too. You really do learn how to be a whaler if you
> read *Moby-Dick*; therefore, there's no reason you
> shouldn't learn how to be a dancer if you read about
> Sassafrass or what you need to do to be a weaver.
> There weren't many black books that taught me
> how to do anything, and I wanted to know how to
> do something. I learned so much from reading po-
> etry and novels; in fact, literature was the founda-
> tion of my education. There might be other people
> like that out there. Just because I'm writing for the
> twentieth century doesn't mean I shouldn't try to
> perform the same functions that other novelists and
> poets performed for me: give me clues and methods
> and ways of behavior and thought processes and
> activities and moments that were pleasurable and
> therefore exciting.[17]

Okra's childhood recollection offers a tonal and subject contrast to
her and Greens' account of the injustices of growing up black and
poor in North America. Shange takes the incident of the 1979-81

Atlanta [male] child murders and the inadequate and suspicious investigations into those murders as a reminder that being black and poor is for some synonymous with being inconsequential victims, a variation on Ralph Ellison's metaphor of invisibility when describing blacks' existence in racist North America. Shange changes the gender of the twenty-nine young black boys mysteriously murdered to that of a single black girl, retaining the immediate pain of those who lost children as well as the anger and frustrations she personally feels about the conveniently and hastily shut case. Shifting attention to black girls thereby makes her political attack three-pronged:

> cuz she's black & poor
> she's disappeared
> her name is lost   games weren't played
> nobody tucks her in / wipes traces of
> cornbread & syrup from her lips
> cuz she's black & poor / she's not
>
> just gone   disappeared one day
> & her blood soaks what's awready red in atlanta
> . . . .
> cuz they're black & poor   they gone
> took a bus / was never heard of again
> . . . .
> . . . when yr black & poor /
> who knows what cd happen to you
> we dont seem to be here no way
> how cd we disappear if we aint even here
> who cd hear us screamin? (33-35)

Shange opines that black children vanishing and then turning up dead is more tragic than cross-burnings or lynchings by the Ku Klux Klan; at least Klan activity left signs and implied motives. The short-lived investigation ceased when one person, ironically a black man, was arrested for all of the murders, despite the paucity of solid evidence against him. Yet the case did not attract further investigation because, as Shange and other leaders in the African American community argue, all involved—the victims, as well as the alleged perpetrator—were poor and black, their lives meaningless to mainstream America. Okra's comments move from the third-person narrative to first-person plural as she reveals broader economic, social, and political implications surrounding these murders. She dramatizes the grief and pain of the dead children's mothers—most of whom were the single heads of their homes—and questions the plausibility of accepting these deaths quietly as God's will. Her call is for vocal and political outrage, for overt displays of anger rather than Biblically prescribed stoicism and Christian passivity.

As a collective voice for women, children, and the poor, Shange also attacks global exploitation of the poor. Illustrating that such racial exploitation is not unique to the United States, she moves through the pages of Haitian history to demonstrate similar patterns. In Okra's account of Haitian poverty (28-31),[18] Shange summons the statues of Haiti's past liberators—Dessalines, Petion, and L'Ouverture—to restore hope for those still economically and politically oppressed. Okra pleads desperately and angrily before the seemingly unresponsive leaders, dramatized on stage by three male dancers. She details the starvation and suffering of the poor and stresses the urgency of her invocation:

> will you come again/ some one of you
> sweep thru the alleys & the stink/ come here
> with yr visions
> la liberte, l'egalite, la fraternite.
> come visit among us that we might know
> again/ some hope. (29)

That Shange considers past and present social and economic conditions of people of color globally establishes for African Americans in North America a community with other peoples of color. To celebrate Haiti's past liberators is to presume that such leadership is no longer necessary and immediate. And just as Mary and Martha are instructed to change their weeping and mourning to shouts and screams, here the narrator screams and shouts to provoke protest and action tantamount to racial and gender liberation.

While black life remains insignificant to white America, both Okra and Greens recall a time when blacks in America were more

politically conscious and more culturally proud. Arming herself with
the vibrancy of a richly textured African American past in much the
same way that Okra can and does when her world suffocates her
culturally, Shange looks to a racial and cultural past that nurtured
and nourished her own political and creative awareness. Documenting a moment in her personal biography, Shange credits her keen
cultural and racial insights to having grown up in a "race family,"
albeit middle class, that refused to accept political apathy in the face
of external restricting cultural aggressions:

> it hasnt always been this way
> ellington was not a street
> robeson no mere memory
> du bois walked up my father's stairs
> hummed some tune over me
> sleeping in the company of men
> who changed the world
>
> it wasnt always like this
> why ray barretto used to be a side-man
> & dizzy's hair was not always grey
> i remember   i was there
> i listened in the company of men
> politics as necessary as collards
> music even in our dreams. (38)

Paradoxically, Shange would argue, the same concessions for which
blacks risked their lives thirty years ago have forced blacks consciously or unconsciously to accept cultural and racial assimilation
and to adopt values and ideals of Anglo-America as the measure of
blacks' worth. Greens then functions as a mouthpiece for Shange,
who was influenced artistically and politically not only by a race-
conscious father and grandmother but also by black "greats" during
her formative years. She often recalls her childhood acquaintance
with Miles Davis, Charlie Parker, Chuck Berry, Muhammad Ali,
Dizzy Gillespie, and W.E.B. DuBois. Her use of negative cataloguing allows her to revisit historical moments when blackness was
reason for celebration rather than a source of self-alienation.

Nevertheless, Shange affirms the notion that blacks as a group seem compelled to assimilate for economic and social survival in a racist society. In a poem sequence entitled "Improvisation" that appears in *A Daughter's Geography* (14-18) as one female voice, Shange articulates a black female's continual struggle for person-hood. In *Okra*, however, the emphasis shifts from the oppressed female perspective to the oppressed racial perspective, indicated by the fact that Greens joins Okra in this editorial. Social injustice and racial oppression are like phlegm is acid caught in their throats:

> there is something caught in my throat
> it is this place
>
> . . . .
> how it sears the membranes
> eats the words right outta your mouth
> leaves you suckin' pollutants impotence
> & failure/. (39)

Greens understands a woman of color's double oppression. Not only must she meet with unjust social treatment by a white patriarchy, but she also must contend with those black men who look upon women solely as sexual pawns and scapegoats. Okra complains about a man who takes female identity for granted while seeking his own physical pleasures:

> some man/ wants to kiss my thighs
> roll his tongue around my navel
> put his hands all up my ass
> & this place is in my throat
>
> how can i tell him
> there is nothing up my behind/ that
> will get this place
> out of my throat. (39-40)

The woman here is doubly angered and frustrated. While she works toward equality and positive selfhood in the face of racism and sexism, her politically unconscious and self-absorbed male companion can consider only his sexual needs. Greens, as sympathetizer and ally, offers Okra advice:

> you cd tell him a few things
>> there are dead children out here
>> there are desperate women out here
>> the sky is falling
> & i am choking to death
> cuz of where i am & who we are.
> this is the twentieth century. (40)

Despite the fact that Americans are more technologically advanced and allegedly sophisticated in their thinking, treatment of oppressed peoples remains essentially unchanged. Such an assessment of modern society allows Shange to attack other social evils, the root of which she would argue lies in men's lust for power, its manifestations spanning the gamut from political aspirations to be masters of the universe through escalating military power to child molestation. An avid crusader against both child pornography and molestation, Shange recognizes that these threats are triple-barreled for female children. As both a literal and a metaphorical mother, Shange, through Greens and Okra, speaks out against child molestation:

> OKRA.
> . . . my daughter . . . is still sleeping
>> GREENS.
> she thinks unicorns & magnolias
> are things to put in her mouth
> she dont know where she is yet
> she dont know alla black kid's gonna get
> is a fist in her mouth or a white man
> who says she's arrogant / cuz
> she can look him in the eye/ cuz
> she dont know where she is.
>> OKRA.
> . . . .
> i told this man my daughter didnt know
> where she was/ where i keep my child

> there are no white men   with sexual thoughts
> about infants/ she'll know better next time
> cuz she aint having this place. (40-41)

She decries the injustice of men who abuse children sexually and questions the integrity of men whose political power controls the fate of human existence. In this poem, child molestation becomes Shange's metaphor for the broader issue of sexism that plagues North America. Until full respect for human life is achieved, the only ideal way that the narrators can keep their female child safe from the world presented in "it's not so gd to be born a girl/ sometimes" (*boogie woogie landscapes* 135-36) is to create, give birth to, and nurture her within the safe boundaries of the responsible parents' creative imaginations.

Despite Okra and Greens' openness and mutual commitment, their marriage is not without conflict. Greens' infidelity—he falls prey to the sexual allure of glamorous women—allows them both a chance to reassess their relationship. According to Greens, adventure in romance distances him only temporarily from a more sustaining love he feels for Okra. Both Okra and Greens call his amorous dalliances a case of "greens overdose," allowing fantasies and dreams—in Greens' case, romantic adventures—to control his life. Greens does not enjoy this life away from Okra; he acknowledges:

> . . . most victims smile
> without knowing why/ but i know   i gotta
> o.d. of greens/ i'm sufferin so
> my pods are gleamin/ ready to jump out
> the vertical/ into the greens diagonal. (45)

When Greens abandons her, Okra's loss reaches the core of her existence. Explaining her emptiness during Greens' first absence, she again searches for words to express her pain:

> when you disappeared
> a tremendous silence shook
> my body til my bones split
> i hadta   grab my sinews from the mouths of bats

. . . .
my hair turned back
i looked like the child found in
the chicken coop after 13 years
i knew no language
my fingers had never held bread
i cd not walk
when you disappeared
the moon cracked in a ugly rupture. (46)

As in the dramatization of the crooked woman's life in Greens'
opening monologue, Okra's pain is described through physical
images: splitting bones, lack of sinews, unmanageable hair, weak
fingers and legs, and rupturing. Without Greens, Okra is the crooked
woman before she finds a male companion. Once again, such a move
is not Shange's prescription that a woman must have a man in her life
romantically in order to be whole. Rather this emptiness is a vulnerability of anyone who finds love and experiences the feelings associated with losing that love. Notice once again that Okra questions the
adequacy of verbal language to express pain and loss. Yet their
relationship survives his disloyalties; he returns to Okra with humble
apologies. Just as their relationship began with a sexual encounter,
Greens offers his renewed faithfulness through lovemaking. As he
beckons Okra "to make love tonite" (47), he admits that the glamour
and allure of other women do not compare to the sustaining force of
the affection he feels for and receives from Okra. In accepting his
apology, Okra admits an infidelity also; she has fantasized being
married to "Bob Marley/ for at least 17 years" (47). Okra, however,
does not act out her romantic fantasies with another lover. Although
Okra details a fictitious on-going romance with Marley, Shange's
sympathies, here, are clearly with the female and not with the male
transgressor. The characters' infidelities become another reminder of
Shange's feminism: women, just as men, are tempted by extramarital
affairs. Okra therefore represents the more sensitive partner, repress-
ing her personal fantasies out of respect and loyalty to her man.
Granted, Okra's is a fantasy that cannot be easily acted out. Dramatically, her monologue relieves the tension of the moment in a tit-for-
tat, playful manner. In this test of their relationship, Okra and Greens

find renewed strength in their understanding of themselves and each other. With humor and their willingness to forgive and empathize with the other—evidenced in their interchanging voices—they survive marital and romantic difficulties that can plague any couple. They speak almost incantatorily and with encouragement to each other and to other couples with similar experiences:

> rise up fallen fighters
> unfetter the stars
> dance with the universe. (50)

Making mistakes, acknowledging them to oneself and to one's partner, practicing forgiveness, understanding, tolerance, then moving on in the relationship is the advice that Greens and Okra offer to other lovers committed to maintaining a mutually satisfying relationship.

Shange particularly emphasizes artistic creation within this male-female relationship by making both Okra and Greens poets. Especially sensitive to the lives of articulate artists, she uses Okra and Greens' romance to distinguish between male and female perspectives artistically. Throughout Okra and Greens' relationship, Okra seems the more openly intimate partner, often professing physically the emotions she is unable to express verbally. While Greens views sex as the primary means of expressing love, he seems focused on an external environment rather than an immediate, on the international rather than the local. One such example occurs early in their courtship when they spend a day at Asbury Park in New Jersey. In their conversation, Okra, despite Greens' efforts to teach her about the landscapes of South America, concentrates on their immediate existence as lovers. While Greens talks of death and starving children in other lands, Okra's concern is that their "smiles swallowed the sky" (14). Indeed, Shange is not suggesting Okra's ignorance of issues outside her realm of personal existence. Instead, Greens' eventual infidelity in one sense results from his attraction to the world outside their relationship as Okra works to hold their life together. Such a representation offers potentially another gender stereotype: man's province as the world, woman's the home. Shange reiterates the historically documented political responsibilities and opportunities for both individuals to be equally responsive to worldly issues as well as issues at and in the home.

  Okra's pregnancy, whether metaphorical or literal, is first an occasion for her to present her husband, Greens, with the ultimate expression of her love for him—a child. Although each partner has equal responsibility and power in the creation of that child, Okra's physical nurturing of the fetus inside her body makes the actual birth a kind of gift-giving process alluded to in the choreopoem's title, "From Okra to Greens." Shange affords this pregnancy a literary context and equates Okra's giving of a child to her giving of a poem, "a feminist poem," to Greens. Using gynecological terminology to describe the child's birth, Shange proclaims herself an artist continually pregnant with feminist gospel. Shange's definitive feminist poem is therefore one that shows

> our [women's] language is tactile
> colored & wet
> our tongues speak
> these words
> we dance
> these words
> sing em like we mean it/
> . . . .
> our visions are our own
> our truth no less violent than necessary
> to make
> our daughters' dreams
> as real as mensis. (50-51)[19]

Through Okra's poem, Shange offers another distinction between characteristically male poetic vision and feminist poetic vision. While Greens has consistently shown his concern with the physicality of lovemaking, geographic landscapes, and political concerns outside his immediate relationship with Okra, Okra has consistently expressed herself in the abstract. Still, she is aware of the powers of sexuality as one of many avenues in successful romantic communications; Greens, however, seems the more limited in his emotional perceptions because of social conditioning and constructed gender roles. Shange even proposes here that verbal language is used differently by males and females:

> I have a problem with a lot of male writers in that there is always *the idea*. I never really feel the person; . . . . In works by men there's usually an *idea* as opposed to a *reality*. So that the main character sometimes just embodies a notion or a philosophical perspective, as opposed to being a feeling and thinking person. Men also generally approach character in a way that allows them to skim over whatever the real crisis is. In Amiri Baraka's *The Toilet*, for instance, or in Richard Wesley's *The Mighty Gents*, or in Baraka's *Sidnee Poet Heroical*, there are sexual innuendoes respectively about homosexuality, getting raped, and fear of women; but they are just skimmed over, when the whole play could have been about those things. Respect for that focus is going to take a lot more emotional growth [for men].[20]

In response to Claudia Tate's assertion that

> Women's writing tends to focus on very vivid emotional descriptions of sexual intimacy; whereas, that of men tends to focus on physical movement in the sense of an oncoming train [and i]n women's writing you have the sensation of psychic contact among people[,][21]

Shange adds:

> That is because women are more in touch with their feelings; therefore, they're able to identify what it is they're doing and feeling. I also think that women use their feelings to a greater degree and in more varied ways than men do. Then, on the other hand, I know so many men—poets, painters, among

> others—with whom I feel perfectly comfortable in
> any situation, as friends, lovers and as peers.[22]

Okra is an embodiment of the complex emotional realities for a female endeavoring to articulate and communicate effectively her love, passion, and pain to her male companion and to a global patriarchy at large. That Greens is a poet affords him in this instance a degree of sensitivity and awareness that other males might not possess.

Okra and Greens' parenting continues in their "acknowledgment of their global offspring" (52). This section of *Okra* is another move by Shange to remind her audience that as persons of color, Okra and Greens are not politically or culturally privileged to disconnect themselves from a global community of oppressed peoples of color. Continuing the parenting metaphor, Shange speaks against the imperialistic victimization of Latin America and Africa and suggests that all oppressed must unite for survival. The irony of internal struggle when there is a greater threat of democracy versus tyranny underlines the section. Shange's analogy of the political strife between Salvador and Johannesburg, Santiago and Brixton, and Cape Town and Palestine highlights the irony that besets all minorities who "cannot speak the same language/ but . . . fight the same old men" (55). The analogy further recognizes that both home and abroad sexism within the black race indirectly assists a dominant white culture in maintaining racial oppression and inequality.

As Okra and Greens' relationship is more realistic than idyllic and romantic, their traditional honeymoon comes after a series of personal and political obstacles. Just as the women in *for colored girls* triumph amid nature's responses to their now realized "possibilities" as black women, here, the couple basks on a Caribbean beach. Their communion with nature and the natural elements reveals a hopeful confidence in Okra and Greens' mutual commitment as a married couple. While there is no suggestion that Okra and Greens will continue their married life free of internal and external problems, their quiet reverie in this final moment is a reaffirmation that their relationship can survive if both partners are willing to work at it. The sun is an approving nurturer smiling down on her own; even the sea responds approvingly to their union. Okra and Greens' delight in the natural setting recalls the Lady in Red's account of nature's response to the seven women's personal victory: ". . . the only tree i cd see // took me up in her branches // held me in the breeze // made me dawn dew // . . . the sun wrapped me up swingin rose light everywhere" (*for colored girls* 66-67). The women and the couple are for the moment one with themselves, each other, and with nature, an ideal Beau Willie and Crystal can not even imagine.

From Okra to Greens, as an experiment with the choreopoem form, succeeds as a commentary on the complicated lives of females in a male-dominated society. Rather than present a woman's view of a woman's world, however, as in *for colored girls* and *boogie woogie landscapes*, Shange here offers a feminist text within the boundaries of a romantic heterosexual relationship between two African Americans. Emphasizing her characters' racial identity, Shange shows the inseparability of race and gender issues and national and international political concerns. A study of both female victimization and positive female identity in the face of external oppositions, *Okra* submits on the stage what *A Daughter's Geography* renders on the page—the purpose of Shange's entire literary canon: a glimpse into the unadorned realities of "bein alive & bein a woman & bein colored" in the modern world. *Okra* admittedly seems Shange's only choreopoem wherein a black female finds the spiritual love she desires from a sensitive black man. Continuing to celebrate sexuality and female identity, Shange posits that matters of racism and sexism inevitably represent broader socio-political issues which cannot and should not be ignored even in successful heterosexual relationships.

NOTES

1. Most recently, Shange has taken her last poetry volume, *The Love Space Demands: A Continuing Saga* (New York: St. Martin's, 1987), and transformed the poems into a performance piece in the manner of *From Okra to Greens*. This piece was performed first at New Jersey's Crossroads Theater (March 1992) and later at Philadelphia's Painted Bride Art Center (February 1993). According to Susan Howard's "Feeling the Pain of Black Women: Ntozake Shange Again Puts Her Poetry on Stage" (*New York Newsday*, 5 March 1992), Shange describes this piece as an "advanced form of the choreopoem." Shange was one of six dancers/performers, Mickey Davidson choreographed the piece, William "Spaceman" Patterson created an original jazz score for the piece, and Adal's black-and-white photographs were part of the set (81). Reviews of this production were unavailable. However, reviews for the Painted Bride's production were decidedly unfavorable: "This show . . . was announced as a 'theatrical dramatization' of the book. What I saw was neither theatrical nor dramatic. What I saw was choreography . . . comprised of undulating . . ., strutting and arm-waving. . . . [M]ost of the time we [audience] were sloshing around in adolescent self-absorption" (Toby Zinman, "*The Love Space Demands*," *Philadelphia City Paper*, 16 February-5 March 1993, 22).

2. Ntozake Shange, *The Southern Register: The Newsletter of the Study of Southern Culture*, The University of Mississippi, volume 3, number 4 (Spring/Summer 1985).

3. Shange's list of specific song titles and their artists "suggested" for performance appears on page 58 of the Samuel French edition. Dance movements and style and choices of music in *for colored girls* are not as restricted and depend primarily on a director's and actors' preferences.

4. Ntozake Shange, *A Daughter's Geography* (New York: St. Martin's, 1983). Further references to this volume will appear in the text parenthetically by page number and title.

5. Ntozake Shange, *From Okra to Greens/ A Different Kinda Love Story: A Play/ With Music & Dance* (New York: Samuel French, 1985), 7-8. Subsequent references to this play will appear

parenthetically in the text by page number. Rosalee Alfonso dances to this poem in a videotape of Shange's reading at San Francisco State University (17 November 1976).

6. Shange's technique of connecting language and imagery with graphic sexuality is evident in the last segment of "some men" (to be discussed later) and in "'if i go all the way without you/ where would i go?'—The Iseley Brothers," from her most recent volume of poetry, *The Love Space Demands* (New York: St. Martin's, 1991).

7. Ntozake Shange, "She Who Comes from Herself," Iowa State UP (1984), audiocassette, side A.

8. Ntozake Shange, Dedication to *Some Men* (May 1981). Neither publisher nor publishing place is indicated. Borrowed through Interlibrary Loan from Sonoma State College Library, 1801 East Cotati Avenue, Rohnert Park, California 94928. The pages of this text are unnumbered.

9. This idea also brings attention to the fact that specific socially constructed gender realities—conscious and subconscious—are established as soon infants come into the world and genitalia has been identified.

10. Recall both Richard and Lyle's comments on their lovemaking skills, particularly with women not of their own race, in Baldwin's *Blues for Mister Charlie* (1964).

11. Lakoff, *Language and Woman's Place*, 43.

12. Tate, 151-52.

13. Recall Earl's reactions to Claire's newfound independence as a model in *a photograph*.

14. This same violent scenario is repeated in Spike Lee's first movie, "She's Gotta Have It" (1986), an allegedly feminist celebration of a black woman's sexual liberation amid three competing black males. As Nola Darling beckons an angry and insecure Jamie to make love to her, he responds: "I'll fuck you but I won't make love to you." With this comment, he abruptly pushes her onto a bed, then turns her around to penetrate her anally. Lee's stage direction describes this moment: "[Jamie's] frustrated and he's treating her rough. While Jamie is doing this he's yelling all kinds of stuff at her. He's trying his best to hurt her feelings [and her physical person], he's demeaning her" (Spike Lee, *Spike Lee's* Gotta Have It: *Inside Guerrilla Filmmaking* (New York: Fireside Book, 1987), 349. Black

feminist theorist bell hooks addresses this clearly violent moment in her essay, "'Whose Pussy Is This': A Feminist Comment," in her collection *Talking Back: Thinking Feminist, Thinking Black* (Boston: South End, 1989), 134-41.

15. Personal interview, *Black American Literature Forum.*

16. Perhaps this explains Greens' potentially ambiguous comments about being pregnant and having a gynecologist examine the walls of his "swollen cervix" (51). Since the poem/baby analogy does work in the final moments of the play, however, this detail reveals Shange's belief that a politically and emotionally sensitive male can become pregnant with poetic and black feminist vision in much the same way that some expectant fathers allegedly respond sympathetically physically to a woman's body's responses during pregnancy.

17. Personal interview, *Studies in American Drama.*

18. This section is entitled "A Black Night in Haiti, Palais National, Port-au-Prince" in *A Daughter's Geography*, 33-36.

19. This poem appears as "New World Core" in *A Daughter's Geography*, 52.

20. Tate, 160.

21. Ibid., 161.

22. Ibid.

CONCLUSION

Ntozake Shange is a writer enraged by and committed to writing about the injustices suffered by oppressed peoples of color, women and children. Long before the emergence of *for colored girls* as a theater piece, Shange, as dancer, poet, scholar, and cultural and political activist, crusaded for raised gender and race consciousness in her personal living. With *for colored girls*, she brought to the stage a distinctly black feminist perspective that manifested itself in the choreopoem, a genre which she feels most effectively explores, presents and legitimizes the interdisciplinary and non-European texture of African American culture, a form closely akin to performance in its open integration of music, song, and dance. Since *for colored girls*, Shange has continued to create and recreate mythologies that validate rather than negate her existence as a woman generally, her existence as an African American woman particularly. Emerging from an African tradition of movement, music, and dance, and emotional catharsis, Shange's choreopoem embraces those elements that accentuate a richness and variety of African American life. Shange's development of this form in American and world theater parallels her growth as a writer exploring her own personal life as a black female artist. While broadening existing forms of Westernized American theater, she affords people of color and women alternative possibilities for existence, working toward an ideal where one's potential for development as a complete individual assuming his or her rightful place in the social and world order is not dictated by race or gender, or by Eurocentric ideals.

As her writings for the stage reveal, Shange moves with ease from the intensely personal pains of her own suicide attempts to anger at political injustices in Haiti and South Africa, to the potential threat of violence any female might feel in the presence of any male. Having described herself on several occasions as a "war correspondent . . . in a war of cultural and aesthetic aggression,"[1] Shange declares war on the patriarchy's universally oppressive system. Toward this end, she arms herself with the rhythms and cadences of black vernacular, black music, and popular culture, and celebrates experiences that positively define and sustain her people. In an interview/conversation with African American political activist Angela Davis, Shange explains her role as a poet writing not only about an oppressive and dominant culture's historical and continued efforts to misrepresent and invalidate African American experience, but also about patriarchal objectifications of women, forthrightly denying the validity of their experiences. Her choreopoem then is not necessarily a conscious move to "challenge" existing European forms of art but to arrive at a form that best allows her and her characters to exist freely and comfortably without shame and fear, a form that allows her characters to celebrate themselves. The empowerment she feels in offering such a form that is definitively her own is her way of not only recording the battles in this cultural war of aesthetics but also aggressively participating in it:

> I do [choreopoem] better than anybody else. They [culturally arrogant and usually white male critics] can't take that from me because I made it up. They can't say it's wrong. They can't say it don't work because I made it up. I know what works in [my own form]. . . . That's true cultural aggression. But that's not exploitative cultural aggression. That's not taking something from somebody. That's giving us something. So we [African American writers and artists] have to be culturally aggressive.[2]

"At war with and making love to the world at the same time,"[3] Shange is passionate about black life and about love, sexuality, self-worth, and the possibilities of creating for women and people of color a language that does not define or restrict. It is as a poet and choreographer that she approaches theater and works first and foremost to elicit emotional responses from her audiences. Believing that emotion transcends racial, gender, and even class boundaries, and that the spontaneity and urgency of poetry particularly allows for easier access to those emotions, Shange moves to effect social and political change at both emotional and psychological levels.

Each of her five published theater pieces reveals Shange's careful blending of autobiographical threads with a comprehensive familiarity with her individual and collective racial and cultural ancestry. Arguing that "timely pieces are important because the history of oppressed people is also oppressed like the people,"[4] Shange, as a black feminist, embraces simultaneously and without personal choice the intensely private and the aggressively public. For Shange, she and all writers of color have a public responsibility "to explore and document our lives. . . . Exploration leads to discovery and documentation leads to history. We need to have a very solid base of understanding about what we've come from and who we are."[5] It is against this wealthy background of historical information, political and creative possibilities that Shange establishes a place for an historically displaced community physically, artistically, and psychologically. Within this landscape, Shange creates and works with forms that allow her characters quite simply to exist though nothing about their existence is simplistic:

> I am interested in . . . creating vehicles for people
> [of color and women] who can't exist in [European
> artistic] forms. My characters cannot exist in those
> forms. So I have to make a place where they can
> live. . . . I try to make a place where my voices can
> be heard, where they can move around, they can
> dance or they can hear music that they want to
> hear. . . . I'm trying to create a land for us where
> we can live.[6]

Shange celebrates in *for colored girls* the social and sexual identity of a black female. Chronicling a movement from physical heterosexual love to sisterly love and eventually to self-love, the choreopoem affirms a black woman's possibilities in the face of racism and sexism. *for colored girls* affords black women access to previously unarticulated—at least in such a public arena as theater—

and innermost desires and feelings while recognizing dance, language, and imagination as vehicles that help them survive their own self-destruction. Still feminist-centered, *spell #7*, continues to exalt blackness amid seemingly inescapable racial and gender stereotypes. A heterogeneous group of performing artists becomes one collective voice of black artist who finds dream and creative imagination fundamental to self-liberation and psychologically healthy living. *a photograph: lovers in motion* explores the ambiguity of male-female sexual identities. The most conventional of Shange's dramas in plot and characterization, *a photograph* examines the life of Sean David as he moves from the sometimes brutal exploitation of his female lovers to emotional and psychological confusion about his manhood and his unresolved relationship with his father. In *boogie woogie landscapes*, Shange presents a psychological self-portrait of a black woman in North America. Using a dream motif and extensive expressionist techniques, Shange explores a colored girl's inner being—her dreams, her fears, and her fantasies—all to validate an African American woman's unique and complex struggles against racism and sexism. *From Okra to Greens: A Different Kinda Love Story* is Shange's most blatant conjoining of poetry with theater. Using poems from a previously published collection, *A Daughter's Geography*, Shange distributes the poems between two voices—the African American male and the African American female. As a love story rendered from a distinctly female's perspective, *Okra* offers a black woman's view of both romantic bliss and turmoil amid rampant political and social injustice.

Characteristic of all of Shange's theater pieces is the notion of "combat breathing," a notion she adopts from philosopher Frantz Fanon. According to Fanon's assessment of the colonies of Francophone Africa,

> There is no occupation of territory, on the one hand, and independence of persons on the other. It is the country as a whole, its history, its daily pulsation that are contested, disfigured, in the hope of final destruction. Under this condition, the individual's breathing is an observed, an occupied breathing. It is a combat breathing.[7]

Shange's characters struggle continually against a society that oppresses, one that offers women and people of color few options for satisfying existence and no territorial claims. Made to feel displaced, insignificant, and marginal, they retreat survive through imagination, dream, dance, language, music, and segregated community. Such avenues are not ways of permanent escape for the characters—for although some of her characters consider suicide, they do not take their own lives—but are accessible means of resting and gaining sustenance needed to continue the struggle toward legitimacy, wholeness, and positive self-identity.

Finding that library books spoke nothing of rape, child molestation, wife battering, abortions, and menstruation, Shange—at an early age—deemed herself a feminist determined to document the complexities of her female world. As a feminist, she is intensely aware of a female's—particularly a black female's—need for options for personal and social survival. Daring to celebrate the realm of a woman's dreams, her fears, and her sexuality,[8] Shange recognizes the inseparability of a female's personal and political existence: "I think the dangerous mistake that women make is to assume the personal is not political. When I make a personal statement, it is to me a political statement."[9] Having acknowledged her feminist determination when she rejected the Black Panther Party for the Young Lords Party because equality for women was part of the Young Lords' platform, Shange recognizes language of the patriarchy as one of women's greatest obstacles to positive selfhood. She credits her steadfast commitment to attacking the patriarchy through language to feminist poet Judy Grahn:

> The language of a white, male-dominated society must be done away with in women's literature.
> We have to murder the King's English before it murders us. I feel dedicated to Judy Grahn, one of the most significant lesbian American poets. Her basic premise is that we have to murder the King's English to express women's thoughts because that particular language can't speak for us. We have to change and distort English so it can express women's feelings. Feminists all over the world are

trying to do that.

I think it's important for us to never forget that language determines how we perceive ourselves and unless women and people of color take charge of the language we are nothing.[10]

Black women particularly, Shange reiterates, have no right to remain passive in this movement toward social and political change:

A lot of Black women don't want to accept our part of the responsibility for our oppression, and I'm just not free to do that. I will not look at my daughter 20 years from now and have her ask me "Well, why didn't you do something to help?" I feel obliged to pay attention to and to be an advocate for, in some artistic way that's satisfactory, the dramatic changes in attitude in the lives of women and children in this country.[11]

For Shange, the same language, awareness, anger, and commitment that moved blacks to the political forefront in the turbulent sixties are needed to liberate women from the same patriarchal oppressor. Yet, while her writings are intended immediately for women, they are also meant to educate men about women's realities:

The same rhetoric that is used to establish the Black Aesthetic, we must use to establish a woman's aesthetic, which is to say that those parts of reality that are ours, those things about our bodies, the cycles of our lives have been ignored for centuries in all castes and classes of our people, are to be dealt with now. . . . One has to speak about things inherently female. And that is my persona. A woman. And she is going to talk the way she understands. Why must I use metaphors because men understand them? . . . I'm not going to change what I write [just] to help a man understand it. They've been here as long as I've been here. They rule the damned world, they rule the household, if not the world, and they can certainly learn who their mother was, and who they sleep with at night.[12]

Because of Shange's intense concern for language, both verbal and nonverbal, her theater pieces reveal her utmost attention to the rhythms of words—through unpredictable usage of dialect, slang, Portuguese, Spanish, alleged profanity—and of the body through improvised dance and physical movement. A master of dramatic monologues, Shange presents characters whose lives are not the least bit tragic. Neither are they necessarily, artificially, or superficially ordered. Hers are characters that crave, struggle against, and embrace life, characters who, if they do nothing else, talk and give voice to their experiences.

Shange, not unlike other black feminist authors, has perhaps been most misunderstood in her portrayal of black men on the stage. As E. Ethelbert Miller avers, "Ntozake Shange is not a radical feminist singling out men as the primary problem in our society; instead she is a Black artist opening our eyes to the totality of our [black women's] dilemma. . . . Shange's play[s] [are] poem[s] and not . . . polemic[s]."[13] Indeed, if there is a message in Shange's dramas, hers is one of political urgency, not one of moralizing or sermonizing. While her plays emphasize the sexuality of female identity, she at no point embraces lesbianism as the solution to women's problems with men, an issue that has separated her from other feminist camps. What she works toward is a level of communication in male-female relationships built upon mutual respect, trust, and individual self-worth. Her attack on men comes in her persistent questioning of some males' exploitative treatments of women, in some men's—and not a few women's—acceptance of society's limiting expressions and definitions of manhood. A politically conscious man with artistic sensibilities seems Shange's ideal man, one who does not lose his perceived masculinity in acknowledging and respecting females' perspectives. Julianne Malveaux's assertion about *for colored girls* applies to all of Shange's theater pieces: "[They] offer a slice of Black life, not [merely] a series of generalizations and statements about black men and women."[14] To those who accuse her of writing to attack black men, Shange responds:

> If you take a definitive look at black women, you
> automatically get into their relations with black
> men, and unfortunately black men can be extremely
> cruel to black women, possibly because they feel
> black women are the only people they are superior
> to. As a black feminist, I naturally resent that atti-
> tude a hell of a lot. [15]

Shange's literary and feminist influences are many, and she continually reminds her interviewers that her rich family background, her formal education in African American history, literature, poetry, and music, as well as her sustaining community of poets and musicians of color all contribute to her own black feminist identity politically and artistically. She identifies her heroes as Toussaint L'Ouverture, Denmark Vesey, Sojourner Truth, Nat Love, Albert Ayler, Jelly Roll Morton, Bessie Smith, and Zora Neale Hurston[16] and adds that Paul Laurence Dunbar, Margaret Walker, Ralph Ellison, Richard Wright, James Baldwin, Ann Petry, Countee Cullen, Jean Toomer, Claude McKay, Langston Hughes, Owen Dobson, Ted Jones, Leopold Senghor, and Aime Cesaire also inspired her work: "all those people gave me something. They made a place for me."[17] Their challenges, their music, their thoughts, their writing, their creative living, and their exemplary lives have allowed Shange a wellspring of knowledge from which to express her own creativity.

Those feminist writers who have nourished her work and her life include Olga Broumas, Thulani Davis, Jessica Hagedorn, Wopo Holup, June Jordan, Susan Griffin, Sandy Esteves, Kitty Tsui, Toni Morrison, Geraldine Kudaka, Gloria Naylor, Adrienne Rich, Audre Lorde, Barbara Smith, Shere Hite, Emily Mann, Andrea Dworkin, Judy Grahn, Lydia Fagundes Telles, Eva Logan, Mary Daly, Carol Le Sanchez, Alice Childress, E. Ethelbert Miller, Judy Chicago, and Susan Brownmiller. According to Shange, each of these writers "has faced down the dragon of patriarchal language and kidnapped the King's English with an eye toward its realignment, if not its destruction"[18] She also respects the artistry of male writers—particularly Latino writers whose struggle for cultural legitimacy she sees as parallel to her own—such as Roberto Mario Vargas, Tom Cusan, Llosa Enfante, Alejandro Murghia, Pablo Neruda, Miguel Asturias,

Gylan Kain, Gabriel Garcia Marquez, Manuel Puig, Leon Damas, Papoleto Melendez, Pedro Pietri, Victor Hernandez Cruz, Clarence Major, who "certainly have a perspective that is less feminist (if at all), but [are also] language warriors."[19] That black women and artists of color are still writing and performing is, according to Shange, reason to continue as a literary and visual artist committed to documenting history that legitimizes the existence of her people and other people of color despite lackluster commercial reception.

Perhaps the most recognizable artistic and political influences on Shange have been the early LeRoi Jones/ Amiri Baraka and Ishmael Reed. Aside from Jones' failure to address issues that legitimized women's lives and experiences in his work, Shange recalls a fascination especially with Jones' use of raw language and imagery as well as his use of history to document and validate the lives of black people. She recognizably has adopted Jones' consistent use of lower case letters, slashes and phonetic spellings, as well as his concern for the visual aesthetics of poems on the printed page. They also share a preoccupation with the syntactical structures of their poems, deliberately and boldly violating the rules of standard English. Shange also responded quite directly to Baraka's early revolutionary insistence that black poets be playwrights:

> What is needed is for many of the Black poets, those with the most true revolutionary fervor, to . . . begin to write, or better, to record improvised dramas, plays, skits, dramatic teaching forms, songs, dances, about the worldwide Black revolutionary struggle. . . . Poets shd begin writing short skits. Actors, singers, dancers cd write them, short musicals describing the need for Black Unity and Self Determination. Plays reach our people better than literature or books. These plays cd have songs, dances, poetry together or have the content through any one of these. . . .
>
> Importantly, revolutionary African governments like Tanzania & Guinea both utilize the arts, but especially drama, dance & song to drive home the revolutionary message.[20]

Baraka's daringness to confront, indeed his calculated confrontations with audiences to arrive at gut responses also finds its way into Shange's dramas. Both playwrights' use and manipulations of language and imagery privilege their focus on emotion over intellect and cerebreality. And while Shange as a budding artist and author might have considered "every word outta imamu's mouth [as] gospel" (*for colored girls* 12), she also recognized the absence of women's complex perspectives in this revolutionary sermons.

Ishmael Reed's use of fantasy with history and myth influenced Shange, as did his explorations with diction. She acknowledges her literary debts:

> The two books that changed my entire perspective
> of the world were Ishmael Reed's *Yellow Back*
> *Radio Broke-Down* and *Preface to a Twenty Volume*
> *Suicide Note* by Amiri Baraka (then LeRoi Jones). I
> have to pay homage to both of these men, because
> if it weren't for them I wouldn't have the courage to
> do what I do, even though we're so disparate in
> terms of style and politics. Ishmael gave me the
> right to use history and fantasy in any way I chose,
> and Amiri gave me the right to be as intimate as I
> felt like being; to use what history I chose to use as
> my jumping-off point; to be as international as I
> wanted, or as obscure as I wanted if the piece de-
> manded it. He also gave me the right to be inso-
> lent.[21]

Shange's lists of influences evidence not only her wide reading and education but also her intense and immediate involvement with literature, music, and poetry of African Americans and of Central and Latin Americans as well. Schooled in her youth by her family in African American history and a frequent traveler with her family to Trinidad, Cuba, Haiti, and currently a regular visitor to Aruba, Jamaica, Bermuda, Martinique, Curacao, Nicaragua, Brazil, Puerto Rico, and Nassau, Shange has enjoyed steady global exposure to and deep communal connections with people of color and their cultures. In addition, she continues to remain active in national and international politics and has successfully produced her choreopoems in such places as London, Brazil, and Jamaica. She elaborates on her varied artistic influences poetically and musically:

> i thot leroi jones (imamu baraka) waz my primary jumping-off point. that i cd learn from him how to make language sing & penetrate one's soul, like in *the dead lecturer, the system of dante's hell,* & *black magic poetry.* then i found myself relating technically to ishmael reed, particularly in terms of diction & myth, as in *yellow back radio broke-down* & *mumbo jumbo.* then i discovered the nostalgia david henderson can make so tangible; our immediate past as myth. & here comes pedro pietri, allowing language to create a world that can't exist outside his poems. i find victor hernandez cruz shows me how to say anything i thot i saw.
> jessica hagedorn on the other hand puts the worlds we both share in a terribly personal & cosmopolitan realm. her book, *dangerous music,* says to me that complicated notions can be explicated by rhythm. we can approach difficult concepts with ourselves; there is no need to go the route of iowa to get a sophisticated poem. all the years i've been writing i've spoken constantly with thulani, whose poetry sustains me as much as my own. thulani teaches me to take risks. her familiarity with the new black music & her understanding of a woman's relationship to the universe continually push me to refuse to be afraid of what i am feeling.
> then there is clarence major who has let fantasy loose for me. let me see language with no more responsibility than to give me an image / however contorted, private & bizarre. clarence's stuff, like his novel *reflex* & *bone structure,* is breaking the linear tradition in black literature, moving us from narrative to the crux of the moment. i've learned so much from latin americans too: julio cortazar, man-

uel puig, octavio paz, mario vargas llosa, miguel
angel asturias, rene depestre, gabriel garcia marquez, jacques roumain, leon damas. i get a western
hemispheric reference that saves me from what is
insidious in north american & european literature /
the suggestion that black people exist only as vehicles for white people's fantasies. the technical skill
& brilliance of the characterizations of garcia
marquez have raised my expectations of how well a
reader shd know a person / place. & then there is
neruda. . . .[22]

As for black women in theater, Alice Childress and Adrienne
Kennedy provided Shange with working models aesthetically and
philosophically. Specifically, Alice Childress established a political
basis for centralizing a black female in theater. In her essay, "A
Woman Playwright Speaks Her Mind" (1966), Childress explains:

> . . . the Negro woman has almost been omitted as
> important subject matter in the general popular
> American drama, television, motion pictures and
> radio; except for the constant, but empty and
> decharacterized faithful servant. And her finest
> virtues have been drawn in terms of long suffering,
> with humility and patience.
> . . .
> The Negro woman will attain her rightful place in
> American literature when those of us who care
> about truth, justice and a better life tell her story,
> with the full knowledge and appreciation of her
> constant, unrelenting struggle against racism and
> for human rights.[23]

Still, in terms of more complicated explorations of black female
existence, Adrienne Kennedy's plays present a closer affinity with
Shange's. Whereas Kennedy's explorations of black female psyche
depict fragmentation resulting usually from race, gender, and cultural
issues, Shange's plays work to celebrate resolution, not just identify-

ing such conflicts. Shange, like Kennedy, is less concerned with resolving conflict particularly between European and African influences on African American female identity. Shange's characters find hope not deterioration and despair in their racially segregated worlds. They do not, as a result of their inability to accept fragmentation, hang themselves as does Sarah in Kennedy's *Funnyhouse of a Negro* (1962) or transform into a screeching owl as does She in *The Owl Answers* (1963). Shange's characters are also not concerned with accepting European influence. Shange's anger is replaced by Kennedy's despair and confusion; Shange's efforts toward resolution replace Kennedy's psychological and physical deterioration.

To absorb the strategies of writers before and around her is to open her work to a world of possibilities technically, aesthetically, and creatively. And while some may insist that Shange's work is too limited in subject matter and intended audience or redundant because of her persistent attention to social injustices, her writings continue to be as forceful, as political, and as private as the poems that first presented to us the lives of her seven colored girls. Because women and people of color are demanding that their lives be recovered, re-examined, validated and hence documented accurately, Shange's work is intensely relevant to our American and global perspectives. As for her commitment to writing as a black woman, she assures us:

> There's little possibility of my exhausting my material. I'm still alive and feeling and seeing,[24] [but more importantly,] I have a daughter [so] I don't have much choice but to write. I can't allow the things that happened to me to happen to her.[25]

Her choreopoems, then, are staged vehicles that acknowledge, voice, and preserve her individual and cultural identity heretofore ill-defined or deliberately misrepresented. Shange's consistent work in a deliberately eclectic "'untranslatable [from Western perspectives and by Western ideologies] form' demands and preserves an artistic integrity of African-American cultural experience."[26] Definitively, the choreopoems aggressively present Shange's political, cultural, and aesthetic marking and making of her own territorial claim, a literary space and place from which she refuses to move.

NOTES

1. Stella Dong, "*Publishers Weekly* Interviews Ntozake Shange," *Publishers Weekly*, 3 May 1985, 75.
2. "Ntozake Shange Interview with Angela Davis," videotape, American Poetry Archives, The Poetry Center, San Francisco State University, 5 May 1989.
3. Halifu Osumare, "Ntozake Shange: Choreopoet," *Arts* (April 1981).
4. Ntozake Shange, Arts and Education Council's Conference on Southern Literature, University of Tennessee at Chattanooga (4 April 1987). While Shange is not generally thought of as a "southern writer" in a literary tradition of William Faulkner, Eudora Welty, Ernest Gaines, Carson McCullers, or Tennessee Williams, she describes herself as a "good southern-northern girl." Despite having spent much of her life in New York, California, and now Philadelphia, Shange maintains that her rich southern sensibilites emerge from her South Carolinean familial ancestry and from living in St. Louis and Texas. Shange appeared at the Conference on Southern Literature with writers Ellen Gilchrist, Louis D. Rubin, Jr., Richard Marius, and Ernest J. Gaines.
5. H. Maria Noel, "Ntozake Shange Writes Characters, Not Messages," *Chattanooga Times*, 4 April 1987, B2.
6. "Ntozake Shange Interview with Angela Davis," 5 May 1989.
7. Frantz Fanon, *A Dying Colonialism* (New York: Grove, 1967). Quoted in Shange's *three pieces*, xii. Sandra L. Richards' article, "Conflicting Impulses in the Plays of Ntozake Shange" in *Black American Literature Forum* 17 (Summer 1983): 73-78, considers the dialectic of combat breathing versus will to divinity using Shange's *spell #7*. Richards explains that "the diametric opposite of Shange's combat breath is the will to divinity whereby individual protagonists seek to transcend corporeal existence in order to merge with natural, cosmic forces" (74). This same idea can be most connected with Layla's experiences in *boogie woogie landscapes*.
8. Shange's most recent poetry collection, *The Love Space Demands (A Continuing Saga)* (New York: St. Martin's, 1991), is a

woman's celebration of her sexuality through language in the face of physical death from physically loving too many, too much.

9. Kathleen Betsko and Rachel Koenig, *Interviews with Contemporary Women Playwrights* (New York: William Morrow, 1987), 370.

10. Charlise L. Lyles, "Black Women's Bard," *Virginian-Pilot*, 3 October 1986.

11. Jewelle Gomez, *"Belles Lettres* Interview: Ntozake Shange," *Belles Lettres: A Review of Books by Women*, September/October 1985, 9.

12. Henry Blackwell, "An Interview with Ntozake Shange," *Black American Literature Forum* 13 (1979): 136.

13. E. Ethelbert Miller, "For ZAKI—Who Dances the Bomba," *New Directions: The Howard University Magazine*, April 1980, 30.

14. Julianne Malveaux, "The Sexual Politics of Black People, Angry Black Women, Angry Black Men," *Black Scholar*, May-June 1979, 33. Quoted by E. Ethelbert Miller in "For ZAKI—Who Dances the Bomba," *New Directions: The Howard University Magazine*, April 1980, 30.

15. Ribowsky, 42.

16. Blackwell, 137.

17. Barbara Lewis, *"for colored girls who have considered suicide/ when the rainbow is enuf*: The Poet," *Essence*, 7 (November 1976): 119.

18. Gomez, 10.

19. Ibid.

20. Imamu Amiri Baraka, "Black 'Revolutionary' Poets Should Also Be Playwrights," *Black World* (April 1972): 4-7.

21. Dong, 75.

22. "Ntozake Shange Interviews Herself," 72.

23. Alice Childress, "A Woman Playwright Speaks Her Mind," in Lindsay Patterson, ed. *Anthology of the American Negro in the Theatre: A Critical Approach* (New York: Publishers Company, Inc., 1976), 75-79. See also Childress' essay, "For a Negro Theatre," *Masses and Mainstream* 4 (February 1951): 61-64.

24. Blackwell, 138.

25. Charlise L. Lyles, "Black Women's Bard."

26. Chezia Thompson-Cager, "Superstition, Magic and the

Occult in Two Versions of Ntozake Shange's Choreopoem *for colored girls.* . . and Novel *Sassafrass, Cypress and Indigo*," *MAWA: Quarterly Publication of the Middle Atlantic Writers Association* 4 (December 1989): 37. Thompson-Cager discusses Shange's use of African American "mystical" elements—dance, magic, and female menstruation—as ways of creating new mythologies for black people generally, for black women particularly. Importantly, Thompson-Cager mentions a first version of *for colored girls* that was published as a poetry anthology by Shameless Hussy Press (1975), a version that included at least two poems—"two" and "dancers"—"about magical phenomenon." These poems were omitted by the 1976 staged publication.

BIBLIOGRAPHY

Primary Sources

Shange, Ntozake. *for colored girls who have considered suicide/ when the rainbow is enuf.* New York: Bantam, 1981.
——. *From Okra to Greens/ A Different Kinda Love Story: A Play/ With Music & Dance.* New York: Samuel French, 1985.
——. *three pieces.* New York: St. Martin's, 1981.

Secondary Sources

Abramson, Doris E. *Negro Playwrights in the American Theater 1925-1959.* New York: Columbia UP, 1969.
Anderlini, Serena W. "*colored girls*: A Reaction to Black Machismo, or Hues of Erotic Tension in New Feminist Solidarity?" *Journal of American Drama and Theatre* 2 (Spring 1990): 33-54.
——. "Drama or Performance Art? An Interview with Ntozake Shange." *Journal of Dramatic Theory and Criticism* 6 (Fall 1991): 85-97.
——. "Gender and Desire in Contemporary Drama: Lillian Hellman, Natalia Ginzburg, Franca Rame, and Ntozake Shange" *DAI* 49 (1988): 809A.
Anderson, Janet. "Many Cutting Edges: Nuances Abound in Musical Drama *Betsey Brown*." *Philadelphia Daily News* 31 March 1989.
Angelou, Maya. *I Know Why the Caged Bird Sings.* New York: Bantam, 1971.
"Ann Waldman vs. Ntozake Shange." World Heavyweight Cham-

pionship Poetry Bout. Taos, New Mexico. Taos Poetry Circus. 20-23 June 1991 (videocassette).

Aponte, Lionel. "'Talkin' White.'" *Essence* January 1989: 11.

"Archie Bunker, Alive and Well." *Newsweek* 21 January 1991: 59.

Arnold, Jay. "Stage Review: *For Colored Girls. . . .*" *Hollywood Reporter* 14 July 1978: 2.

Asquith, Ros. "Black Magic." *(London) Observer* 14 April 1985.

Atwood, Margaret. "What is a Woman's Novel? For That Matter, What Is a Man's?" *Ms.* August 1986: 98.

Austin, William. "Blacks, 'the Great White Way.'" *New York Amsterdam News* 9 October 1976: D11.

Baccolini, Raffaella. "L'identita femminile nel teatro contemporaneo in lingua englese." *Il teatro e le donne: Forme drammatiche e tradizione al femminile nel teatro inglese.* Ed. Raffaella Baccolini, et. al. Urbino: QuattroVenti, 1991.

Bailey, A. Peter. "A Look at the Contemporary Black Theatre Movement." *Black American Literature Forum* 17 (Spring 1983): 19-21.

Baldwin, James. *Blues for Mister Charlie.* New York: Dell, 1964.

Bambara, Toni Cade. "*For Colored Girls*—And White Girls Too." *Ms.* September 1976: 36, 38.

Baraka, Ameer. "The Black Aesthetic." *Negro Digest* 18 (September 1969): 5-6.

Baraka, Imamu Amiri. "Black (Art) Drama Is the Same as Black Life." *Ebony* 26 (February 1971): 74-82.

——. "Black 'Revolutionary' Poets Should Also Be Playwrights." *Black World* 21 (April 1972): 4-6.

——. LeRoi Jones. "The Revolutionary Theatre." *Selected Plays and Prose of Amiri Baraka/ LeRoi Jones.* New York: William Morrow, 1979. 130-33.

Barnes, Clive. "American-style *Courage* Is an Asset for Public." *New York Post* 14 May 1980. *New York Theatre Critics' Reviews* 4 (1980): 184-85.

——. "Stage: Black Sisterhood/ Ntozake Shange's *For Colored Girls* Opens at Papp's Anspacher Theater." *New York Times* 2 January 1976: 4.

——. "Stage: Shange's *For Colored Girls.*" *New York Times* 3 June 1976.

——, ed. "Ntozake Shange: *For Colored Girls Who Have Considered Suicide/ When the Rainbow is Enuf.*" *Best American Plays* (eighth series). New York: Crown, 1982.

Bauer, Grace. Rev. of *Ridin' the Moon in Texas: Word Paintings* by Ntozake Shange. *Library Journal* 112 (1 May 1987): 71.

Baxter, Robert. "New Festival Musical Aims for the Heart." *(Philadelphia, Pennsylvania) Courier-Post* 24 March 1989: 1-2.

Beaufort, John. "Black Cast Electrifies Off-Broadway 'Choreopoem.'" *Christian Science Monitor* 7 June 1979. *New York Theatre Critics' Reviews* 40 (1979): 109.

——. "*For Colored Girls. . . .*" *Christian Science Monitor* 24 September 1976. *New York Theatre Critics' Reviews* 37 (1976): 202.

——. "*Mother Courage and Her Children.*" *Christian Science Monitor* 19 May 1980. *New York Theatre Critics' Reviews* 4 (1980): 186.

Bell, Roseann Pope. "*For Colored Girls Who Have Considered Suicide/ When the Rainbow Is Enuf.*" *Black Collegian* 7 (May-June 1977): 48-49.

Berman, Laura. "The Last Angry Woman? Playwright-poet Isn't Running from the Rage That Inspires Her." *Detroit Free Press* 30 October 1979: C1, A3.

"*Betsey Brown*: Ntozake Shange Play." National Public Radio. *Morning Edition* 31 March 1989 (audiocassette).

"*Betsey Brown*: Semi-Autobiography by Shange." National Public Radio. *All Things Considered* 6 June 1985 (audiocassette).

Betsko, Kathleen, and Rachel Koenig, eds. *Interviews with Contemporary Women Playwrights*. New York: William Morrow, 1987, 364-76.

Bigsby, C.W.E. *A Critical Introduction to Twentieth-Century American Drama (Volume Three: Beyond Broadway).* Cambridge: Cambridge UP, 1985.

"Black Box 13-14/ Double Issue." Washington: Watershed Foundation, 1978 (audiocassette).

"Black in White America." Ray Dunn, producer. American Broadcasting. August 1989 (television documentary).

"*The Black Scholar* Reader Forum: Black Male/ Female Relationships." *Black Scholar* 10 (May-June 1979): 14-62.

"Black Theatre: The Making of a Movement" Woody King, Jr., producer. San Francisco: California Newsreel, 1978 (videocassette).

"Black Women Novelists: New Generation Raises Provocative Issues." *Ebony* November 1984: 59, 60, 62, 64.

"Black Women Writers." Donahue. Show #72089. Transcript #2733. 20 July 1989 (audiocassette).

Blackwell, Henry. "An Interview with Ntozake Shange." *Black American Literature Forum* 13 (1979): 134-38.

Bond, Jean Carey. "*For Colored Girls Who Have Considered Suicide*" *Freedomways* 16 (Third Quarter, November 1976): 187-91.

Bonetti, Kay. "Interview with Ntozake Shange." Columbia, MO: American Audio Prose Library, 1989 (audiocassette).

boogie woogie landscapes. Press Release Fact Sheet. John F. Kennedy Center for the Performing Arts. Washington, D.C.: Press Department (17 June-13 July 1980).

Bovoso, Carole. "Books: Ntozake Shange and Alice Walker Celebrate the Magic and Power of Black Women in Two Exciting, Insightful and Stylish New Novels." *Essence* October 1982: 20.

Bowles, Juliette, ed. *In the Memory and Spirit of Frances, Zora, and Lorraine: Essays and Interviews on Black Women and Writing*. Washington: Institute for the Arts and Humanities, Howard U, 1979.

Bradby, Marie. "Atlanta's Alliance Theatre Brings Music, Dance and Poetry to Lexington." *Lexington Herald* 1981: B1.

Bradley, Linda. "Is a Female Literary Tradition Proper?" Rev. of *Modern American Women Poets*, by Jean Gould. *(Nashville) Tennessean* 10 November 1985.

Bray, Rosemary L. and Karen Fitzgerald. "The Luxury of Summer Reading." *Ms.* June 1987: 16-22.

"'Bride-burning' Said Increasing in India, Though Police Deny It." *Birmingham News* 24 January 1988: H2.

Broumas, Olga. *Beginning with O*. New Haven: Yale UP, 1977.

Brown, Edward K., II. "An Interview with Ntozake Shange." *Poets and Writers* 21 (May/ June 1993): 38-46.

Brown, Elizabeth. "Six Female Black Playwrights: Images of Blacks in Plays by Lorraine Hansberry, Alice Childress, Sonia Sanchez,

Barbara Molette, Martie Charles, and Ntozake Shange." Diss. Florida State U, 1980.

Brown, Sterling A. "Negro Character as Seen by White Authors." *Journal of Negro Education* 2 (April 1933): 179-203.

Browne, Lindsey. "Shows Vivid Color Theme." *(Sydney, Australia) Sun Herald* 1978.

Brown-Guillory, Elizabeth. "Black Women Playwrights: Exorcising Myths." *Phylon* 48 (Fall 1987): 229-39.

Brownmiller, Susan. *Against Our Will: Men, Women and Rape.* New York: Simon and Schuster, 1975.

Buckley, Tom. "The Three Stages of Ntozake Shange." *New York Times* 16 December 1977: C6.

Bullins, Ed. *The American Flag Ritual (A Short Play or Film Scenario). The Theme Is Blackness:* The Corner *and Other Plays.* New York: William Morrow, 1973. 135.

——. *How Do You Do (A Nonsense Drama). The Theme Is Blackness:* The Corner *and Other Plays.* New York: William Morrow, 1973. 595-604.

——. *A Short Play for a Small Theater. The Theme Is Blackness:* The Corner *and Other Plays.* New York: William Morrow, 1973. 182.

Burbank, Carol. "Colored Girl: *Betsey Brown* Breaks and Remakes the Mold." *Philadelphia City Paper* 14 April 1989: 14.

Cain, Scott. *"For Colored Girls. . .* Director Aims for Freshness." *Atlanta Journal and Constitution* 8 March 1981: E4.

Calio, Louise. "A Rebirth of the Goddess in Contemporary Women Poets of the Spirit." *Studio Mystica* 7 (Spring 1984): 50-59.

Caplan, Betty. "Spelling It Out." *(London) The Labour Herald* 4 April 1985.

Carby, Hazel V. *Reconstructing Womanhood: The Emergence of the Afro-American Woman Novelist.* Oxford: Oxford UP, 1987.

Carlos, Laurie. Telephone interview. New York City, 27 August 1986.

Carne, Rosalind. *"Black Power." Arts Guardian* 17 April 1985.

Chenault, Julie. "What I Wanted to Be When I Grew Up." *Essence* May 1986: 80-81, 160.

Childress, Alice. "For a Negro Theatre." *Masses and Mainstream* 4 (February 1951): 61-64.

———. "A Woman Playwright Speaks Her Mind." *Anthology of the American Negro in the Theater: A Critical Approach.* Ed. Lindsay Patterson. New York: Publishers, 1976. 75-79.

Christ, Carol P. *Diving Deep and Surfacing: Women Writers on Spiritual Quest.* Boston: Beacon, 1980.

Clancy, Ambrose. "Trying To Fly By the Nets." Rev. of *Betsey Brown*, by Ntozake Shange. *St. Petersburg (Florida) Times* 15 September 1985. *NewsBank* [microform], 1985, 50: E14, fiche.

Clurman, Harold. Rev. of *for colored girls who have considered suicide/ when the rainbow is enuf*, by Ntozake Shange. *Nation* 22 (1 May 1976): 541-42.

Coleman, Michael. "What is Black Theatre? An Interview with Imamu Amiri Baraka." *Black World* 20 (April 1971): 32-36.

Collins, William B. "American Music Theater Festival Opens Season with *Betsey Brown.*" *Philadelphia Inquirer* 31 March 1989: 14.

"Color Adjustment." Marlon Riggs, producer/ director. San Francisco: California Newsreel, 1987 (videocassette).

"A Colored Girl: Ntozake Shange." Public Broadcasting Service. Washington: WGBH-TV, 1980 (videocassette).

"*Colored Girls* Returns Tonight." *(Nashville) Tennessean* 22 November 1980: 34.

"*Colored Girls* . . . Shocks Savannah." *Savannah Tribune* 4 February 1981: 1, 7.

"*Colored Girls* to Gain Wider Audience." Rev. of *for colored girls who have considered suicide/ when the rainbow is enuf*, by Ntozake Shange. *Theatre News* 12 (April 1980): 4.

Collins, L. M. "New Ntozake Shange Tale Indigestible." Rev. of *Betsey Brown*, by Ntozake Shange. *(Nashville) Tennessean* 12 May 1985.

Conklin, Nancy F., Brenda McCallum, and Marcia Wade. *The Culture of Southern Black Women: Approaches and Materials.* University, Alabama: Archive of American Minority Cultures and Women's Studies Program, U of Alabama, 1983.

Considine, Shaun. "On Stage/ British Theater Had Its Angry Young Men—Off-Broadway Savors Its First Furious Woman, Ntozake Shange." *People Weekly* 5 July 1976: 68-69.

Contemporary Literary Criticism. Vols. 8 and 25. Detroit: Gale Research, 1978, 1983.

Cooper, Priscilla Hancock. *Call Me Black Woman.* Louisville, KY: Doris, 1993.

Coveney, Michael. *"Spell Number Seven/* Donmar Warehouse." *(London) Financial Times* 3 April 1985.

Cronacher, Karen. "Unmasking the Minstrel Mask's Black Magic in Ntozake Shange's *spell #7." Theater Journal* 44 (1992): 177-93.

Cropper, Martin. *"Spell No. 7/* Donmar Warehouse." *(London) Times* 4 April 1985.

Crump, Fred, Jr. *Rapunzel.* Nashville: Winston-Derek, 1991.

Daly, Mary. *Gyn/ Ecology: The Metaethics of Radical Feminism.* Boston: Beacon, 1978.

"The Date Who Rapes." *Newsweek* 9 April 1984: 91.

Davis, Ossie. "The English Language Is My Enemy." *Negro History Bulletin* 30 (April 1967): 18.

———. *Purlie Victorious (A Comedy in Three Acts).* New York: Samuel French, 1989.

Deck, A. Rev. of *See No Evil: Prefaces, Essays & Accounts, 1976-1983,* by Ntozake Shange. *Choice* 22 (October 1984): 271.

de Weever, Jacqueline. *Mythmaking and Metaphor in Black Women's Fiction.* New York: St. Martin's, 1991.

Dickie, Elizabeth D. Rev. of *Betsey Brown,* by Ntozake Shange. *Richmond (Virginia) Times-Dispatch,* 9 June 1985. *NewsBank* [microform], 1985, 124: B2, fiche.

Dong, Stella. *"Publishers Weekly* Interviews Ntozake Shange." *Publishers Weekly* 227 (May 1985): 74-75.

"Donmar Warehouse: *Spell No. Seven." Stage and Television Today* 18 April 1985.

Douglas, Imani. "American Music Theater Festival Presents *Betsey Brown*: A Study Guide." March 1989.

DuBois, W.E.B. *The Souls of Black Folk. Three Negro Classics.* New York: Avon, 1965. 207-389.

Duffy, Mike. "Leaving Behind the 'Aunt Jemima Syndrome': Black T.V. Shows Steer Away from Stereotyped Image." *Birmingham News* 5 April 1994: F20-F21.

Early, James. "Interview with Ntozake Shange." *In the Memory and Spirit of Frances, Zora, and Lorraine: Essays and Interviews on Black Women and Writing.* Ed. Juliette Bowles. Washington: Institute for the Arts and the Humanities, Howard U, 1979. 23-

26.

Ebony Pictorial History of Black America (Volume II): Reconstruction to Supreme Court Decision 1954. Nashville: Southwestern, 1971.

Eder, Richard. "Dramatic Poetry." *New York Times* 4 June 1979: C13.

——. "Miss Shange's Rousing Homilies." *New York Times* 22 July 1979: D3.

——. "Papp Proves Less Is More." *New York Times* 2 April 1978: 11.

——. "A Revised Version: *Spell #7.*" *New York Times* 16 July 1979: C12.

——. "Sovereign Spirit." *New York Times* 22 December 1977: C11.

——. "*Spell #7* by Ntozake Shange." *New York Times*, 16 July 1979. *New York Times Theatre Critics' Reviews* 40 (1979): 107-08.

Elliot, Jeffrey. "Ntozake Shange: Genesis of a Choreopoem." *Negro History Bulletin* 41 (January 1978): 797-800.

Ellison, Ralph. "King of the Bingo Game." *Dark Symphony: Negro Literature in America.* Eds. James A. Emanuel and Theodore L. Gross. New York: Free P, 1968. 271-79.

"*Essence* Main Events/ Theater: *Mother Courage and Her Children.*" *Essence* August 1980: 2.

"Ethnic Notions: Black People in White Minds." Marlon Riggs, producer/ director. San Francisco: California Newsreel, 1987 (videocassette).

Evans, Donald T. "Bring It All Back Home: Playwrights of the Fifties." *Black World* 20 (February 1971): 41-46.

Evans, Everett. "*Ridin' the Moon* Is Much Ado About Nothing." *Houston Chronicle* 11 April 1986, sec. 1: 19.

Evans, Mari. *I Am a Black Woman.* New York: Quill, 1970.

Fabre, Geneviève. *Drumbeats, Masks, and Metaphor: Contemporary Afro-American Theatre.* Melvin Dixon, translator. Cambridge: Harvard UP, 1983.

——. "Ntozake Shange." *Revue Francaise D'Etudes Americaines* 10 (1980): 259-70.

"Fact Sheet: *boogie woogie landscapes.*" John F. Kennedy Center for the Performing Arts. Washington, D.C.: Press Department, 1980.

Fadlman, William. "Shange Records the Agonies of Change." Rev. of *Betsey Brown*, by Ntozake Shange. In *Los Angeles Herald Examiner* 26 May 1985. *NewsBank* [microform], 1985, 124: A11, fiche.

Fanon, Frantz. *Black Skin, White Masks*. New York: Grove, 1967.

———. *A Dying Colonialism*. New York: Grove, 1967.

"Finding the Words to Tell Us, How Writers Develop Their Craft: A Lecture/ Conversation with Ntozake Shange." New York: Mid-Manhattan Library. 29 April 1991 (audiocassette).

Fitzgerald, Karen. "The Good Books: Writer's Choices." *Ms.* December 1985: 80-81.

Fitzgerald, Sheryl. "A Black Girl Learns to Cope." Rev. of *Betsey Brown*, by Ntozake Shange. *(Long Island) Newsday* 25 August 1985. *NewsBank* [microform], 1985, 27: D1, fiche.

Flowers, Sandra Hollin. "*Colored Girls*: Textbook for the Eighties" *Black American Literature Forum* 15 (1981): 51-54.

"*For Colored Girls* . . . Returns to Atlanta" Press Release from Alliance Theatre Company/ Atlanta Children's Theatre, 12 February 1981.

"*For Colored Girls Who Have Considered Suicide/ When the Rainbow Is Enuf*." Los Angeles: Pacifica Tape Library, 1978 (audiocassette).

"*For Colored Girls Who Have Considered Suicide/ When the Rainbow Is Enuf*." Production notes. *Dictionary of the Black Theatre: Broadway, Off-Broadway, and Selected Harlem Theatre*. Allen Woll. Westport, Connecticut: Greenwood, 1973. 65.

For Colored Guys Who Have Gone Beyond Suicide and Found No Rainbow: A Choreopoem/ Drama. Writers Club. (Jessup) Maryland House of Correction for Men, 1986.

"For Shange, Writing's Only Part of Her Life." *Houston Post* 26 May 1985. *NewsBank* [microform], 1985, 124: A9-10, fiche.

Fortune, Marie M. *Sexual Violence: The Unmentionable Sin*. New York: Pilgrim, 1983.

Franklin, J.E. *"Black Girl": From Genesis to Revelations*. Washington: Howard UP, 1977.

Fraser, C. Gerald. "Theater Finds an Incisive New Playwright."

New York Times 16 June 1976: L27.

Freeman, Jo, ed. *Women: A Feminist Perspective*. Palo Alto, California: Mayfield, 1975.

Freud, Sigmund. *Three Contributions to the Theory of Sex*. New York: E.P. Dutton, 1962.

"Future Subjunctive: Shange's New Song." *Horizon* 20 (September 1977): 70.

Gates, Henry Louis, Jr. "T.V.'s Black World Turns—But Stays Unreal." *Reading Culture: Contexts for Critical Reading and Writing*. Eds. Diana George and John Timbur. New York: HarperCollins, 1992. 463-70.

Gayle, Addison, Jr. *The Black Aesthetic*. Garden City, NY: Anchor, 1971.

Geis, Deborah R. "'Distraught Laughter': Monologue in Ntozake Shange's Theater Pieces." *Feminine Focus*. Ed. Enoch Brater. New York: Oxford UP, 1989.

Gelman, David. "Theater: This Time Shange Casts No Spell." *Newsweek* 30 July 1979: 65.

Gillespie, Patti P. "America's Women Dramatists, 1960-1980." *Essays on Contemporary American Drama*. Eds. Hedwig Bock and Albert Werthrim. West Germany: Max Hueber Verlag, 1981. 187-206.

Giovanni, Nikki. "Ego Tripping (There May Be a Reason Why)." *The Norton Anthology of Modern Poetry*. Eds. Richard Ellman and Robert O'Clair. New York: Norton, 1973.

——. *My House*. New York: William Morrow, 1972.

Glastonbury, Marion. "Of the Fathers." Rev. of *Betsey Brown*, by Ntozake Shange. *New Statesman* 110 (4 October 1985): 29.

Gomez, Jewelle. "*Belles Lettres* Interview: Ntozake Shange." *Belles Lettres: A Review of Books by Women* 1 (September-October 1985): 9-10.

Gordon, Alice. "Over the Rainbow." *Texas Monthly* 6 (January 1978): 96.

Gottfried, Martin. "*Rainbow* Over Broadway." *New York Post* 16 September 1976. *New York Theatre Critics' Reviews* 37 (1976): 201.

——. "Theater: Playmaking Is Not Enough." *Saturday Review* 5 (18 February 1978): 42.

Grahn, Judy. *The Common Woman.* Oakland, California: Women's P Collective, 1970.

Griffin, John. "*Colored Girls. . .* Succeeds." *(Lexington) Kentucky Kernel* 1981.

Griffin, Susan. "Rape: The All-American Crime." *Women: A Feminist Perspective.* Ed. Jo Freeman. Palo Alto, California: Mayfield, 1975.

Groome, Clark. "*Betsey Brown* Appealing but Needs Some Pruning." *Chestnut Hill Local* 6 April 1989: 54.

Guerro, Ed. *Framing Blackness: The African American Image in Film.* Philadelphia: Temple UP, 1993.

Gussow, Mel. "Stage: *Colored Girls* On Broadway." *New York Times* 16 September 1976. *New York Theatre Critics' Reviews* 37 (1976): 200.

———. "Stage: *Mother Courage/* Brecht in Old West." *New York Times* 14 May 1980. *New York Theatre Critics' Reviews* 4 (1980): 183.

———. "*Where the Mississippi Meets the Amazon.*" *New York Times* 20 December 1977: 44.

Hackley, Azalia. *The Colored Girl Beautiful.* Kansas City: Burton, 1916.

Hagedorn, Jessica Tarahata. *Dangerous Music.* San Francisco: Momo's, 1975.

———. Telephone interview. New York City, 27 August 1986.

Hall, Joan Joffe. "Good Poems, Bad Poems, Poems That Surprise." Rev. of *A Daughter's Geography*, by Ntozake Shange. *Houston Post* 9 October 1983.

Hansberry, Lorraine. "The Negro in the American Theatre." *American Playwrights on Drama.* Ed. Horst Frenz. New York: Hill and Wang, 1965. 160-67.

Hari. "*Betsey Brown.*" *Variety* 12-18 April 1989.

Harper, Michael S. "Three Poets." Rev. of *Nappy Edges*, by Ntozake Shange. *New York Times Book Review* 21 October 1979: 27.

Harris, Jessica B. "*For Colored Girls . . .* from Ntozake to Broadway" *New York Amsterdam News* 9 October 1976: D10-11.

———. "*For Colored Girls Who Have Considered Suicide/ When the Rainbow Is Enuf*—The Women Who Are the Rainbow." *Essence*

November 1976: 88-89, 102, 104, 112, 122, 147.

Harris, Katherine. "Life As Viewed by a 13-year-old Girl." Rev. of *Betsey Brown*, by Ntozake Shange. *Boston Herald* 2 June 1985. *NewsBank* [microform], 1985, 124: A12, fiche.

Haskins, James. *Black Theater in America*. New York: Thomas Y. Crowell, 1982.

Hay, Samuel A. "On Art, Propaganda and Revolution: Alain Locke and Black Drama." *Black World* 21 (April 1972): 8-14.

Hedgepeth, Chester M., Jr. *Twentieth-Century African-American Writers and Artists*. Chicago: American Library Association, 1991. 271-72.

Helene, Kathryn. "Black Confusion and Runaway Writing." *Welcomat* March 1989.

Heltzel, Ellen Emry. "Shange's Latest Novel Is Heart-tugging Vignette" Rev. of *Betsey Brown*, by Ntozake Shange. *(Portland) Oregonian* 5 August 1985. *NewsBank* [microform], 1985, 27: D2, fiche.

Hennessy, Joan. "News/ Daily Review/ *Educating Rita*: A Real Treat." *Clayton News Daily* 16 May 1983.

Hieronymus, Clara. "*For Colored Girls*: A Telling of Poems." *(Nashville) Tennessean* 11 September 1980: 38, 41.

Hiller, Terry. "The Poet as Professor: Still in Touch with the Unseen." *Fort Worth (Texas) Star-Telegram* 10 October 1982: 1, 8.

"A History of Racist Animation." Ray Atherton, producer. Wavelength Video, 1988 (videocassette).

Holloway, Karla F.C. *Moorings & Metaphors: Figures of Culture and Gender in Black Women's Literature*. New Brunswick: Rutgers UP, 1992.

Holy Bible: King James Version. Camden, New Jersey: Thomas Nelson, 1972.

Homer, Ronald A. "Combatting Racism on the Job." *Business Week Careers* November 1986: 55-56.

hooks, bell. *Ain't I a Woman: Black Women and Feminism*. Boston: South End, 1981.

———. *Feminist Theory: From Margin to Center*. Boston: South End, 1984.

———. "Straightening Our Hair." *Reading Culture: Contexts for*

Critical Reading and Writing. Eds. Diana George and John Trimbur. New York: HarperCollins, 1992. 290-99.

——. *Talking Back: Thinking Feminist, Thinking Black*. Boston: South End, 1989.

——. "'Whose Pussy Is This': A Feminist Comment." *Talking Back: Thinking Feminist, Thinking Black*. Boston: South End, 1989. 134-44.

Howard, Susan. "Feeling the Pain of Black Women: Ntozake Shange Again Puts Her Poetry on Stage." *New York Newsday* 5 March 1992: 55, 81.

Howe, Florence, and Ellen Bass, eds. *No More Masks!: An Anthology of Poems by Women*. Garden City, NY: Anchor/ Doubleday, 1973.

Howe, Joyce. "Talking Black." *Voice* 26 March 1985: 42.

Hughes, Catherine. "Theatre: Three New Musicals." *America* 135 (27 November 1976): 373.

——. "Theatre: Two Black Plays." *America* 135 (9 October 1976): 214.

Hughes, Langston. *Simply Heavenly (A Comedy)*. *Five Plays by Langston Hughes*. Ed. Webster Smalley. Bloomington: Indiana UP, 1963. 113-81.

——. *The Ways of White Folks*. New York: Vintage, 1990.

——. *Selected Poems of Langston Hughes*. New York: Alfred A. Knopf, 1959.

Hurston, Zora Neale. *The Sanctified Church: The Folklore Writings of Zora Neale Hurston*. Berkeley: Turtle Island, 1981.

——. *Their Eyes Were Watching God*. Chicago: U of Illinois P, 1978.

"Is the Pen Mightier Than the Ayatollah?" Donahue. Show #22489. Transcript #2629. 24 February 1989.

Isaacs, Edith J.R. *The Negro in the American Theater*. New York: Theater Arts, 1947.

"It's That Old Black Magic." *London Week* 19 April 1985.

Iverem, Esther. "Theater Black to Black: It May Not be 'High Art' but Plays Aimed at African-Americans Are Finding an Audience." *Birmingham News* 3 April 1994: F1, F3.

James, C.L.R. "Black Ink: On Toni Morrison, Alice Walker, and Ntozake Shange" *Cultural Correspondence*. Ed. Jim Murray.

New York: n.d. 22-25.

Jones, LeRoi. *Preface to a Twenty Volume Suicide Note . . .* New York: Totem P in Association with Corinth, 1961.

Jordan, June. *On Call: Political Essays.* Boston: South End, 1985.

——. "Second Thoughts of a Black Feminist" *Ms.* February 1977: 113-115.

——. "Shange Talks the Real Stuff." *The Dial* February 1982: 11-13.

"Just Shuffling Along: The Black Stereotype in Motion Pictures." Ray Atherton, producer. Wavelength Video, 1988 (video-cassette).

Kalem, T.E. "He Done Her Wrong." *Time Magazine* 14 June 1976: 74.

Keating, Douglas J. "The Birth of an R & B Musical: How Two Women Have Taken *Betsey Brown* from Book to Stage." *Philadelphia Inquirer* 26 March 1989: H1, H7.

Keller, Karl. "A Performing Playwright/ Poet Who Records the Pulse of a People" *Los Angeles Times* 29 July 1984. *NewsBank* [microform], 1984, 19: E12, fiche.

Keller, Krys. "Theater: *Colored Girls* Is Big Success." *Savannah Morning News* 31 January 1981.

Kendall, Tina. "*Spell #7/* Donmar Warehouse." *Spare Rib* May 1985.

Kennedy, Adrienne. *Funnyhouse of a Negro. In One Act.* Minneapolis: U of Minnesota P, 1988. 1-23.

——. *Lesson in Dead Language. In One Act.* Minneapolis: U of Minnesota P, 1988. 47-53.

Kent, Assunta. "The Rich Multiplicity of *Betsey Brown.*" *Journal of Dramatic Theory and Criticism* 7 (Fall 1992): 151-61.

Kerr, Walter. "From Brilliance to Bewilderment to a Blunder." *The New York Times* 13 June 1976: 1.

Keyssar, Helene. "Communities of Women in Drama: Pam Gems, Michelene Wandor, Ntozake Shange." *Feminist Theatre.* New York: Grove, 1985.

——. "Rites and Responsibilities: The Drama of Black American Women." *Feminine Focus: The New Women Playwrights.* Ed. Enoch Brater. Oxford: Oxford UP, 1989.

Kidd, Helen. "'. . . if it's a statistic, it's not a woman': a look at 'serious lessons learned' by Ntozake Shange." *Contemporary Poetry Meets Modern Theory.* Eds. Anthony Eastope and John O. Thompson. London: Harvester Wheatsheaf, 1991. 195-207.

Kissel, Howard. *"Mother Courage." Women's Wear Daily* 14 May 1980. *New York Theatre Critics' Reviews* 4 (1980): 185.

Kline, Betsey. *"Betsey Brown* Insights Outweigh Its Few Faults." *Kansas City Star* 30 June 1985. *NewsBank* [microform], 1985, 5: G8, fiche.

Kownacky, Michael. *"Betsey* Crowded, but Good." *(Philadelphia) Times* 4 April 1989: B5.

Kramer, Gloria Hayes. "American Music Theater Festival Premieres *Betsey Brown." (West Chester, Pennsylvania) Daily Local News* 3 April 1989: D5.

Kroll, Jack. "Women's Rites." *Newsweek* 14 June 1976: 99.

Kuel, Patty Joan Farris. "Remembering the Goddess Within: The Functioning of Fairy Tale and Mythic Motifs in the Novels of Hurston, Walker, Morrison and Shange." Diss. U of Tulsa, 1991.

"Ladies of the Rainbow." Press Release from Alliance Theatre Company/ Atlanta Children's Theatre, 1981.

Lakoff, Robin T. *Face Value: The Politics of Beauty.* Boston: Routledge and Kegan Paul, 1984.

——. *Language and Woman's Place.* New York: Octagon, 1976.

Lardner, James. "The Great Black Hope." *Washington Post* 15 June 1985: G1, G5.

Latour, Martine. "Ntozake Shange: Driven Poet/ Playwright." *Madmoiselle* September 1976: 182, 226.

Lee, Carmen. Rev. of *Betsey Brown,* by Ntozake Shange. *Shooting Star: Black Literary Magazine* (Autumn 1988): 38.

Lee, Catherine Carr. "Ntozake Shange." *Contemporary Authors, Bibliographical Series: American Dramatists.* Detroit: Gale, 1989. 305-24.

Lee, Felicia. "Ntozake Shange Goes Beyond the Rainbow." Rev. of *Betsey Brown,* by Ntozake Shange. *USA Today* 4 June 1985: D6.

Lee, Spike. *Spike Lee's Gotta Have It: Inside Guerrilla Filmmaking.* New York: Fireside, 1987.

Lee, Wayne. "A Sense of Wonder at the Creative Essence: Interview" *Washington Times* n.d.

LeSeur, Greta. "From Nice Colored Girl to Womanist: An Exploration of Development in Ntozake Shange's Writings." *Language
and Literature in the African American Imagination*. Eds. Belay
Blackshire and Aisha Carol. Westport, CT: Greenwood, 1992.
167-80.

Lester, Neal A. "African American Renderings of Traditional
Texts." *Global Perspectives on Teaching Literature: Shared
Visions and Distinctive Visions*. Ed. Sandra Ward Lott, et. al.
Urbana: NCTE, 1993. 239-53.

———. "At the Heart of Shange's Feminism: An Interview." *Black
American Literature Forum* 24 (Winter 1990): 717-30.

———. "An Interview with Ntozake Shange." *Studies in American
Drama, 1945-Present* 5 (1990): 42-66.

———. Personal Interview with Ntozake Shange. Houston, Texas.
August 1986. Unpublished.

———. "Shange's Men: *for colored girls* Revisited, and Movement
Beyond." *African American Review* 26 (Summer 1992): 319-28.

Levin, Tobe, and Gwendolyn Flowers. "Black Feminism in *For
Colored Girls Who Have Considered Suicide When the Rainbow
Is Enuf*." *History and Tradition in Afro-American Culture*. Ed.
Gunter H. Lenz. Frankfurt: Campus, 1984.

Levine, Jo Ann. "'Bein' a Woman, Bein' Colored': A Black Artist
Looks At Her New Success." *Christian Science Monitor* 9
September 1976: 23.

Levine, Josie. Rev. of *for colored girls who have considered suicide/
when the rainbow is enuf*, by Ntozake Shange. *School Librarian*
27 (March 1979): 83.

Levine, Lawrence W. *Black Culture and Black Consciousness: Afro-
American Folk Thought from Slavery to Freedom*. New York:
Oxford UP, 1977.

Lewis, Barbara. "*for colored girls who have considered suicide/
when the rainbow is enuf*: The Poet." *Essence* November 1976:
86, 119-120, 122, 147.

Lewis, Claude. "Too Many Blacks Don't Speak English Correctly."
Birmingham News 30 June 1989: A9.

Lindsey, Kay. "The Black Woman as Woman." *The Black Woman:
An Anthology*. Ed. Toni Cade Bambara. New York: Mentor/
Penguin, 1970. 85-89.

Loney, Glenn. "Other Stages." *After Dark* 10 (April 1978): 80.

Lorando, Mark. "Hope of More and Better Balanced Black Representation on TV Fades." *Birmingham News/ Birmingham Post-Herald* 4 June 1994: B4

Low, Denise. "Poet Maps Women's Anguish, Joys." Rev. of *A Daughter's Geography*, by Ntozake Shange. *Kansas City Star* 23 October 1983. *NewsBank* [microform], 1983, 39: G11, fiche.

Lyles, Charlise L. "Black Women's Bard." *(Norfolk) Virginian-Pilot* 3 October 1986. *NewsBank* [microform], 196, 39: E12-13, fiche.

Lyons, Brenda. "Interview with Ntozake Shange." *Massachusetts Review* 28 (Winter 1987): 687-96.

Mackenzie, Suzie. "*Spell Number 7* (Donmar Warehouse)." *Time Out* (April 1985).

Major, Clarence, ed. *Juba to Jive: A Dictionary of African-American Slang*. New York: Penguin, 1994.

Malcolm X. *The Autobiography of Malcolm X (as Told to Alex Haley)*. New York: Ballantine, 1964.

Malveaux, Julianne. "Political and Historical Aspects of Black Male/ Female Relationships/ The Sexual Politics of Black People: Angry Black Women, Angry Black Men." *Black Scholar* 10 (May-June 1979): 32-35.

Mapplethorpe, Robert. *Black Book*. Foreword by Ntozake Shange. New York: St. Martin's, 1986.

Martin, Judith. "A Scattered *Landscape*." *Washington Post* 27 June 1980.

Martin, Reginald. *Ntozake Shange's First Novel: In the Beginning Was the Word*. Fredericksburg: Mary Washington C, 1984.

Maupin, Elizabeth. "Shifting Views Skew Shange's *Betsey*." *St. Paul (Minnesota) Pioneer Press* 29 June 1985. *NewsBank* [microform], 1985, 5: G7, fiche.

McCauley, Robbie. Personal letter. 27 August 1986.

McCulley, Cecil. "A Play that Sings One's Possibilities." *William and Mary News* 10 February 1981.

McGrath, Sandra. "Black Is Not Quite White For Oz Scott." *(Sydney) Australian* 13 March 1978: 7.

McIntyre, Dianne. Personal letter. 11 June 1991.

McKenley, Jan, and Suzanne Scafe. "Theatre: Cooling Out."

(London) *City Limits* 29 March 1985.

McLellan, Joseph. "Bungled *boogie*: Ntozake Shange's Lower-Case Editorials." *Washington Post* 20 June 1980: C6.

Miles, Jack. Rev. of *Ridin' the Moon in Texas: Word Paintings*, by Ntozake Shange. *Los Angeles Times Book Review* 19 July 1987: 6.

Miller, Cristanne. Rev. of *Black Women Writers (1950-1980): A Critical Evaluation*, by Mari Evans. *Library Journal* 109 (August 1984): 1450.

Miller, E. Ethelbert. "For Zaki—Who Dances the Bomba." *New Directions: The Howard University Magazine* April 1980: 29-31.

Miller, Jeanne-Marie A. "Black Women Playwrights from Grimke to Shange: Selected Synopses of Their Works." *All the Women Are White, All the Blacks Are Men, But Some of Us Are Brave: Black Women's Studies*. Ed. Gloria T. Hull, et. al. Old Westbury, New York: Feminist, 1982. 280-96.

———. "Images of Black Women in Plays by Black Playwrights." *CLA Journal* 15 (September 1971): 494-507.

———. "Ntozake Shange." *Dictionary of the Black Theater: Broadway, Off-Broadway, and Selected Harlem Theater*. Ed. Allen Woll. Westport, CT: Greenwood, 1983. 248-50.

———. "Three Theatre Pieces by Ntozake Shange." *Theatre News* 14 (April 1982): 8.

Miller, Lynn F. Rev. of *for colored girls who have considered suicide/ when the rainbow is enuf*, by Ntozake Shange. In *Educational Theatre Journal* 29 (May 1977): 262-63.

Milner, Ron. "Black Theater—Go Home!" *The Black Aesthetic*. Ed. Addison Gayle, Jr. Garden City, NY: Anchor, 1971. 288-94.

Mitchell, Carolyn. "'A Laying on of Hands': Transcending the City in Ntozake Shange's *for colored girls who have considered suicide/ when the rainbow is enuf*." *Women Writers and the City: Essays in Feminist Literary Criticism*. Ed. Susan Merrill Squier. Knoxville: U of Tennessee P, 1984. 230-48.

Mitchell, Kendall. "Past, Present, Future Explored by Novelists In Three Uneven Works." Rev. of *Betsey Brown*, by Ntozake Shange. *Chicago Tribune* 8 September 1985. *NewsBank* [microform], 1985, 27: C14, fiche.

"Mo' Funny: Black Comedy in America." Yvonne Smith, producer.

Home Box Office, 1992 (videocassette).

Molette, Barbara. "They Speak: Who Listens? Black Women Playwrights" *Black World* 25 (April 1976): 28-34.

Monroe, Sylvester. "Brothers." *Newsweek* 23 March 1987: 54-86.

Morris, William, ed. *The American Heritage Dictionary of the English Language.* Boston: Houghton-Mifflin, 1978.

Morrison, Toni. *The Bluest Eye.* New York: Washington Square, 1970.

Morse, Pamela. "*For Colored Girls* Tells Tales of Love, Laughter and Pain." *Birmingham News* 29 September 1989: D6.

Mort, Mary Ellen. Rev. of *Sassafrass, Cypress & Indigo,* by Ntozake Shange. *Library Journal* (August 1982): 1484.

——. Rev. of *See No Evil: Prefaces, Essays & Accounts, 1976-1983,* by Ntozake Shange. *Library Journal* 109 (August 1984): 1451.

Murdin, Lynda. "The Colors of Bitterness" *The Standard* April 1985.

Murray, Timothy. "Screening the Camera's Eye: Black and White Confrontations of Technological Representation." *Modern Drama* 28 (March 1985): 110-24.

Myles, Eileen. "The Art of the Real." Rev. of *The Love Space Demand (A Continuing Saga),* by Ntozake Shange. *(Village) Voice Literary Supplement* September 1991: 13.

Nankoe, Lucia and Essa Reijmers. "Identiteit van zwarte vrouwen in romans." *Forum der Letteren: Tijdschrift voor Taal en Letterkunde* 29 (September 1988): 179-91.

Nathan, Hans. *Dan Emmett and the Rise of Early Negro Minstrelsy.* Norman, OK: U of Oklahoma P, 1962.

Nelsen, Don. "Shange Casts a Powerful *Spell.*" (New York) *Daily News* 16 July 1979. *New York Theatre Critics' Reviews* 40 (1979): 108.

Njeri, Itaberi. "People Use Stereotypes in the Absence of Real Understanding." *Birmingham News* 10 June 1988: A9.

Noel, H. Maria. "Ntozake Shange Writes Characters, Not Messages." *Chattanooga Times* 4 April 1987: B1-B2.

Norman, Diane. "*For Colored Girls* . . . Is Painful but Powerful." *Beaufort Gazette* 5 March 1981.

"Ntozake Shange." *Current Biography.* New York: H.W. Wilson,

1978. 380-83.

"Ntozake Shange." *Dictionary of Literary Biography. Afro-American Writers after 1955, Dramatists and Prose Writers.* Detroit: Gale, 1985.

"Ntozake Shange." *New Yorker* 2 August 1976: 17-19.

"Ntozake Shange Adapts Comedy at the Alliance/ *Educating Rita.*" Press Release from Alliance Theatre Company/ Atlanta Children's Theatre to *Atlanta Daily World* 28 April 1983.

"Ntozake Shange Adapts Willie Russell's *Educating Rita*: World Premiere in the Alliance Studio Theatre." Press Release from Alliance Theatre Company/ Atlanta Children's Theatre, 14 April 1983.

"Ntozake Shange: *for colored girls who have considered suicide/ when the rainbow is enuf.*" Los Angeles: Pacifica Tape Library, 1978 (audiocassette).

"Ntozake Shange Interviews Herself." *Ms.* December 1977: 35, 70, 72.

"Ntozake Shange on *Mule Bone (A Comedy of Negro Life)*, by Langston Hughes and Zora Neale Hurston." *The New Theater Review (A Lincoln Center Theater Publication).* New York City, 1991.

"Ntozake Shange: Playwright." *Ebony* August 1977: 136.

"Ntozake Shange: *Sassafrass, Cypress & Indigo.*" Interview by Ginny Z. Berson and Pam Scola. Los Angeles: Pacifica Tape Library, 1983 (audiocassette).

"Ntozake Shange Talks with Angela Davis" San Francisco State University: American Poetry Archives, 5 May 1989 (video-cassette).

"Ntozake Shange Talks with Marcia Ann Gillespie." *Essence* May 1985: 122-24, 203, 205.

"Ntozake Shange: This Side of the Rainbow" Press Release from Alliance Theatre Company/ Atlanta Children's Theatre, 1981.

"Ntozake Shange with Syllable: Live at the Victoria Theater, San Francisco." San Francisco State University: American Poetry Archives, Spring 1989 (videocassette).

"Ntozake Shange: Working Woman's 'Woman of the Week'." Working Woman. Show #35. Fran Murphy, producer. Washington: Allbritton Television Productions, 12 December 1991 (videocassette).

O'Connor, Mary. "Subject, Voice, and Women in Some Contemporary Black American Women's Writing." *Feminism, Bakhtin, and the Dialogic.* Eds. Dale M. Bauer and Susan Jaret McKinstry. Albany: State U of New York P, 1991. 199-217.

O'Conner, Patricia T. "New & Noteworthy: *Betsey Brown* by Ntozake Shange." *New York Times Book Review* 6 April 1986: 38.

Oetter, Joana. "Black Girl's St. Louis Blues." Rev. of *Betsey Brown*, by Ntozake Shange. *St. Louis Post-Dispatch* 16 June 1985. *NewsBank* [microform], 1985, 5: G9-10, fiche.

Oliver, Edith. "The Theatre/ Off Broadway: *A Photograph* and *Where the Mississippi Meets the Amazon.*" *New Yorker* 2 January 1978: 48-49.

——. "The Theatre/ Off Broadway: *For Colored Girls Who Have Considered Suicide/ When The Rainbow Is Enuf.*" *New Yorker* 14 June 1976: 77-78.

——. "The Theatre/ Off Broadway: *Mother Courage.*" *New Yorker* 26 May 1980: 77.

——. "The Theatre/ Off Broadway: *Spell #7.*" *New Yorker* 9 July 1979: 73.

O'Neill, Eugene. *Long Day's Journey into Night.* New Haven: Yale UP, 1955.

Orth, Kevin. "Shange's Latest Touching." Rev. of *Betsey Brown*, by Ntozake Shange. *Columbus (Ohio) Dispatch* 5 May 1985. *NewsBank* [microform], 1985, 124: A14, fiche.

Ostriker, Alicia. "American Poetry, Now Shaped by Women." *New York Times Book Review* 9 March 1986: 1, 28, 30.

Osumare, Halifu. "Ntozake Shange: Choreopoet" *Arts* April 1981.

Palmer, Trudy Christine. "'As Steady and Clean as Rain': The Function of Artistic Vision in Contemporary Afro-American Women's Fiction." Diss. Stanford U, 1991.

Pawley, Thomas D. "The Black Theatre Audience." *Players* 46 (August-September 1971): 257-61.

Peavy, Charles D. "Satire and Contemporary Black Drama." *Satire Newsletter* 7 (Fall 1969): 40-49.

"Performance Probes Heart of Women." *Beaufort Gazette* 3 March 1981: A9.

Peters, Erskine. "Some Tragic Propensities of Ourselves: The Occasion of Ntozake Shange's *For Colored Girls Who Have Considered Suicide/ When the Rainbow Is Enuf.*" *Journal of Ethnic Studies* 6 (Spring 1978): 79-85.

Peterson, Maurice. "On the Aisle/ Theater: *For Colored Girls Who Have Considered Suicide/ When the Rainbow Is Enuf.*" *Essence* October 1976: 48.

Phillips, Deborah C. "Ntozake Shange: Basement Workshop." *Art News* May 1982: 163.

Pinkney, Mikell. "Theatrical Expressionism in the Structure and Language of Ntozake Shange's *Spell #7.*" *Theatre Studies* 37 (1992): 5-15.

"Play Radiates with Themes of Hope, Pride." *Augusta Chronicle/ Augusta Herald* 27 January 1981: B1, B3.

"Presenting Ntozake Shange." Program Corporation of America, 599 West Hartsdale Avenue, White Plains, New York 10607, n.d.

Prettyman, Quandra. "Photograph (For L. Mel.)." *The Poetry of Black America: Anthology of the Twentieth Century.* Ed. Arnold Adoff. New York: HarperCollins, 1973.

Probst, Leonard. "*For Colored Girls Who Have Considered Suicide/ When the Rainbow Is Enuf.*" Unidentified radio station 15 September 1976. In *New York Theatre Critics' Reviews* 37 (1976): 202.

"A Question of Color." Kathe Sadler, producer. San Francisco: California Newsreel, 1992 (videocassette).

Radic, Leonard. "Adelaide Festival: Look Back in Feminist Anger at White America" *The Age* 1 March 1978.

———. "A Woman's Cry that All Can Hear." *The Age* 6 March 1978.

Ramsey, Sheila. "It's All Relative." Rev. of *Betsey Brown*, by Ntozake Shange. *Dayton (Ohio) Daily News* 16 June 1985.

Rankin, Edwina. "Much of Poet Ntozake Shange Is in *Betsey Brown.*" *Pittsburgh Press* 7 July 1985.

Reed, Ishmael. *Conjure: Selected Poems, 1963-1970.* Amherst: U of Massachusetts P, 1972.

———. *Yellow Back Radio Broke Down.* Chatham, New Jersey: Chatham Bookseller, 1969.

"Relationships Turned into a Rainbow." *Birmingham News* 17 November 1991: F6.

Rev. of *Betsey Brown*, by Ntozake Shange. *Essence* June 1985: 36.

Rev. of *Betsey Brown*, by Ntozake Shange. *Jet* 4 November 1985: 62.

Rev. of *A Daughter's Geography*, by Ntozake Shange. *Choice* 21 (January 1984): 708.

Rev. of *A Daughter's Geography*, by Ntozake Shange. *Ebony* November 1983: 26.

Rev. of *Educating Rita*, adaptation by Ntozake Shange. *Variety* 311 (15 June 1983): 76.

Rev. of *for colored girls who have considered suicide/ when the rainbow is enuf*, by Ntozake Shange. *Booklist* 73 (15 November 1976): 451.

Rev. of *for colored girls who have considered suicide/ when the rainbow is enuf*, by Ntozake Shange. *Choice* 14 (November 1977): 1216.

Rev. of *for colored girls who have considered suicide/ when the rainbow is enuf*, by Ntozake Shange. *Kirkus Reviews* 45 (1 April 1977): 1300.

Rev. of *for colored girls who have considered suicide/ when the rainbow is enuf*, by Ntozake Shange. *Nation* 222 (1 May 1976): 542.

Rev. of *Nappy Edges*, by Ntozake Shange. *Booklist* 75 (October 1978): 271-72.

Rev. of *Nappy Edges*, by Ntozake Shange. *Kirkus Reviews* 46 (15 October 1978): 1129-130.

Rev. of *Nappy Edges*, by Ntozake Shange. *School Library Journal* 25 (May 1979): 37.

Rev. of *Sassafrass*, by Ntozake Shange. *Booklist* 73 (15 November 1976): 451.

Rev. of *Sassafrass, Cypress & Indigo*, by Ntozake Shange. *Daedalus Books/ Literature and General Interest* n.d.: 21.

Rev. of *Sassafrass, Cypress & Indigo*, by Ntozake Shange. *Ebony* September 1982: 26.

Rev. of *Sassafrass, Cypress & Indigo*, by Ntozake Shange. *Publishers Weekly* 221 (25 June 1982): 104.

Rev. of *Sassafrass, Cypress & Indigo*, by Ntozake Shange. *Wilson*

Library Bulletin September 1982: 80-81.

Rev. of *See No Evil: Prefaces, Essays & Accounts, 1976-1983*, by Ntozake Shange. *Publishers Weekly* 225 (16 March 1984): 81.

Rhodes, Don. "Drama: Play Radiates with Themes of Hope, Pride." *Augusta (Georgia) Chronicle/ Augusta Herald* 27 January 1981: B1, B3.

Ribowsky, Mark. "A Poetess Scores a Hit with Play on 'What's Wrong with Black Men.'" *Sepia* 25 (December 1976): 42-46.

Rich, Adrienne. *Of Woman Born: Motherhood as Experience and Institution.* New York: Norton, 1976.

Rich, Alan. "Theater: For Audiences of Any Color When *Rex* Is Not Enuf." *New York* 14 June 1976: 62.

Rich, Frank. "Stage View: *Mother Courage* Transplanted." *New York Times* 15 June 1980: D5, D33.

Richards, Beah. *A Black Woman Speaks. Nine Plays by Black Women.* Ed. Margaret B. Wilkerson. New York: Mentor, 1986. 27-39.

Richards, Sandra L. "Conflicting Impulses in the Plays of Ntozake Shange" *Black American Literature Forum* 17 (Summer 1983): 73-78.

———. "Ntozake Shange." *Contemporary Dramatists.* New York: St. Martin's, 1977. 711-713.

"A Rising Star Illuminates Theatre in Atlanta/ *Educating Rita.*" Press Release from Alliance Theatre Company/ Atlanta Children's Theatre to *Atlanta Daily World* 27 April 1983.

Rodgers, Curtis E. "Black Men View *For Colored Girls/* Good Theatre but Poor Sociological Statement." *New York Amsterdam News* 9 October 1976: D11.

Rosenberg, Karen. "Ntozake Shange: She's Striving to Create Messages from beyond the Rainbow." *Boston Globe* n.d.

Rushing, Andrea Benton. "For Colored Girls, Suicide or Struggle?" *Massachusetts Review* 22 (Autumn 1981): 539-50.

Russell, Kathy, et. al. *The Color Complex: The Politics of Skin Color Among African Americans.* New York: Doubleday, 1992.

"Saint Louis Novel about 1950's Desegregation: *Betsey Brown.*" National Public Radio. *Morning Edition* 26 September 1985 (audiocassette).

Salaam, Kalamu ya. "Making the Image Real: Black Producers of

Theater, Film and Television." *Black Collegian* 7 (March-April 1977): 56-58.

Sandburg-Wright, Mercy. "Theatre: *Educating Rita.*" *Creative Loafing* 28 May 1983: A28.

Sanders, Kevin. *"For Colored Girls Who Have Considered Suicide/ When the Rainbow Is Enuf."* WABC-TV 7, 19 September 1976. *New York Theatre Critics Reviews* 37 (1976): 202.

Saunders, Barry. *"Colored Girls'* Villains Humanized by Director." *Atlanta Constitution* 12 March 1981: B6.

Schindehette, Susan. Rev. of *Betsey Brown*, by Ntozake Shange. *Saturday Review* 11 (11 June 1985): 74-75.

Schroeder, Scott. *"For Colored Girls* Celebrates Equality at PBK." *Flat Hat* (Student Newspaper at William and Mary College) 20 February 1981: 11.

Scott, Vernon. "Feminist Sees Progress for Women." *(Nashville) Tennessean* 10 November 1985: E12.

"Shange to Write for Festival." *Houston Chronicle* 11 October 1985, sec. 6: 10.

Shange, Ntozake. Arts and Education Council/ Conference on Southern Literature. U of Tennessee at Chattanooga. 4 April 1987 (audiocassette).

———. "aw, babee, you so pretty." *Essence* April 1979: 87, 145-46.

———. "Beneath the Necessity of Talking: A Performance Piece." With John Purcell and Jean-Paul Bourelly. Columbia, MO: American Audio Prose Library, 1989 (audiocassette).

———. *Betsey Brown.* New York: St. Martin's, 1985.

———. *Between the two of them: a painted poem.* New York: Denneny-Shange Publications, 1983.

———. *Black & White Two Dimensional Planes: A Choreopoem.* Unpublished manuscript. New York City, 1981.

———. "Christmas for Sassafrass, Cypress and Indigo." Rprt. *Essence* December 1982: 68-70, 116-17, 120-21.

———. "Coming to Terms." *Erotique Noire: Black Erotica.* Ed. Miriam DeCosta-Willis, et. al. New York: Doubleday, 1992. 335-38.

———. Conference on Common Differences: Third World Women. U of Illinois at Champaign, April 1983 (audiocassette).

———. *Curriculum Vitae.* January 1985 (personal file).

———. *Daddy Says: A Play. New Plays for the Black Theatre.* Ed. Woodie King, Jr. Chicago: Third World, 1989.

———. *A Daughter's Geography.* New York: St. Martin's, 1983.

———. *Educating Rita: A Play in Two Acts by Willy Russell, Adaptation.* Unpublished manuscript. New York, 3 November 1982.

———. *for colored girls who have considered suicide/ when the rainbow is enuf.* Public Broadcasting Service. American Playhouse. 14 June 1983 (videocassette).

———. "*For Colored Girls Who Have Considered Suicide/ When the Rainbow Is Enuf.*" *TV Guide* 20 February 1982: 14-15.

———. *For Colored Girls Who Have Considered Suicide/ When the Rainbow Is Enuf: A Screenplay.* Unpublished manuscript/ shooting script. New York City, 1 May 1981.

———. *For Colored Girls Who Have Considered Suicide/ When the Rainbow Is Enuf,* Original Broadway Cast Recording. New York Shakespeare Festival. Buddah Records, BDS95007-OC, 1976.

———. "Fore/ Play." *Erotique Noire: Black Erotica.* Ed. Miriam DeCosta-Willis, et. al. New York: Doubleday, 1992. xix-xx.

———. *From Okra to Greens/ A Different Kinda Love Story: A Play/ With Music and Dance.* Videorecording of play rehearsal at the U of Mississippi (from Ntozake Shange's personal collection), n.d.

———. *from okra to greens: poems.* St. Paul: Coffee House, 1984.

———. "However You Come to Me." *Wild Women Don't Wear No Blues: Black Women Writers on Love, Men and Sex.* Ed. Marita Golden. New York: Doubleday, 1993. 203-11.

———. "I Live in Music." Washington: Watershed Tapes, 1984 (audiocassette).

———. "Interview with Toni Morrison." *American Rag* (Winter 1978): 48-52.

———. *It Has Not Always Been This Way: A Choreopoem.* Unpublished manuscript. New York, June 1981.

———. *It Has Not Always Been This Way: A Choreopoem. Yellow Silk: Journal of Erotic Arts.* Issue 2 (Winter 1982): 12-13.

———. *La Luta Continua* (excerpt from novel-in-progress). Columbia, MO: American Audio Prose Library, 1989 (audiocassette).

———. Letter to Dr. Hill. University of Houston (Texas). 16 April 1985. Unpublished.

————. *Liliane*. Unpublished notes on novel-in-progress. Houston, August 1986.

————. *The Love Space Demands (A Continuing Saga)*. New York: St. Martin's, 1991.

————. *melissa & smith*. St. Paul: Bookslinger Editions, 1976.

————. *Mother Courage and Her Children*. Production details. John Willis. *Theatre World* 36 (1979-80): 150.

————. *Mother Courage and Her Children, Adapation*. Unpublished manuscript. New York, December 1979.

————. *Mouths: A Daughter's Geography/ A Performance Piece*. Unpublished manuscript. New York, April 1981.

————. *Nappy Edges*. Great Britain: Methuen, 1987.

————. "oh she gotta head fulla hair." *Black Scholar* 10 (November-December 1978): 13-14.

————. "People of Watts (a poem)." *Vibe* 1 (November 1993): 79.

————. *A Photograph: A Still Life with Shadows/ A Photograph: A Study of Cruelty: A Play*. Unpublished manuscript. New York, (Revised) 14 December 1977.

————. *A Photograph: Lovers in Motion*. New York: Samuel French, 1981.

————. *Ridin' the Moon in Texas: A Performance Piece*. Unpublished manuscript. Houston, 1 May 1986.

————. *Ridin' the Moon in Texas: Word Paintings*. New York: St. Martin's, 1987.

————. "Sassafrass." *Ms.* August 1976: 82-85, 90-93.

————. *Sassafrass*. San Lorenzo, California: Shameless Hussy, 1976.

————. *Sassafrass, Cypress & Indigo*. New York: St. Martin's, 1982.

————. "Serial Monogamy." Performance with Billy "Spaceman" Patterson. New York: WNYC-TV. December 1989 (video-cassette).

————. *Some Men*. New York, May 1981.

————. *She Who Comes from Herself*. Ames, Iowa: Iowa State U. Women's Week, 8 October 1984 (audiocassette).

————. "Tócame." *Erotique Noire: Black Erotica*. Ed. Miriam DeCosta-Willis, et. al. New York: Doubleday, 1992. 176-79.

————. *Triptych and Bocas/ A Performance Piece*. Unpublished manuscript. Los Angeles, 22 February 1982.

————. *Three Views of Mt. Fugi: A Play*. Unpublished manuscript.

Houston, 1987.

——. "Who Says Black Folks Could Sing and Dance?" *Dance Magazine* 57 (August 1983): 78-80.

——. *Word-paintings: Poetry & Prose.* Unpublished manuscript. Houston, 26 March 1986.

——, writing as Paulette Williams. Poems. *Phat Mama: Her Black Mind* New York 1.1 (March 1970): 1-8.

Shange, Ntozake, and Jessica Tarahata Hagedorn. "A Mouth That Speaks: A Poetry Gathering." U of California Extension Media Center Distribution by Poets' Audio Center, 1974 (audiocassette).

——. *where the mississippi meets the amazon and other poems.* Unpublished manuscript. (New version) 5 May 1978.

Shange, Ntozake, in Collaboration with Diane McIntyre. *And How Shall We Know Him/ Is This the Prince?: A Choreopoem.* Unpublished manuscript. New York, January 1982.

Shange, Ntozake, Thulani (Davis) Nkabinde, and Jessica Hagedorn. *where the mississippi meets the amazon and other poems.* Unpublished manuscript. New York, (Version A/ Revised) 6 December 1977.

Sharp, Christopher. "*Spell #7*: A Geechee Quik Magic Trance Manual" *Women's Wear Daily* 4 June 1979. *New York Theatre Critics' Reviews* 40 (1979): 109.

Sherbert, Linda. "Theater Review: *Rita* Is Warm, Comic Collision with Success" *Atlanta Journal/ Atlanta Constitution* 13 May 1983.

Shinn, Thelma J. "Living the Answer: The Emergence of African American Feminist Drama." *Studies in the Humanities* 17 (December 1990): 149-59.

Shorter, Eric. "At Sea with Racial Satire" *(London) Daily Telegraph* 3 April 1985.

"Show Business: Welcome to the Great Black Way!" *Time* 1 November 1976: 72, 75.

"Shows Vivid Colour Theme." *(Sydney, Australia) Sun Herald* 5 March 1978.

Shulson, John. "*For Colored Girls*: Provocative, Faultless." *(Newport News, Virginia) Daily Press* 16 February 1981.

Simon, John. "Fainting Spell." *New York Magazine* 30 July 1979:

57.

——. "On Stage: *Enuf* is Not Enough." *New Leader* 59 (5 July 1976): 21.

——. "Theater: Avaunt-Garde and 'Taint Your Wagon,'" *New York* 26 May 1980: 79-81.

——. "Theater: A Touch Is Better Than None." *New York* 16 January 1978: 57-58.

"Six Women Playwrights: Honor Moore, Ruth Wolf, Alice Childress, Tina Howe, Corrine Jackson, and Myrna Lamb." Los Angeles: Pacifica Tape Library, n.d. (audiocassette).

"A Slim Volume Full of Insight." Rev. of *See No Evil: Prefaces, Essays & Accounts, 1976-1983*, by Ntozake Shange. *San Francisco Chronicle* 28 June 1984. *NewsBank* [microform], 1984, 19: E13, fiche.

Smith, Barbara. "Toward a Black Feminist Criticism." *All the Women Are White, All the Blacks Are Men, But Some of Us Are Brave: Black Women's Studies*. Ed. Gloria T. Hull, et. al. Old Westbury, New York: Feminist, 1982. 157-175.

Smith, Helen C. "*Colored Girls* Shines As Brightly as a Rainbow." *Atlanta Journal and Atlanta Constitution* 13 March 1981: B1, B11.

——. "*Rita* Adapts to Life in the States." *Atlanta Journal/ Atlanta Constitution* n.d.: H3-H4.

Smith, Yvonne. "Ntozake Shange: A 'Colored Girl' Considers Success." *Essence* February 1982: 12, 14.

Smitherman, Geneva. *Talkin and Testifyin: The Language of Black America*. Boston: Houghton Mifflin, 1977.

Southern Register: The Newsletter of the Study of Southern Culture. U of Mississippi 3 (Spring-Summer 1985): 1-11.

"Spell Bound!" *(London) Voice* 6 April 1985.

"*Spell No. 7.*" *Camden News* 2 May 1985.

"*Spell #7.*" Production notes. *Dictionary of the Black Theatre: Broadway, Off-Broadway and Selected Harlem Theatre*. Allen Woll. Westport, CT: Greenwood, 1973. 157.

Spillers, Hortense J. "Black/ Female/ Critic." *Women's Review of Books* September 1985: 9-10.

——. "Kinship and Resemblances: Women On Women." *Feminist Studies* Spring 1985: 111-25.

Splawn, P. Jane. "Rites of Passage in the Writing of Ntozake Shange: The Poetry, Drama, and Novels." *DAI* 50 (1989): 687A.

Squire, Rosemary. "*Spell* Bound!" *The Voice* 6 April 1985.

"Stanley Kauffman on Theater: *For Colored Girls Who Have Considered Suicide/ When the Rainbow Is Enuf.*" *New Republic* 175 (10 July 1976): 20-21.

Staples, Robert. "The Myth of Black Macho: A Response to Angry Black Feminists." *Black Scholar* 10 (March-April 1979): 24-33.

Stasio, Marilyn. "Shange Casts a Mixed *Spell.*" *New York Theatre Critics' Reviews* 40 (1979): 108-09.

———. "Tell It, Sisters!" *Cue* 26 June 1976.

Statistical Abstract of the United States. Washington, D.C.: Bureau of the Census, 1978.

Stearns, David Patrick. "On Stage: *Brown* Takes a Frank Look at Black-on-Black Racism." *USA Today* 6 April 1989.

Steinberg, Sybil. Rev. of *Betsey Brown*, by Ntozake Shange. *Publishers Weekly* 227 (22 March 1985): 53.

Stewart, Judith. "Growing Up Black in the Tumult." Rev. of *Betsey Brown*, by Ntozake Shange. *Grand Rapids (Michigan) Press* 2 June 1985. *NewsBank* [microform], 1985, 124: A13, fiche.

Stone, Elizabeth. "This Colored Girl Considers Digging It." *Village Voice* 4 October 1976: 133-134.

Strandness, Jean. "Reclaiming Women's Language, Imagery, and Experience: Ntozake Shange's *Sassafrass, Cypress & Indigo.*" *Journal of American Culture* 10 (Fall 1987): 11-17.

Struthers, Ann. "'Hollar!' she says 'Holllar!'" Rev. of *A Daughter's Geography*, by Ntozake Shange. *Des Moines Register* 7 October 1984: F11-F12.

Stuart, Andrea. "We Are Feeding Our Children the Sun: Talking with Ntozake Shange." *Spare Rib* no. 178 (May 1987): 14-17.

"Studio Theatre Premieres American Adaptation of British Award-Winning Drama." *Alliance Theatre News* March 1983.

Sullivan, Dan. "'Colored Girls': They Can Cope." *Los Angeles Times* 14 July 1978: 1, 25.

———. "At Huntington Hartford/ 'Colored Girls': They Can Cope." *Los Angeles Times* 14 July 1978: 1, 25.

Sulter, Maude. "Casting a *Spell*: Buzzz Profile of America's Leading

Black Woman Playwright, Ntozake Shange." *(London) The Voice* 30 March 1985: 22.

"Surviving Rape: Facts and Feelings." Pamphlet published by Rape Response, 3600 Eighth Avenue South, Birmingham, Alabama 35222.

Sykes, Jill. "A Black Girl's Song." *Sydney (Australia) Morning Herald* 4 March 1978.

Talbert, Linda Lee. "Ntozake Shange: Scarlet Woman and Witch/ Poet." *Umoja* Spring 1980: 5-10.

"The Talk of the Town." *The New Yorker* (2 August 1976): 17-19.

Tate, Claudia P. "Ntozake Shange." *Black Women Writers at Work.* New York: Continuum, 1983. 149-74.

Taylor, John Russell. Rev. of *For Colored Girls Who Have Considered Suicide/ When the Rainbow Is Enuf,* by Ntozake Shange. *Plays and Players* 27 (December 1979): 16-17.

Teer, Barbara Ann. "The Great White Way Is Not Our Way—Not Yet." *Negro Digest* 17 (April 1968): 21-29.

Tenzer, Lawrence R. *A Completely New Look at Interracial Sexuality: Public Opinion and Social Commentaries.* Manahawkin, NJ: Scholars' Publishing, 1990.

"Theatre: News and Reviews." *Time Out* 4-10 April 1985.

"Theatre Off Broadway." *The New Yorker* 14 June 1976: 77.

Thompson-Cager, Chezia, dir. *For Colored Girls Who Have Considered Suicide/ When the Rainbow Is Enuf.* Smith C Theater Department. Northampton, Mass. February 1987 (Program notes).

——. "Superstition, Magic, and the Occult in Two Versions of Ntozake Shange's Choreopoem *for colored girls. . .* and Novel *Sassafrass, Cypress and Indigo.*" *MAWA: Quarterly Publication of the Middle Atlantic Writers Association* 4 (December 1989): 37-41.

Timpane, John. "'The Poetry of a Moment': Politics and the Open Form in the Drama of Ntozake Shange." *Studies in American Drama, 1945-Present* 4 (1989): 91-101.

Toll, Robert C. *Blacking Up: The Minstrel Show in Nineteenth-Century America.* New York: Oxford UP, 1974.

"Tom Sutcliffe on *A Raisin in the Sun* at the Tricycle, and Rosalind Carne on *Spell #7* at the Donmar Warehouse: Black Power."

Arts Guardian 17 April 1985.

Toomer, Jean. *Cane.* New York: Liveright, 1975.

Trescott, Jacqueline. "Ntozake Shange: Searching for Respect and Identity." *Washington Post* 29 June 1976: B1, B5.

Truss, Lynne. "Being Black and Loving It." *(London) Times Higher Education Supplement* 12 April 1985.

"Trying to Be Nice." *Time* (19 July 1976): 44-45.

"Uggams (Leslie) Sees Little Change." *Birmingham News* 18 October 1989: A2.

Valentine, Dean. "On Stage/ Theater of the Inane." *New Leader* 61 (2 January 1978): 28-29.

Van Peebles, Melvin. *Ain't Supposed to Die a Natural Death.* New York: Bantam, 1973.

Vincent, Mal. "*For Colored Girls* for Everyone." *Virginian Pilot* 19 February 1981.

Walker, Alice. "The Abortion." *Breaking Ice: An Anthology of Contemporary African-American Fiction.* Ed. Terry McMillan. New York: Penguin, 1990. 630-38.

——. *Possessing the Secret of Joy.* New York: Harcourt Brace Jovanovich, 1992.

Wallace, Michele. *Black Macho and the Myth of the Superwoman.* New York: Dial, 1979.

——. "Ntozake Shange: *For Colored Girls,* the Rainbow Is Not Enuf." *Village Voice* 16 August 1976: 108-09.

Wambu, Onye. "Broken Spell: *Spell Number 7* at the Donmar Warehouse" *(London) The Voice* April 1985.

Ward, Douglas Turner. "American Theater: For Whites Only?" *Anthology of the American Negro in the Theatre: A Critical Approach.* Ed. Lindsay Patterson. New York: Publishers, 1967. 81-84.

——. *Day of Absence (A Satirical Fantasy).* *Contemporary Black Drama from* A Raisin in the Sun *to* No Place to Be Somebody. Eds. Clinton F. Oliver and Stephanie Sills. New York: Charles Scribner's Sons, 1971. 340-64.

Waters, Kate. Rev. of *Nappy Edges,* by Ntozake Shange. *School Library Journal* 25 (April 1979): 77.

Watt, Douglas. "Brecht's *Mother Courage* Scalped Out West." *Daily News* 14 May 1980. *New York Theatre Critics' Reviews* 4

(1980): 184.

——. "Here's to the Ladies Again." *Daily News* 16 September 1976. *New York Theatre Critics' Reviews* 37 (1976): 199.

Weathers, Diane, Diane Camper, Vern E. Smith, Brenda Russell, and Sylvester Monroe. "A New Black Struggle." *Newsweek* 27 August 1979: 58-60.

Weaver, Carolyn. "*Betsey Brown*: A Novel by Ntozake Shange." *Mother Jones* June 1985: 58.

Weaver, Michael. "Authors Outline the Coming of Age of Two Black Girls." *(Baltimore, Maryland) Sun* 21 April 1985. *News-Bank* [microform], 1985, 103: G6, fiche.

Weinrub, Judith. "A Touring Black Troupe Begins Its Journey." *Washington Star* 15 June 1980: H1-H2.

Welch, Adrienne Y. "*Betsey Brown* Ends Too Soon." *Omaha (Nebraska) World-Herald* 16 September 1985. *NewsBank* [microform], 1986, 50: F1, fiche.

——. "Shange's *Betsey Brown* Mixes Poetry, Humor." *Miami Herald* 11 July 1985. *NewsBank* [microform], 1985 16: B4, fiche.

Welsh, Anne Marie. "Theater: *landscapes* of Authentic Voice." *Washington Star* 20 June 1980: C11-C12.

Wiley, Catherine. "*Spell #7.*" *Theatre Review* 43 (October 1991): 381-84.

Willard, Nancy. "Life Abounding in St. Louis." Rev. of *Betsey Brown*, by Ntozake Shange. *New York Times Book Review* 12 May 1985: 12.

Williams, Juan. *Eyes on the Prize: America's Civil Rights Years, 1954-1965.* New York: Blackside, 1987.

Williams, Mance. *Black Theater in the 1960s and 1970s: A Historical-Critical Analysis of the Movement.* Westport, CT: Greenwood, 1985.

Williams, Shirley Anne. "Roots of Privilege: New Black Fiction." Rev. of *Betsey Brown*, by Ntozake Shange. *Ms.* June 1985: 69-72.

Williams, Valencia. Rev. of *Betsey Brown*, by Ntozake Shange. *Library Journal* 110 (15 May 1985): 80-81.

Wilson, Edwin. "*For Colored Girls.*" *Wall Street Journal* 21 September 1976. *New York Theatre Critics' Reviews* 31 (1976): 199-

200.

Wilson, Harriet E. *Our Nig; or, Sketches from the Life of a Free Black.* New York: Vintage, 1983.

Winer, Linda. ". . . the stage is set for a hit season." *Chicago Tribune* 26 January 1977: 3, 12.

———. "Theater: On Broadway. . . Profits Earn Top Billing." *Chicago Tribune (Arts and Fun)* 23 January 1977, sec. 6: 2-4.

Witchel, Alex. "Back on the Bus." *Elle* April 1988: 52.

Wolfe, George C. *The Colored Museum.* New York: Broadway Play, 1987.

———. "The Colorization of American Culture, or One Playwright (of Color)'s Not-So-Humble Opinion." *Performing Arts: The Theatre and Music Magazine for California and Texas* (June 1988): 6-7.

Woll, Allen. *Dictionary of Black Theater: Broadway, Off-Broadway, and Selected Harlem Theater.* Westport, CT: Greenwood, 1983. 65.

"Women and the Creative Process: A Discussion by Susan Griffin, Norma Leistiko, Ntozake Shange, and Miriam Schapiro." *Mosaic* 8 (n.d.): 91-117.

"The Women of Eritrea Literally Are Fighting to Gain Their Equality." *Birmingham News* 28 February 1988: E8.

"Women Playwrights: Themes and Variations." *New York Times Arts and Leisure* 7 May 1989: H1, H42.

"Women's Rites." *Newsweek.* 14 June 1976: 99.

Woodis, Carole. "*Spell No. 7,* by Ntozake Shange." *(London) City Limits* 12 April 1985.

———. "*Spell No. 7*: Donmar Warehouse." *Plays and Players* June 1985.

"Words Alive!" Museum of Fine Arts, Houston, Texas. Brown Auditorium. 10 April 1986. Program of Houston Festival 1986.

Wright, Richard. "The Ethics of Living Jim Crow." *Uncle Tom's Children.* New York: Harper and Row, 1965. 3-15.

Wyckoff, Peter C. "Tempo's Just Right in Rhythmic Novel About Growing Up." Rev. of *Betsey Brown,* by Ntozake Shange. *Houston Post* 26 May 1985. *NewsBank* [microform], 1985, 124: B1, fiche.

Zancanella, Don. Rev. of *Betsey Brown,* by Ntozake Shange. *English Journal* 74 (November 1985): 91-92.

INDEX

Angelou, Maya, 72n30,
77n53, 127n24,
130n35, 131n40,
132n44, 218n18

Baldwin, James, 13; *Blues for
Mister Charlie*, 13,
129n34, 218n19,
265n10
Baraka, Amiri Imamu (LeRoi
Jones), 11-12, 67,
70n22, 109, 133n51,
140, 179, 261, 275, 277
Beau Willie Brown and
Crystal, *for colored
girls* . . ., 61-65, 103,
142, 173n16
Betsey Brown (novel), 47, 91,
127n21, 217n12,
221n37, 222n40
Bigsby, C.W.E., 11-12,
18n15
black women, 5, 99-100,
130n38, 216n9; and
beauty ideal, 61; and
intellect, 120; and
physical bodies, 44, 59-
60, 77n53, 98

Brown, Sterling A., 132n47
Brownmiller, Susan, 50,
76n45, 76n46, 274
"built metaphors," 11, 17n13
Bullins, Ed, 109, 133n51,
172n12

Caldwell, Ben, 109
Carlos, Laurie, 5, 109
children, 64, 89, 111, 189,
240-41; deaths of, 62,
65, 103, 213-14, 252,
256; *see also* Sue-Jean;
girls, 27-28, 33, 199-
201, 203-04, 215, 256-
57; play songs, 37,
73n31, 87
Childress, Alice, 274, 278
choreopoem, 3-4, 11-13,
16n7, 267-68;
interdisciplinary, 13-14,
140; and emotion, 3, 5,
106; and language, 5;
and musical forms, 3,
12; and poetic
traditions, 3, 11-12
Christ, Carol P., 24, 26
Colon, Willie, 39-40, 113,

17n9, 68, 75n40,
77n57, 98, 119-20, 142,
148, 219n31, 273-74,
see also Beau Willie
Brown and Crystal;
white men, 98-99
Milner, Ron, 109, 133n51
Minstrelsy, 7-8, 82-84, 86,
89, 107, 111, 123n5,
124n7, 132n48, 132n49
Morrison, Toni, 72n30,
79n59, 137n71,
126n14, 126n17,
131n41, 131n43,
137n71, 274
*Mother Courage and Her
Children* (adaptation),
133n52, 133n54

names and naming, 10-11, 30
Nappy Edges (poems), 16n5,
35, 125n12, 127n24,
220n35
"negative cataloguing," 115,
136n65, 254

Passion Flower *(for colored
girls)*, 53-55, 103
play productions, 21-22, 81,
122n1, 139, 175, 223-
24
Prettyman, Quandra, 141

Reed, Ishmael, 222n41, 275-
76
religion, Christianity, 7, 187-
190, 222n40, 253;
conversion/ rebirth, 7,

66, 185-87; dance, 212;
God/ god, 45, 67, 148-
49, 186, 212, 218n17;
Neo-HooDoo, 85,
222n41
Rich, Adrienne, 28, 51, 181-
82

Sanchez, Sonia, 11, 70n22,
140
Sassafrass, Cypress & Indigo
(novel), 74n33, 74n37
Sechita *(for colored
girls . . .)*, 45-46, 53
sexuality, 244-45, 255, 258;
abortion, 51-53, 76n50;
ambiguity, 152-55, 168-
70; dance, 43; females,
6, 32, 38-39, 45, 101-
02, 131n40, 158, 160,
193-96; objectification
of women, 77n52, 236,
239; sexual violence
against women, 47-52,
75n42, 157, 196-204,
220n32, 242-45; as
female power, 53-55,
101-02; and men/
manhood, 129n34, 143,
145, 150, 154, 156,
232-46, 261
Shange, Ntozake
(autobiography), 10-11,
16n4, 29, 44, 90-91,
127n21, 132n45,
135n62, 161, 190-93,
208-09, 254, 267, 276-
79